First Love

"This book is engaging, respectful, and well-written. It provides the reader with perceptive, dignified, and thoughtful insights into the mystery of adolescent love. I recommend it to everyone who believes in the vitality of youth, the power of the romantic pulse, and the union of two in young love."

John J. Mitchell, Professor of Education,
Okanagan University College, British Columbia;
Author, The Mental and Emotional Life of Teenagers

"*First Love* is a book of greatest magnitude about a subject that is of greatest magnitude to all humans. This scholarly portal into the abiding concern of the significance of adoration, affection, and devotion in young people's lives opens up the question of the meaning of love relations for people of all ages.... Love, that four-letter word, represents a subject that is still being shunned by serious scholars in the social and human sciences. But in this rich, deep, and eloquent exploration into the manifold theories and narrative perspectives on adolescent love, Wendy Austin demonstrates the timeliness and relevance for the study of love in people young and old. Her research is both learned and passionate. She spell-binds her readers with insights, reminiscences, and portrayals that cannot help but prompt us to reflect on the formative experiences in our own lives."

Max van Manen, Author, Researching Lived Experience:
Human Science for an Action Sensitive Pedagogy

First Love

AC / SS Adolescent Cultures, School & Society

Joseph L. DeVitis & Linda Irwin-DeVitis
General Editors

Vol. 18

PETER LANG
New York • Washington, D.C./Baltimore • Bern
Frankfurt am Main • Berlin • Brussels • Vienna • Oxford

WENDY AUSTIN

First Love

The Adolescent's Experience of Amour

PETER LANG
New York • Washington, D.C./Baltimore • Bern
Frankfurt am Main • Berlin • Brussels • Vienna • Oxford

Library of Congress Cataloging-in-Publication Data

Austin, Wendy.
First love: the adolescent's experience of amour / Wendy Austin.
p. cm. — (Adolescent cultures, school and society; vol. 18)
Includes bibliographical references and index.
1. Love in adolescence. I. Title. II. Adolescent
cultures, school & society; vol. 18.
BF724.3.L68 A97   306.7'0835—dc21   00-036397
ISBN 0-8204-5003-0
ISSN 1091-1464

Die Deutsche Bibliothek-CIP-Einheitsaufnahme

Austin, Wendy:
First love: the adolescent's experience of amour / Wendy Austin.
–New York; Washington, D.C./Baltimore; Bern;
Frankfurt am Main; Berlin; Brussels; Vienna; Oxford: Lang.
(Adolescent cultures, school and society; Vol. 18)
ISBN 0-8204-5003-0

Cover design by Joni Holst
Cover art: Gustav Vigeland, *The Kiss,* 1921
© Vigeland Museum/SODART 2002

The paper in this book meets the guidelines for permanence and durability
of the Committee on Production Guidelines for Book Longevity
of the Council of Library Resources.

© 2003 Peter Lang Publishing, Inc., New York
275 Seventh Avenue, 28th Floor, New York, NY 10001
www.peterlangusa.com

Printed in the United States of America

This is dedicated to the ones I love
And to young lovers everywhere

Table of Contents

Acknowledgments

I am deeply indebted to many people for their contributions to this study of adolescent love. I wish to acknowledge at least some of them here.

- Liane Faulder and *The Edmonton Journal* for the article that introduced the study to many participants;
- The participants themselves for opening up their intimate experiences of love for me to explore, for their rich and delightful conversation;
- Max van Manen for his thoughtful, tactful guidance through the realm of phenomenology;
- Other distinguished scholars at the University of Alberta who, like Max, so generously shared their wisdom with me: Len Stewin, Vangie Bergum, Gretchen Hess, and the late Wilfred Schmidt;
- My favorite cadre of researchers, Brenda Cameron, Susan James, Michele Samuel, April Buchanan, Roberta Hewat, Casey Boodt, Serge Hein, and Rauno Parrila, for their good and stimulating company;
- Helen Raboud and Robert and Cheryl Austin for kindly providing places where I found solitude to think and write;
- Kevin Austin for coaxing my computer into action on more than one occasion;
- Linda Ogilvie and Pauline Paul for their acts of friendship which peaked when I was racing to meet a submission deadline;
- Yves Paradis for his enthusiastic support of this work; My interest in adolescent love germinated on a trip to France as a parent chaperone with twenty teenagers in 1986. Yves was the brave teacher on that journey and later, as a fellow graduate student, he shared this research journey. As on that first trip, he has been a great traveling companion, from helping me to prepare for my proposal defense to editing the final draft.
- My children, Mark and Kara Hurtig, for the chance to get a second look at adolescence through their young eyes, for their love, patience, and support.

My heartfelt gratitude goes out to them all.

I would also like to acknowledge the financial support for my studies that I received from the Social Sciences and Humanities Research Council of Canada, the University of Alberta, the Heritage Fund of the Province of Alberta, the Alberta Association of Registered Nurses, and the Alberta Foundation for Nursing Research. Their support made this study possible.

1
A Question Arises

I remember watching for him daily from a window in my parents' bedroom. His paper route was on the next block and, if I timed it right, I could see him pass between the houses across the way as he made his deliveries. His name was Sean; he was 14 years old—a year older than I was. This was a secret watch. If discovered, I would not have truthfully explained why I was in my parents' room, waiting by this window. Even my closest friends who knew I had a "crush" on this boy did not know that I would watch for him like this. A glimpse of him from the window or in the hallway at school was the measure of my day: a day was good if I saw him. A sighting brought a kind of contentment. I was embarrassed that this was so. Why did he have the power to make my pulse quicken? My experience of him was almost totally through sight. It was by his physical appearance that I knew him. I loved his eyes, his smile, and the way a lock of his dark hair would fall across his eyes. I knew how he moved and could easily find him in the crowded corridors at school. I knew that he was a "nice guy" only by reputation. Why, then, if I came upon him unexpectedly, did my heart seem to stop? The awkwardness and selfconsciousness that came with the maturing of my body peaked painfully at his glance. I felt terribly transparent and vulnerable in his presence. Why should this boy affect me so? Anxiety normally made me talkative, but near him I couldn't say a word. We met only occasionally and then within a group—we never did speak directly to one another. At the end of that year, I left to attend another school.

Looking back I can clearly remember the raw, overwhelming sense of emotion I felt for this boy I really didn't know—was it love? It seemed such a delicate memory that I always hesitated to examine it closely. When I watched my teenage daughter flush at the mention of a certain boy's name and heard her voice change whenever she spoke of him, those days came back to me. I wondered and wanted to remember: What is it like to be an adolescent in love? The question began to occur to me again and again. It came when I saw a boy and girl standing at a corner, speaking animatedly, their bodies moving closer together and then quickly apart. It came when I noticed the look on a young man's face as he glanced at a girl near him. There were both tenderness and fear in that glance. She did not notice his look. They were sitting with their friends, laughing, talking. I saw his hand gently touch the ends of her long brown hair where it hung over the back of a chair. He is in love, I thought to myself. What is this love that I can see from all the way across the room? Gadamer (1960/1990) describes how a question occurs to us, how it presents itself more than we do: It "presses itself on us" (p. 366). The pressing question for me became *What is the experience of the adolescent in love?*

When my children reached adolescence, one of the greatest changes in their world seemed to be that romantic love, or at least the expectation of it, was present in a strong way. It was in the songs that they sang, in the movies that they saw, in the gossip that they shared with their friends. Much of the excitement, laughter, and turmoil in their lives seemed related to it. I have been awakened by the sound of six boys with one guitar serenading my daughter from the street. I have listened to the back seat teasing of her friends as I, the silent driver, chauffeured them to a school dance. I have seen her distress on receiving a poem—an avowal of love—from a boy she valued as a friend. Her recognition of his vulnerability (and her own) was apparent. So was her annoyance. "Love can mess everything up," she told me. I realized too that my daughter, poem in hand, was mindful of another young man. Sixteen, in her grade at school, he had killed himself the previous summer "over a girl." Like other parents, I try to help my children as they learn about and experience life. It can be difficult to know the best way to "be there" for your adolescent. When my son sat at the end of my bed in the early morning hours after a date, talking around his feelings, I was not sure how to guide him, or even if I should. But I knew that I needed to understand his experience to be understanding with him.

In our society today it seems agreed that our youth must be taught about their sexuality; we are less sure about acknowledging that they fall in love. In Victorian times, love and sexuality were severed. The young were denied a conscious understanding of sexuality. Perhaps something similar is happening in our own time. While the language of romantic love was once a means of obscuring sexuality, our focus on sexuality may serve to repress love. Denial may have just changed its appearance (Alberoni, 1983). Roland Barthes (1977/1978) believes that there has been a historical reversal of values—the sexual is no longer indecent; it is the sentimental that is obscene. Love's sentimentality is discredited; it constitutes a "powerful transgression" (p. 175).

The experience of being *in love* is a transforming one—the lover can rupture the existing ties that anchor him or her in the world. In love, the emotional and ethical center of the person shifts and becomes oriented toward another. Love's rules, not society's, take precedence (Sarsby, 1983). "Love tends to separate the law from the person; it wants to establish other laws, other norms"(Alberoni, 1983, p. 30). What is important to the person changes. No wonder we are uneasy and hesitant about accepting this experience as strong, real, or legitimate in our adolescents.

They want to learn about love. This was movingly evident to me most recently when "young offenders" at a local psychiatric hospital asked that love be included as part of their learning group on sexuality. It was what they most wanted to discuss. These teens are in trouble with the law and are being assessed or treated for serious mental problems. Many are "street kids"; all are coping with very difficult life circumstances. Love in the broadest sense is obviously at issue for these adolescents. It is love in the passionate sense, however, that they are trying to understand right now. With all its complexities—the joys, the jealousies, the elation, the sorrow—it is in their thoughts and their lives, even while they are incarcerated in a forensic psychiatric facility. In speaking with them I was struck by their openness and vulnerability to the question of love, by how much they were like my own children in this. Teens are telling us (as I heard it expressed by a teen at a televised forum on sexual health called *Teen Talk*):

> Don't talk about sex without love. Just, you know, boy puts penis in vagina. You teach a sex class. You've got to teach a love class too.[1]

Falling in love seems a significant happening in the life passage of teenager to adult. In medieval times, when the stages of life were conceived of as seven (to correspond with the number of known planets), adolescence was the third stage (Ariès, 1960/1962).[2] Its essence was named by Shakespeare[3] as "the lover, / Sighing like a furnace, with a woeful ballad / Made to his mistress' eyebrow." It is true that a 5 year old may ask, "What does it mean when you get a funny feeling in your stomach when a girl smiles at you?" (Sutton, 1974, p. 93). We know first kisses are often experienced in the elementary school yard. It is in adolescence, however, that an intense desire for intimacy, physical and emotional, with another individual (outside of kinship bonds) first occurs.

Martin Buxton (1987), a child psychiatrist, describes the clinical challenge—and clinical headache—of treating adolescents whose "developmental propensity is to seek love relationships" (p. 75). In "Adolescent Couples in a Psychiatric Hospital: 'I'll Never Forget What's Her Name'," he describes how these teen relationships may be clinically problematic. He gives some examples:

> A psychological assessment had to be understood in the context of the patient's precipitous mood changes when he saw his girlfriend talking to another male just

before the patient was to be tested. Teachers had to allow students to make up exams because they were unable to prepare satisfactorily, secondary to acute depressions set in motion by the prospective transfer of a boyfriend to another unit. Staff were perceived as ruthless, insensitive, and capricious for discharging a youngster before his or her mate was also ready to leave hospital. (p. 75)

Buxton says he has at times felt like "a UBoat commander who has torpedoed the Love Boat." He recognizes, however, that these experiences can be growth enhancing for the teens. What better way to learn about yourself than through relationships? How are teens to achieve the developmental tasks of adolescence (which he identifies as separationindividuation, identity formation, and preparation for successful adult sexual relationships) without such experiences?

In trying to understand adolescent love, I have looked back upon my own teen years and have tried to remember what love was like for me then. I think about the yearlong "crush" I had on a boy I barely knew. Though I smile to myself now at the memory, a part of me is very reluctant to get in contact with the feelings that I had then. They were so intense. I remember feeling exposed, defenseless against something I did not understand. I realize that I am still trying to understand it.

Adolescence has been called a developmental ontological revolution (Fischer & Alapack, 1987). It is a time of separation, of breaking away from the familiar, of the discovery and creation of a new self. Love seems to play a role in that. For Francesco Alberoni (1983), adolescence is "the age of continual dying and rebirth of something else, of continual experimentation with the frontiers of the possible" (p. 81). Alberoni notes that falling in love is particularly suited to adolescence: Love involves a rebirth, too. I began this study with the thought that if I learned about the lived experience of adolescent love, I might as a nurse, as an educator, as a parent, as a person, assist at this "rebirthing" in a better way.

Studying Love

When I made the decision to study teenagers' experience of love, I found I was hesitant, even defensive, in acknowledging the topic to my colleagues. Coming across Robert Burton's (1621/1977) discourse on "lovemelancholy," I felt a rush of kinship. Burton prefaces his work with a justification for it, in the certainty that he will be censured for writing on "too light" or "too comical" a subject—one fit only for "a wanton poet, a feeling lovesick gallant, an effeminate courtier or some such idle person" (p. 3). He defends himself as a grave, discreet man who has no choice but to discourse on "lover matters" because love is a species of melancholy. Like Burton, I think I have been concerned that, with love as my subject, I may not be taken seriously.

In the past, psychologists have avoided this area of study "for fear of risking alienation and ridicule from the general scientific community" (Kazak & Reppucci, 1980, p. 211). Ellen Berscheid (1988), speaking from experience, made explicit that in the recent past one's scientific mantle was stained if one was frivolous enough to do research on love (p. 360). It seems paradoxical that the study of love and its manifestations is so suspect. Have not all great thinkers, at least since Plato, considered love as central to the human condition? Can the study of the *psyche* be accomplished if love is out of bounds? Even B. F. Skinner, the eminent behaviorist (and staunch opponent of intervening variables), believed that love is an important factor in understanding human behavior (Evans, 1968).

Much of the hesitancy regarding this focus of research came from the way in which we think about science. Science is about the scientific method (problem solving), experimental procedures, hypothesis testing, control of variables, rigor. A philosophy of science is evolving, however, in which the study of human perceptions, intentions, and real-life situations is viewed as authentic research (Howe & Eisenhart, 1990; House, 1991). This perception is propitious to the study of love. There has also been a change within psychology from an exogenic model of knowledge to an endogenic one (Gergen & Davis, 1985). With this change in focus from the external environment of the human body to what is happening within it, psychologists became more interested in emotion. The publication in 1988 by Yale University Press of a landmark book, *The Psychology of Love* (edited by an eminent cognitive scientist, Robert Sternberg), further legitimized research on love. According to Berscheid (1988), the book's very existence was more remarkable than anything between its covers. Love is becoming more acceptable as a focus of inquiry (Bierhoff, 1991; Hendrick & Hendrick, 1989; Lazarus, 1991; Sternberg & Barnes, 1988).

There is, however, more than the scientific approach at issue when studying love. Martha Nussbaum (1990), a philosopher, raises a question, not about *how* or *who* should write about love, but *whether*. She supports the idea that she finds illustrated within Marcel Proust's work that it is through narrative art that life can assume a shape and become real. She says that we must consider Samuel Beckett's stance as well: Art forces life to assume a shape rather than letting it be as it is—messy and formless. Should we let love be?[4]

A U.S. senator once protested federal research funds being used to study romantic love, with this statement:

> I believe that 200 million Americans want to leave some things a mystery, and right at the top of the list of the things we don't want to know about is why a man falls in love with a woman and vice versa. (quoted in Murstein, 1988, p. 34)

Should we leave love's mystery be? Research has the potential to help people understand their experiences, but it may also serve to prescribe some version of love as *real* love, *true* love. Psychologists have in their work subtly—and not so subtly—endorsed their own idea of what is socially desirable (Prilleltensky, 1990). Underlying the scientific research on a phenomenon is the implicit understanding that one may find ways of manipulating it (Ridley, 1991). (We may think here of computer dating.) Nussbaum asks this:

> Could it be that to write about love, even to write humbly and responsively, is itself a device to control the topic, to trap and bind it like an animal—so, of necessity, an unloving act? (Nussbaum, 1990, p. 321)

I have overcome my own doubts about disturbing love's mystery by finding a method of study that allows that mystery to remain. Rather than approaching the study of love as a problem to be solved—"A problem is something which I meet, which I find complete before me, but which I can therefore lay siege to and reduce" (Marcel, 1950, p. 260)—I take a phenomenological approach in which I attempt to bring the mystery more fully present, to evoke it, recapture it rather than dispel it (van Manen, 1990).

The use of a methodology grounded in the philosophic traditions of phenomenology means also that one must address one's own perspectives on the phenomenon, that one must strive to be aware of one's own preunderstandings. There is a commitment to enter a phenomenological study with a sense of self-questioning. This, I believe, is a particularly helpful approach when studying love. Stendhal's (1822/1957) ninth chapter in *Love* consists entirely of this:

> I am trying extremely hard to be *dry.*[5] My heart thinks it has so much to say, but I try to keep it quiet. I am continually beset by the fear that I may have expressed only a sigh when I thought I was stating a truth. (p. 57)

Stendhal recognizes the difficulty of being objective when writing about love. Within contemporary phenomenology the impossibility of being objective about any human phenomenon is made explicit. This seems a more possible approach: acknowledgment of the personal, rather than a struggle to appear *dry*. The personal will be there anyway; it will leak out. It cannot be set aside. "When a psychologist undertakes to address the subject of love, he cannot avoid telling the world about himself" (Branden, 1980, p. 3).

The remaining *whether,* for me, has been grounded in my doubts as an individual: Given the boundaries of my own skills, the research process, and the intricacy of the subject, could I do justice to love? "To try to write love is to confront the muck of language: that region of hysteria where language is both *too much and too little*, excessive…and impoverished"(Barthes, 1977/ 1978, p. 99).[6] There is Wittgenstein's (1961) contention that unsayable things do exist—like our experience of the mystical—and that to attempt to speak of them only causes confusion. Will my attempt to describe the experience of adolescent love cause confusion rather than bringing it closer to understanding? My doubts rose during my conversations with study participants who shared their adolescent love experiences with me. There seemed to be an unspoken statement—*here is my experience, I trust you to use it well*. I recognize the seriousness of that responsibility. I also recognize that the greatest limitation of this research lies here, in my ability to write their experience.

I have created this text to follow the course that I took in trying to answer the question: What is the experience of the adolescent in love? In Chapter Two, I review the research literature on love to discover love as the psychologist sees it. I then explore in Chapter Three some of the theories developed by scholars to explain love and tell us what it is. In Chapter Four, I go outside the scientific and scholarly discourses to contemplate another way in which our understandings of love are shaped. I look at some of the great stories of love that have been told and retold across time, and in the telling have surely influenced our perception of it. With these influences on our understanding of love made explicit, I outline the way in which I studied the phenomenon of adolescent love in this work. This research process, based in hermeneutic phenomenology, is presented as Chapter Five. The heart of this work, a description of adolescent love, lies in the chapters entitled, "Awakening," "Falling," "Possessed," and "Becoming." The final chapter, "The Sentimental Education," is a reflection on the pedagogical considerations of what I have learned about adolescent love.

Notes

1 Unfortunately, I do not recall the details (e.g., date, channel) of this television show.

2 Ariès (1960/1962) in *Centuries of Childhood* writes that in the Middle Ages, "age" was a scientific category (as speed or weight is today) forming part of a system of physical description and explanation derived from Ionian philosophers of sixth century b.c. They

became so commonplace that they passed from science to everyday experience. These categories were *childhood, puerility, adolescence, youth, senectitude* or *(gravity), old age, senies.*

3   One man in his time plays many parts,
    His acts being seven ages. At first the infant,
    Mewling and puking in the nurse's arms.
    Then the whining school boy, with his satchel
    And shining morning face, creeping like a snail
    Unwilling to school. And then the lover,
    Sighing like a furnace, with a woeful ballad
    Made to his mistress' eyebrow.

    Shakespeare (*As You Like It*, 2.7.143–150)

4   Nussbaum answers this question by addressing in *Love's Knowledge* (1990) the uses of literature in understanding ourselves and the human condition and in answering the philosophical question: What is a good life?

5   Italics in original.

6   Italics in original.

2
Love and Psychology

Theodor Reik (1941), who wrote an early, major psychological treatise on love, *Of Love and Lust,* did so because he couldn't shake off the question he heard posed one night at the opera:

> You who do know
> All the heart's turns,
> Say is it love now
> That in me burns?[1]

Reik heard it as a challenge to psychologists and analysts who claim to be in the know: What is love? Do you really know? In his era the psychological perspective was primarily psychoanalytical, that is, love was a goal-inhibited form of the sex drive. Reik, however, believed love was different from sex and noted, "Psychologists discuss sex very fully nowadays, but there is a conspiracy of silence about love" (p. 10–11). Reik broke the silence, but not many voices followed him.

In 1973, Mary Ellen Curtin surveyed 23 volumes of the *Annual Review of Psychology* and did not find love mentioned. It is increasingly mentioned today—although "mentioned" remains the operative word. In over 135,000 references indexed in the *Psychological Abstracts* from 1992 to 1995, only 88 articles, 15 books, and 19 chapters are indexed under *love*. For 1996 to April 2000, *PsychINFO*[2] has 280 citations for the search term, *love*. Hans Bierhoff (1991), reviewing love research, summarizes the reasons given for the "considerable reserve" toward the topic as the "complexity of the issues" and "the question of how to define love" (p. 95).

Irving Singer (1987) believes that it is methodological qualms that keep many scientists from researching love, as if this aspect of human nature is too delicate or elusive to warrant scientific analysis. When I examined the way in which psychologists are attempting to make sense of love, I appreciated their qualms. Though Ethel Person (1988) has suggested that to study love psychologists should follow William James' approach to studying religion (find the most religious man in his most energetically religious mood), this has not been done.

Within psychology, the conceptualizations of love as a human phenomenon have been shaped by the parameters of the scientific method, by the measuring tools of natural scientific analysis. For love to become valid as an area of study, it had to become an operational concept and a measurable variable. It did. What does love look like under the glare of scientific scrutiny? B. F. Skinner's definition might serve as an example: "Love is a heightened probability of positively reinforcing a loved person" (quoted in Evans, 1981, p. 11). There is also Donn Byrne's (1971) Law of Interpersonal Attraction:

$$ y = m \left(\frac{\sum PR}{\sum PR + \sum NR} \right) + k $$

This is a linear equation where y = attraction; PR = positive reinforcement; and NR = negative reinforcement. There is the research on the biochemical basis of love (Walsh, 1991) with its application to the treatment of the lovesick with monoamine oxidase inhibitors. One of the first research investigations in this area was that of Rubin (1970): he devised scales to measure love and liking.

An example of an investigation of love within the discipline is a study by Marshall Dermer and Tom Pyszczynski (1978). They used Rubin's Love and Liking Scales to examine the effects of erotica on responses to loved ones. Male undergraduate psychology students participated in the study in exchange for extra credit. Fifty-one who rated the extent of their love for a woman as being between 30 and 135 mm on a 172 mm line were recruited for a study on "information-processing." After completing a placebo scale, they either read a "Collegiate Fantasy" (erotic condition) or a description of the mating behavior of herring gulls (control condition). They then described their loved ones on measures that included Rubin's scales. A behavioral analysis of the results indicated that men are more likely when sexually aroused to express statements similar to the Love than to the Liking items on Rubin's scales. Although this study was carried out nearly twenty years ago, the guiding paradigm remains current. In fact, a report of an attempt at its replication was published in *Psychological Reports* in December 1992 (Amelang & Pielke, 1992).

The paradigm is also evident in a study that was focused on adolescent love. Hatfield, Brinton, and Cornelius (1989) tested the hypothesis that anxious adolescents are more likely than others to experience passionate love. Forty-one children between 12 and 14 years of age completed a trait anxiety measure. They were asked, if they could have anyone in the world as a boyfriend or girlfriend, whom would they pick? They then completed the Juvenile Love Scale (JLS). Hatfield and her colleagues define passionate love as a "state of intense longing for union with another"; "It is a state of profound physiological arousal" (p. 271). The JLS is designed to "tap the cognitive, physiological, and behavioral indicates of 'longing for union' in children" (p. 271). Multiregression analysis was used to explore the relationships between anxiety, gender, age, and JLS scores. Anxiety scores were significantly related to the JLS scores. The researchers concluded that adolescents who are anxious are "also especially likely to have experienced passionate love" (p. 287). Despite the adherence to the scientific model evident in this study, I do wonder if these researchers have truly discovered that anxious 12-year-olds have experience with passion?[3]

The works indexed in *Psychological Abstracts/PsychINFO* under *love* are, on the whole, focused on scale development, cross-cultural comparisons, attachment and love-styles, correlates of satisfactory relationships, and love as experienced within special groups, for example, the obese, drug abusers, parents of a disabled child, the depressed, or workplace colleagues. Transference and counter transference issues are listed here, as well. By far the most studied group is that of college and university students.

Overall, love research is suggestive of several things: that psychologists aspire to do socially relevant research; that they look to explain and predict; that they continue to use scales to measure love and to consider it in relation to other phenomena and across cultures; and that psychologists have approached love, as might be expected, from the vantage point of the dominant psychological model. The review that follows is focused on the work related to what has been variously termed romantic, erotic, passionate, or amorous love. As defining love has always posed a problem for the researcher, it is a fitting place to start.

The Research on Love

Love's Definition

It seems to me that love is so complex a sentiment that one cannot define it without betraying it.

—Chapsal

A classical type of definition of love (that is, one in which all experiences named love share a common essence) has yet to evolve within psychology. There is no agreement upon a definition of *romantic* or *passionate* love. Hatfield (1988), with her colleague Berscheid, distinguishes between *passionate* and *companionate* love. "Passionate love involves ecstasy/misery. Companionate love flourishes in a mixture of pleasure sprinkled occasionally with real-life frustrations" (p. 207). The difference here is one of emphasis, unlike Rubin's (1970) distinct differentiation between *loving* and *liking*. Dorthy Tennov (1979) originated the concept of *limerence* to distinguish between love and "being in love" (limerence). She characterizes people as limerents or nonlimerents (those that love without ever being "in love"). John Lee (1973, 1998) developed research-based descriptions of love-styles. Using a color analogy to facilitate understanding of his concept, he describes primary styles (*Eros, Storge, Ludus*) and secondary styles (*Pragma, Mania, Agapé*). His taxonomy has been used as a basis for psychometric measures of love.

Beverly Fehr and James Russell (1991) take a prototypic approach to love's definition. They believe that love, as a concept, has an internal structure but "fuzzy borders" (p. 426). Experiences identified as love (love for a child, love for a romantic partner, love for a friend) share a family resemblance: There are no sharp boundaries between members and nonmembers of categories of love. This may explain the inability to achieve consensus on a definition of love. Psychologists are contending with the fact that people can comprehend and use the concept of love without identifying necessary and sufficient features of it. Alan Soble (1990), a philosopher, notes that though Capellanus's definition of love in the twelfth century (*a certain inborn suffering derived from the sight of and excessive meditation upon the beauty of the opposite sex*) and Descartes' five centuries later (*an emotion of the soul caused by a movement of the spirits which impels the soul to join itself willingly to objects that appear to be agreeable to it*) are disparate and say little, we know that they are dealing with the same thing. We know what human phenomenon they have in mind.

The Measure of Love

How do I love thee? Let me count the ways.

—Browning

Psychometrics is, perhaps, the dominant method in psychology's pursuit of romantic or passionate love. (It parallels the research on intelligence.) In this method, the researcher tries to determine the dimensions adequate to describe individuals' experiences. The dimensions are measured relative to one another, and measures with low variability (poor predictors) are discarded. Zick Rubin's (1970) measurement of romantic love is a landmark work that stimulated the development of several other tools. Tools that psychologists use to measure love include the Love Attitude Scale (LAS), the Relationship Rating Form, the Passionate Love Scale (PAS), and the Triangular Theory of Love Scale. A factor analysis of the subscales of these self-report love measures generated five factors: passionate love, closeness, ambivalence, secure attachment, and practicality (Hendrick & Hendrick, 1989). Aron and Westbay (1996) did a factor analysis of 68 prototypical features of love as identified by Fehr and found a three-dimensional structure they labeled passion, intimacy, and commitment. Can there be a general factor in love? Bernard Murstein (1988) reviewed the literature and found all factor analyses of love measures have yielded a unity factor. This factor involved *glorification of the other*. It is interesting that Stendhal put this factor forward in his work of 1822, *Love*, with his concept of *crystallization* (Stendhal, 1822/1957, p. 45). His idea is cogently (and delightfully) argued, but the contemporary psychologist may place more trust in Murstein's statistical approach.

Love as Biology

Love is nothing else but an insatiate thirst of enjoying a greedily desired object.

—Montaigne

That love is correlated with physiological changes has long been accepted. (The pulse as a diagnostic sign of love was an ancient discovery by Erasistratus, a famous physician of Alexandria [Gonzalez-Crussi, 1988].[4]) Today researchers are exploring the neurobiology of love (Carter, 1998; Marazziti, Akiskal, Rossi, & Cassano, 1999). For some (Buss, 1988; Fisher, 1993; Mellen, 1981; Rizley, 1980), the relationship between love and biology is a causal one. Love is seen as a genetic phenomenon with evolutionary, biological significance. This model emphasizes action: "Love is not simply a state; love *acts*" (Buss, 1988, p. 100, italics in original). It posits consequences, social and biological. The consequences of "love acts" influence resource acquisition and allocation, strategies that achieve reproductive success (Buss, 1988). In this approach, love is not simply an internal state of feelings, drives, and thoughts: Love's existence and urgency are founded in prior evolutionary forces.

Love as a Commodity

They do not love that do not show they love.

—Shakespeare

B. F. Skinner defined love as "a heightened probability of positively rein-forcing a loved person" (quoted in Evans, 1968, p. 11). The idea of the love relationship being essentially an exchange of rewards has been explored within psychology. Harold Kelley and John Thibaut (1978) developed an interde-pendence matrix for a dyad that shows how partners control each other's outcomes. Using the matrix, the behaviors and consequences of all possible behaviors in an interaction can be assessed. L. Rowell Huesmann (1980) also conceived of love as based on exchange: Love is "a state of deep mutual in-volvement in which exchange of rewards take place that are highly satisfying to both" (p. 156). Huesmann believes his incremental exchange model ac-counts for numerous phenomena of love, is more precise and unambiguous than other approaches, and is in accord with "the cognitive view of man as an information processor" (p. 171)—a predominant metaphor in psychology at the time of his work. This conception of love, based on the assumption that "individuals look for the maximum rewards at the lowest possible costs" (Vanyperen & Buunk, 1991), can be used to predict and measure outcomes and fits well with the rational and capitalistic tradition that has molded mod-ern psychology. Recent research shows, however, that this model does not fit if a cross-cultural perspective is taken. Dutch psychologists (Vanyperen & Buunk, 1991) found that equity theory fitted the American experience but not the Dutch, and then only fitted Americans who were low in communal orientation. "Some modern romantic love research is so devoid of historical awareness that the reader might conclude that romantic love was an Ameri-can invention" (Lee, 1988, p. 58). Culture does shape the way one imagines and experiences love. Some, like Stever Seidman (1991), a sociologist, find this so true that they assume love has no essential or unitary identity. Seidman says his analysis is of *American* love.

Love as Cognition

Love looks not with the eyes, but with the mind.

—Shakespeare

Kenneth Livingston (1980), a cognitive psychologist, sees romantic love as a process of reducing uncertainty, "The eventual loss of the experience of uncertainty reduction that produces the decline of passionate feeling" (p. 146). Sandra Murray (1999) agrees. She argues further that it is processes of motivated construal that allow individuals to link faults to greater virtues and thus maintain positive perceptions of partners. Sternberg's work yielded a model of love as a set of cognitions, motivations, and affects. He approached the study of love as he had approached intelligence (Sternberg & Grajek, 1984). Comparing structural models of love based on three psychometric conceptions of intelligence, he decided a Thomsonian "bonds" model fitted best. His rather elegant triangular theory presents love as a combination of passion, intimacy, and commitment. He has described love as a story (Sternberg, 1995) and produced a book, *Cupid's Arrow* (1998), in which he gives a psychological account of love over time.

Love as Pathology

Love is a sickness full of woes.

—Samuel Daniel

A clinical orientation developed within psychology during the aftermath of World War II (Sarason, 1981) when psychological states became something from which a person *suffered* (Leary, 1987). It is not too surprising, then, that a diagnostic and treatment paradigm has been used to conceptualize amorous love. This is evidenced in Sternberg's ideas (see Sternberg & Barnes, 1988) for the application of his triangular theory of love: the diagnosis of components of a particular love relationship and therapy for areas that need change. The author of *Love and Addiction*, Stanton Peele (1988), finds that while social psychologists tend to emphasize romance and the positive aspects of love, clinicians find pathology "passing" as love. For Peele, Romeo and Juliet represent love addiction. This is self-absorption in another, idealization and total acceptance of the other, a private world, painful or a refuge from pain, accidental, volatile, and incommensurable. (In this view, all Tennov's limerents are experiencing pathology.) True love for Peele is a helping relationship, an experience continuous with friendship and affection. Myron Weiner (1980) is less zealous in identifying lovesickness, but believes that any human attribute can become a perversion and gives submissiveness, bondage, and masochistic attachments as examples. The love addict for Weiner is someone who repeatedly falls, or seeks to fall, in love because he/she needs to be part of a union to feel alive.

Summary

Psychologists are studying love. They are, however, choosing explanatory models and research methods that do not seem to reach love's essence. After reading the well-written and procedurally correct studies, I was left wondering if psychology has achieved in its study of love that which Gordon Allport has described as a "situation of ignorant expertise" (quoted in Lubek, 1979). I think, at times, the research tells us more about psychology than it does about love.

Adolescent Love

As to the sentiment of love in the adolescent, we still know too little.
—G. Stanley Hall

Though Hatfield and her colleagues are studying teenage passion, this research focus seems rare. Adolescent love research literature is usually found as an adjunct to teenage sexual issues. Some examples of studies follow.

Joseph Scott (1983) interviewed students at a School-Age Mothers (SAMs) program in the U.S.A., finding that love was a major (not dominant) motive for initiating sexual intercourse (the motive for 40% of white SAMs and 35% of black SAMs) and strongly associated with pregnancy. White SAMs were in love with their sex partners at the onset of pregnancy 89% of the time, as were 80% of the black SAMs.

Philbrick and Stones (1988) examined love-attitudes of white South African adolescents using the Munro-Adams Love-Attitude Scale. Boys were found to be more romantic than girls. These adolescents endorsed the *romantic power* sub-factor on this scale (love has a potent influence on a person's life and surmounts all obstacles) over *conjugal love* (love should have a calm, sober, and stabilizing influence and demands serious thought and consideration).

Robin Simon, Donna Eder, and Cathy Evans (1992), using data from interviews, naturally occurring discourse and field notes, studied early adolescent female peer groups. These authors argue "adolescence is a period during which females acquire cultural knowledge about romantic love, including the social norms that guide romantic feelings" (p. 43). Knowledge and norms about romance were transmitted within the group—though the girls did not always abide by the norms and sometimes intentionally defied them. Highly developed and accepted norms were those of heterosexuality, exclusivity, and monogamy. Two norms revealed the high salience of romance for girls: norms concerning the importance of romantic relationships (a boyfriend enhances popularity) and the importance of being in love continually (a means to validate self-worth).

Richard Alapack studied first love in adolescence using a phenomenological approach (Fischer & Alapack, 1987). He found essential characteristics that differentiate this relationship from other intense personal-sexual involvements. Adolescent first love was experienced as absolute (omnipresent and eternal), unique, perfect and ideal, and compatible with one's roots. There was a sense of heartfelt communication and exclusive "togetherness." Love for Alapack's teens was reciprocal, innocent, and oriented to the future. Its meaning was neither a fantasy projection nor a correlate of needs or intentions. The signs of love seemed to pivot around the other as a real partner and around the shared relationship.

Line Robitaille and Francine Lavoie (1992) studied the adolescent amorous relationships of 15-year-old francophone students in Québec. They used focus groups to elicit boys' and girls' opinions about love. There were four groups: older boys (16–18 years of age), younger boys (14–16), older girls (15–19), and younger girls (14–15). Discussion included love's definition, becoming a couple, couple-activities, and being a couple within a group of friends. Conflict and breakups were also addressed. In all groups, some teens idealized love as magical. The older girls, for instance, said love was giving yourself without expecting anything in return. Within both boys' groups love was described as infinite, encompassing everything. It was inexplicable. The boys related feeling inadequate in regard to ever living such a real love. The idea of finding a predestined, lifelong love was shared as a hope by some teens. Boys perceived girls as romantic, and many girls described themselves as such. In the older boys' group, Harlequin romances were decried as playing a role in girls' expectations of love, but the boys were unable to elaborate on this in any detail. Communication was seen as crucial by both groups of girls and by the younger boys. The difficulty of opening to the other was discussed, including the fact that friends often remained the privileged confidants. One girl said she was never able to tell her boyfriend what she felt about him, about being in love with him, but that her entire gang knew it all. The teens discussed the beginning of love relationships, saying that intense feelings and idealization of the other characterizes this time. Serial monogamy seemed to be the norm. Some differences in the way the sexes spoke about love (e.g., boys emphasized the sexual aspects; girls talked about respect) were noted, but both girls and boys believed that the sexes defined and thought about love in the same way.

Social, academic, and job competence and rule-breaking conduct were studied by Jennifer Neemann, Jon Hubbard and Ann Masten (1995) by assessing children from ages 8 to 22. Early romantic involvement had negative consequences for all but social domains. Later in adolescence, however, romance lost its negative significance.

The experience of being "in love" for early and middle adolescents was explored by Marilyn Montgomery and Gwendolyn Sorell (1998). They found teens are actively thinking about the nature and meaning of romance, with boys falling in love earlier and more often than girls.

Maggie Kirkman, D. Rosenthal, and A.M.A. Smith (1998) interviewed Australian teens to explore, as a basis for safe sex education, the way they understand love and sex. Sexual relationships were seen as part of the quest for love, with males and females having well-defined roles to play. Females were expected to value intimacy while males sought coitus as an end in itself. The researchers argue that the teens' dominant romantic narrative promotes the use of condoms for contraception but not for preventing sexually transmitted disease, as use for the latter would suggest distrust or promiscuity. They conclude that health educators must take into account romantic narratives and their influence when developing programs.

Though these studies are few in number, their results seem to indicate that amorous love is a potentially serious, intense, and prominent component of adolescents' lives. What is it like for them? What is it like to be a teenager in love? What is this love?

Notes

1   A verse from Da Ponte's libretto written in 1786 for Mozart's *The Marriage of Figaro* (Ewen, 1963).

2   The electronic version of *Psychological Abstracts.*

3   Paradigm issues aside, there seems to me an alternate explanation for their results: The physiological arousal items on the anxiety measure correlated with the ones on the JLS.

4   This observant physician noted that the pulse of a young prince, intent on starving himself to death, became lively when his stepmother was in the room and slothful when she left. As well as the quickened pulse, there were other signs of physiological turmoil: perspiration, trembling limbs, flushed face. The story has a happy ending for the prince: the king, rather than lose his son, appointed him as king, and his stepmother as his queen (Gonzalez-Crussi, 1988).

3
What Love Is

I noticed the girl right away. She stood at the corner of the street, balanced on the very edge of the curb. She appeared vigilant, rather nervous and in another foreign city, I might have guarded my purse as I went by her. This was Kyoto, however, and so I wondered why a girl her age was alone, and not in school. Her face brightened suddenly, so much that I turned to see the cause. A boy on a bike whizzed past me, and I watched him stop just long enough for her to hop on, and they were off. I had to smile. "That explains the unsettled look in her eyes." To my surprise, I saw her with him again. They were sitting side by side in a nook near the bell of the Myoshinji Temple. They seemed quietly intense with one another, speaking softly, an obvious world of two.

I saw in this pair of young adolescents an amorous couple, looking and acting as teenagers might in my own society across the ocean. There the setting would be different, of course, and the aura of secrecy less pronounced. It was the way they were with one another that seemed familiar, recognizable. What was it I was seeing? Was this love I saw?

A World of Two

Is there an essence to young love that is shared across cultures and societies, perhaps even across time? Is there not a poem from the culture of these young Japanese, written over a thousand years ago, that echoes the sentiments of a contemporary Bruce Springsteen song[1]

> To meet my love
> I have no way
> Like the tall peak
> of Fuji in Suruga
> Shall I burn forever?
>
> *Anon (quoted in Bownas & Thwaite, 1964)*

What is it that makes us *burn for* one another? What is this love? Plato thought to answer the question in his *Symposium*: Love is the desire for beauty and excellence. Is that what I recognized in my young teens? *They* seemed beautiful to me. For Plato, love was about the good. It was the good and beautiful qualities of our lover that we loved. Another with the same excellence and beauty would be as lovable. I wonder, would a different, but also excellent, boy bring the same unsettled look to the young girl's eyes?

Sigmund Freud gave an answer from his work in psychoanalysis: Love is a striving for an object representing a source of primitive pleasure. Yes, their pleasure at being together was evident. Freud meant something more. He would say that their moments together—riding; talking; sitting—were a sublimation of their real purpose: sex. Was sex the reason sitting close on a wooden bench was enticing? Is love civilized sex? What would happen if one of these teens thought another might be a potentially greater source of sexual pleasure?

The philosopher Robert Solomon (1988) argues that it is sexual desire that is universal but that *I love you* is not in a universal language. For Solomon there is nothing like it in most societies, and no emotion quite to compare with it. Romantic love, he writes, is "anthropologically speaking quite rare" (p. 38). Is it romantic stirrings I see in these adolescents? Am I distorting their togetherness? How different are they from a teenage couple back home in Canada?

Perhaps it is neurochemistry creating the synergy I see between them. Liebowitz (1983) and his colleagues believe that it is the action of phenylethylamine (PEA)—the neurotransmitter Helen Fisher (1992) calls *attraction juice*—on the limbic system that causes the symptoms of infatuation. These symptoms can be treated with monoamine oxidase inhibitors. Would a regimen of antidepressants remove the pull between these teens?

I wonder how their parents would feel about these meetings of their children. This was only the first time I came across them. Staying at an inn of the temple, I discovered that theirs was a regular rendezvous. Would their parents smile and see innocent promise in this learning to be together? Would they be afraid for their children and insist they keep apart? Parents have hopes and expectations for the future of their offspring. There are obligations to family and society that one day must be fulfilled. Do we trust that learning about love, particularly the amorous kind, will help them with that? Our religions, in sanctifying coupling, share a common mistrust of passion. Would their secretive sharing be seen as wrong?

Dante called it *l'amor che move il sole e l'altre stelle.*[2] Beatrice, the love of his life, was loved from afar. He never touched her. Dying young she became his muse and he immortalized her in *La Vita Nuova* (Bergin, 1968). This early love infused his entire life. In his poetry he tells us that the greatest happiness love can bring is in a spiritual union after death, that love is divine. I think my teens, in life, have something of the divine about them. Despite the everydayness of their situation—teenagers all over the world are sharing a similar intimacy—I am moved by their togetherness. I see it. I have been *there*. It seems a place of grace.

A more earthbound approach to love is that of La Rochefoucauld. He tells us, "Some people would never have been in love if they hadn't heard love talked about" (quoted in Handley, 1986, p. 22). Have these Japanese adolescents been watching too many Western movies? Are they trying to emulate the love relationships portrayed on the screen? Certainly, romantic love is the entertainment business's most lucrative theme. Is that so because romance is vastly entertaining, or does romance speak to everyone? Was I seeing something recognizable, familiar, in this teenage couple because it is being sold everywhere?

Romance is "existential fraud" (Morgan, 1986). In the feminist literature there are warnings that romantic love is a patriarchal myth, a myth destructive to women (Greer, 1971; Loudin, 1981). Is love—the unsettling, "you take my breath away" kind—a male conspiracy used to keep females in their place? Shulamith Firestone (1971) asserted this and added that it ought to be done away with. Is this possible? The existence of books like Lowndes' (1997) *How to Make Anyone Fall in Love with You* or Sayles' (1994) *How to Marry the Rich* suggests that there are also other motivations to loving behavior. Are these teens, nestled together by the bell, succumbing to the lure of a harmful form of relationship? Will the quickening, the excitement of their attraction for one another, become a conflict over power?

When we ask "What is love?" we call into question something basic to the way we are relationally in the world. We are wondering about our very existence. Is love a possibility for every human being? Must "love" happen to me if I am to be fully human? Is it as Kahil Gibran (1992) has written, that only with love will I laugh all of my laughter, cry all of my tears? Is love *real*? Could it be that love is a type of self-deception, a futile wish for something divine? Is romantic love a fairytale thing, a foolish thing? Could it be biology: an incentive, a lure toward the procreation of the human race? Is it an artifact of culture, prescribed and constructed for various societal purposes? Is it a hoax perpetrated on the unsuspecting? Is love all these things? And more? Is "What is love?" an absurd, unanswerable question?

Scholars have certainly dared to say what love is and their beliefs and disbeliefs have influenced our perception of love. Many explanations have been offered for "an obvious world of two." Considering these explanations seems an important step on the way to understanding the experience of adolescent love.

The Theories

Love Is Singing the World

For many scholars, romantic love comes directly from the troubadours of the eleventh or twelfth centuries (Valency, 1958; Lewis, 1936; de Rougemont, 1940/1956; Loudin, 1981; Seidman, 1991). The songs of these wandering poets of Provence celebrated *fin' amors* (pure love). The troubadours' poetry told of love in many forms—sexual, coarse, spiritual, idealistic—but in their *canso maestrada*, the doctrine of love was the song of a suppliant knight to an unattainable lady (Valency, 1958). Sometimes the knight fell in love with his lady without seeing her; news of her charms was enough. He pledged himself to her, and lived to be worthy of her love. This total devotion to an ideal of female goodness and beauty was the reversal of the real relation of man and woman in society. These were feudal times.

We can see this vision of love most clearly in the court of Eleanor, Queen of England and Duchess of Aquitaine. It was Eleanor's chaplain, Andreas Capellanus, who wrote *Tractatus amoris & de amoris remedio* (later translated as *The Art of Courtly Love*). Eleanor's daughter, Countess Marie of Champagne, was the patron of Chretien de Troyes, a writer of passionate love stories (Loudin, 1981). His chivalrous stories told of the conflicts between love and society. They always ended happily with heroic, if simple, solutions (Singer, 1984b). Eleanor and Marie established a kind of a game they called a Court of Love. They created a code of manners, a set of rules for this Court. When court was called, everyone would gather to consider some problem of love, to debate and banter. Consider this example of a love problem: Eleanor was asked to choose her preference in a lover between a young man of no virtue and a virtuous old man. Her answer was the latter, of course: Love is based on merit and virtue is to be prized (Ackerman, 1994). Love was about virtue but, according to this Court, not about marriage. Capellanus wrote:

> We consider that marital affection and the true love of lovers are wholly different and arise from entirely different sources, and so the ambiguous nature of the word prevents the comparison of the things and we have to place them in different classes. (quoted in Singer, 1984b, p. 81)

Marriage was a forced choice based on economics, politics, and familial obligations; lovers' feelings were free and personal.

How did this vision of amorous relations come to be so influential? It was actually Gaston Paris, a French medievalist, who in 1883 coined the term *amour courtois* (courtly love) and argued that it was a social ideal, a system of love (Singer, 1984b). C. S. Lewis in his 1936 work, *The Allegory of Love*, popularized that view for us today. Lewis told us that the French poets of the eleventh century "discovered or invented or were the first to express" the romantic species of passion nineteenth-century poets still write about (p. 4). Denis de Rougemont (1940/1956), in *Love in the Western World*, decries the way the stories of the troubadours, like the story of Tristan and Isolde, have led us to embrace passion. He believes we are desiring suffering, separation, and death. Romantic love, for him, calls to the dark side of human nature and leads us away from the life-enhancing love of marriage.

Maurice Valency (1958), an eloquent scholar and expert on the lyric tradition of the troubadours, finds the suggestion that they invented love to be extraordinary. He can tell us how the love poetry of the troubadours differs in important ways from the "amatory patterns" found in the literature of antiquity, but he finds the idea that a momentous psychological phenomenon was created rather ludicrous. Such a revolution would have made the Renaissance seem a very minor event. There is no sign in the economic, political, or social life of the Middle Ages that any foundational change in the relations of men and women was occurring (Valency, 1958).

We can see that the songs of the troubadours have roots in foreign places. The Crusades gave men a glimpse of a different world and they brought some of that world home with them. The influence of Arab poetry (such as that of Ibn Hazm), in which lovers are transformed in a merger of souls more delightful than any physical union, is evident in the ballads of Provence (Ackerman, 1994). There is also good evidence that romantic love was occurring outside the boundaries of Europe at this time. William Jankowiak and Edward Fisher (1992), in a cross-cultural look at romantic love, cite the most popular tale of the Sung Dynasty (928--1233), "The Jade Goddess." In this story, Chang Po loves a woman already engaged to another. His despair closely resembles that of the Romance ballads. Eloping, Chang and his lover suffer poverty and isolation and eventually are forced to return home. Chang tells her, "since heaven and earth were created you were made for me and I will not let you go. It cannot be wrong to love you" (p. 153). Words for a troubadour.

Love Is Universal

William Jankowiak and Edward Fisher (1992) tell us that the anthropological study of romantic love is virtually nonexistent due to a widespread belief that love is unique to Euro-American culture. Questioning the truth of this, they used data from works of the Standard Cross-Cultural Sample to identify those cultures in which romantic love was present or absent. Is it possible that romantic love[3] exists as a human universal?

Jankowiak and Fisher's research, the presence of romantic love in a culture, was accepted only if the ethnographer made a distinction between love and lust, and then noted the presence of love. The exception to this was if the ethnographer claimed romantic love was not present and yet provided a folktale or incident that belied this claim. Then the negative interpretation was rejected. In many ethnographies there were no detailed illustrations of romantic love so other clues were used, for instance, specific acts like elopement. Folklore proved to be the richest source of documentation. The presence of any of the following indicators in a culture qualified it to be coded as *love present* (pp. 151–152):

- accounts depicting personal anguish and longing;
- love songs or folklore that highlight the motivations behind romantic involvement;
- elopement due to mutual affection;
- native accounts affirming the existence of passionate love;
- the ethnographer's affirmation that romantic love is present.

At least one incident of passionate love was found in 88.5% of the 166 cultures studied. The remaining 19 cultures were coded as *romantic love not present*. Jankowiak and Fisher believe, however, that it was most likely that the negative cases arose "from ethnographic oversight rather than any set of cultural norms that prevent an individual from experiencing romantic affection" (p. 153). These researchers conclude that romantic love is a near-universal—which is universal enough.

Has romantic love always been a human possibility? John McGraw (1994) in an article on the universe and universality of love writes that a sign of love's significance and universality is that it is indisputably the dominant theme in all non-didactic and imaginative literature. "Of all the phenomena associated with human consciousness, love has been consistently the most universally compelling and celebrated" (p. 11). Martin Bergmann (1987) accepts the existence of love poetry 3,500 years ago in ancient Egypt as evidence of love's universality. Solomon (1988), on the other hand, disputes such claims. He believes that love is to be found only in the past few centuries and only in certain parts of the world. Examples of passionate love from the past that conflict with his belief—like ancient Egyptian poems or the Japanese poem quoted earlier in this chapter—Solomon explains away. He claims, "the rare emotion of one or two exceptional individuals (typically kings or queens or otherwise very privileged persons) hardly points to a general conception" (p. 25).

William James, considered the father of American psychology, argues that human love could not be a modern invention. Though James (1887/ 1987) writes little about romantic love, we find in his review of an 1887 book, *Romantic Love and Personal Beauty*, that he challenges the author's position that romantic love in its "bare existence" and not just its "fashion" is a late product of evolution. James writes that though "Mr. Finck devotes nearly two hundred pages of historical review to showing that love, as a cultivated modern person feels the passion, was unknown in any previous age," he fails to do so. "So powerful and instinctive an emotion can never have been recently evolved" (p. 404). As James points out, it is the ideas about our emotion and the esteem in which we hold them that differ from generation to generation.

Diane Ackerman echoes James' view in her 1994 work, *A Natural History of Love*. She argues that if you took a woman from ancient Egypt and put her in a Detroit automobile factory she would certainly be disoriented, but if she saw a man and woman stealing a kiss, she would smile and understand (p. xx). What would we find scholars saying of love if we went back to ancient times?

Love Is the Good

"Love is the only thing I profess to know about," says Socrates in *Symposium* (Plato, 1956b, p. 75). (Such a statement from *this* philosopher—it grasps us immediately.) The banquet is a celebration at the home of Agathon, the playwright, in honor of the successful opening of one of his tragedies at the Theater of Dionysos. After dinner, the guests decide against a bout of heavy drinking. Eryximachos, a physician, advises them that drunkenness is a dangerous thing, especially if one has a headache from yesterday—and many of these guests have already been celebrating. They decide, instead, to entertain one another with talk. It is proposed that they talk of love, "for we should find plenty to amuse us in the speeches" (p. 75). There are no women here; even the female flute players and dancers have been dismissed. This is how the most significant philosophical work on love is set: Male friends in the aftermath of excited celebration, full of dinner, speak of it.

Through the speeches of the guests, Plato explores and exposes various ideas about love. We recognize, however, that it isn't until the final oration, that of Socrates, that we are getting Plato's preferred rendering of love. Though he will affirm that love exists, Socrates claims he has learned about the affairs of love from Diotima of Mantineia.[4] It is this woman who has taught him—in a dialogue, not by experience—about love affairs. Love, Socrates has learned, is the desire for the perpetual possession of the good. It is excellence and beauty that we love.[5] Through love we move toward a vision of the world as it truly is. For the author of *Symposium*, the world is better understood by the lover than the non-lover (Gould, 1963). Plato envisioned lovers seeking the good from one beloved and then another, always in a quest for the higher good. Through Socrates he tells us that the right way to go to love is to begin with a beautiful thing and then:

> to mount for that beauty's sake ever upwards, as by a flight of steps, from one to two, and from two to all beautiful bodies, and from beautiful bodies to beautiful pursuits and practices and from practices to beautiful learnings, so that from learnings he may come at last to that perfect learning which is the learning solely of that beauty itself, and may know at last that which is the perfection of beauty. (1956b, p 105–106)

Aroused by the magnificence of another, the lover finds inspiration for his soul. Passion provides the energy for our journey toward perfection.[6]

Though true lovers experience physical passion for one another, they resist acting upon it, for doing so would stop them in their progress toward the highest good. The love of which the minstrels of France will later sing is similar to this, except that a beautiful and good woman is the beloved and the inspiration for a transcending existence.[7] In another work, *Phaedo*, Plato (1956a) tells of a Socratic encounter in which passion and rationality are debated. Socrates meets Phaedrus going off to memorize a speech by the great orator Lysias. The speech is the persuasive appeal of a man to a boy in which the boy is asked to yield and become the man's lover. The man argues that he does not love the boy; he espouses the merits of the non-lover. The man's admiration is rational; his friendship is available; he is in control of his emotions. On hearing this, Socrates (of course) wants to define the exact nature of the subject addressed in the speech, and he engages Phaedrus (and us) in an exploration of love. Socrates arrives eventually at the idea that man needs to love with passion and spirit—he harnesses these metaphorically together as the black (sensory desires) and white (spirituality) winged horses of the psyche. Driven by the charioteer of reason, they may take him to the summit to view the Forms (which are what a good life is all about).

Platonic love is conditional. Plato believed that what true love demands from us is recognition of the good, the ability to determine what—who—has moral excellence. The beloved must possess intrinsic value. It is that value, that goodness, which the lover seeks to possess. For Plato, then, love is not for an individual self, but for universally good qualities.

The idea that love is based essentially on qualities possessed by the beloved continues to be debated. Blaise Pascal (n.d./1966), the French philosopher and mathematician, also believed that we love qualities, not the self of another individual. Pascal argued that one's self is not the sum of one's qualities: There is a self that exists even if the qualities perish. One may lose one's judgment or one's beauty and not lose one's self. A body or soul can only be loved for the sake of qualities, not, Pascal wrote, for some abstract substance. *We*, as our *selves*, are not loved.[8]

Nussbaum (1990), in a moving and evocative piece on "Romantic Rightness and Platonic Aspiration," argues the opposite: When we love we love more than qualities (goodness); we love an individual. She holds that "love is in its essence a relationship with a particular person and that the particular features of the other person are intrinsic to its being the love that it is" (p. 334). Nussbaum imagines going out looking for someone with the good qualities of justice and wisdom or perhaps even advertising for him. The limited potential for success in this shows us that it fails to capture the way love happens. Determining the qualities of an individual is a complex thing: We become known to one another through more obvious properties and through the filters we put between others and ourselves (images, masks, and disguises). "Often I will know only that this person is beautiful and exhilarating in some way I cannot yet describe" (p. 328). Nussbaum argues for love as incommensurable. Loving someone who is intelligent and sensitive does not mean that we could love another in his or her place as long as this other has the same degree of intellect and sensitivity. Nussbaum finds that non-repeatable properties are essential to love—and there are properties necessary for a particular love, not in the qualities of the beloved, but in the love relation itself.

Brown (1987), in *Analysing Love*, takes a similar position: To love someone is to love the person as irreplaceable and to do so within a unique love relationship. Brown, too, rejects the idea that the love is based on a set of properties. Soble (1989) takes Brown to task for this, claiming that Brown has asked the right questions about love (e.g., What is the *object* of love?)[9] but finding his account of how the beloved becomes irreplaceable to be counterintuitive. Soble reaches a different conclusion in his analysis of the *eros* and *agapé* traditions of love: The eros tradition he delineates as property based: x loves y as y has S. This love is founded on the perceived merit of y, and thus is not inherently irrational, but dependent upon reasoning. The agapé tradition, on the other hand, is irrational. In this opposing view, y is attractive to x because x loves y. Love is based in x, not in y. If so, Soble argues, love is incomprehensible. To him, no love is subject-centered.

Love Is Lust

Ovid considered love "a shudder in the loins" (quoted in Singer, 1984a, p. 122). Unlike Plato, who saw love as a spiritual force and the truest reality, Ovid reacted against such idealism and claimed love as lust and carnal desire. He saw love as based in the same reproductive zest as that of other beasts. He declared, nevertheless, that humans should express themselves as lovers with civilized taste, style, and even panache. He set about to teach them how to do so. Conquest was the ruling metaphor in his "Art of Love": pursuit, capture, and surrender.

> Love, like war, is a toss-up. The defeated can recover,
> While some you might think invincible collapse;
> So if you've got love written off as an easy option
> You'd better think twice. Love calls
> For guts and initiative. (Ovid, 15 B.C./1982, pp. 101–102)

This early Roman (43 B.C.–A.D. 17/18) saw the participants in the war games of love as equals. Unlike Plato, who saw love as the prerogative of men (Singer, 1987), Ovid thought women had the right to love—that is, indulge themselves in the joys of the flesh—and that they made worthy opponents.[10] His poems of love are sophisticated, even by contemporary standards. Full of wit and humor (often black), in them eros is depicted as a dangerous pleasure, one that makes life worth living. He writes of the details of finding, stealing, and securing a lover. He advises, in "Cures for Love," how to deliver oneself from love as well. His practical approach includes a poem (unfinished), "On Facial Treatment for Ladies."

Ovid provides a perspective of love as the serious, yet paradoxically frivolous, game of life. Love is not about finding universally good qualities in a beloved as a means of achieving a spiritually fulfilled life. Good qualities in a lover for Ovid mean finesse in lovemaking: "Technique is the secret." "Technique can control Love himself" (Ovid, 15 B.C./1982, p. 166).

This cynical proponent of love as seduction at one time held a different view. When Ovid was an adolescent lover and being tutored as a rhetorician, he wrote a *controversia* advocating the passionate marriage. He argued that true love knew neither sense nor moderation and that to be calculating in love, to even weigh one's words, was *sic senes amant* (Green, 1982).[11] Scholars suggest that the girl Ovid married at the age of 16 (and left at 18), probably the Corinna of his "Amores," betrayed him (Green, 1982). In his works (e.g., "Heriodes" and "Metamorphoses") there is evidence that he had an authentic understanding of the poignancy of love and of the ways in which love can be constant and beneficial (Singer, 1984a). His philosophy of love, however, does not go beyond the lover as conquistador.

Arthur Schopenhauer (1818/1966) shares the basic proposition of Ovid that love is entirely rooted in the sexual impulse. Love for Schopenhauer is also essentially about the qualities of the lovers. This is so because love, Schopenhauer believes, is nature's cunning device. In *The World as Will and Idea,* he tells us love causes so much trouble because what is decided by it is nothing less than the next generation. His argument is that no matter how ethereal and individual love seems it is *the will to live* of the whole species. He does not deny that people fall in love or that they act as the poets say. His point is that love is a biological stratagem. Passion is the way nature ensures that the right man mates with the right woman for the benefit of the species. Random sexual behavior does not produce the kind of offspring required for the next generation. So lovers are filled with hunger for one another, tormented until they come together. Once sexual intercourse has taken place, however, things are different. The passion dissipates. Lovers discover they have deluded themselves: Love as happiness is an illusion. Schopenhauer says love never dies: Every generation will be duped in the same way.

He is preemptive of our contemporary sociobiological explanations for adultery. Schopenhauer maintains that men fall in love easily because they have the capacity to procreate many times. A woman, on the other hand, needs to fasten onto the father of her offspring for protection and care. Why are we surprised, he asks, that all societies censure adultery in women more than in men? A happy marriage according to this philosopher—and he did believe it possible, if unlikely—is one of convenience; the choices are made consciously and in the absence of desire. He leaves us one consolation: Sometimes friendship can exist between the lovers unconsciously driven together by the will of the world (cited in Singer, 1984b).

It was Schopenhauer, Freud claimed, who first showed us how much our lives were determined by sexual impulses (Singer, 1984b). For Freud, too, love was actually sex, what he termed *aiminhibited sex.* He saw love as a type of delusion. His explanation was that love is our attempt to find again the bliss of infancy when sexuality and tenderness were one. Our attempts to recover what he termed *infantile narcissism* were always doomed to failure, but out of them evolved civilization: art, culture, living successfully together. Striving for a futile goal, we soon learn to satisfy our desires through fantasy. We learn to take our pleasure in socially acceptable ways, and, by the mechanism of sublimation, turn primal sexual energy toward other less dangerous but creative pursuits, for example, composing a symphony, devising a method of psychotherapy. It is our suppressed desires—our frustrated sexual longings—that create civilization.

This propulsion by love toward a higher type of existence is likely the basis for Freud's claim that his concept of sexuality coincides with the eros of Plato. It is difficult to see any other similarity. Plato saw love as real, as the goodness of the lover must be. For Freud love was a fantasy: There is no love that is not based in sexual aggression.[12] Being in love means that one has made a misperception, a sexual overvaluation of a love-object (Theweleit, 1994). When this happens, one is regressing, going back to childhood, and idealizing the object-choice in the same way the mother was once idealized. As being in love (complete object love rather than narcissistic love of oneself) originates in a little boy's love for his mother, girls do not experience it. Freud—and here he is like Plato—believed that only men experience the state of being in love (Singer, 1984a; Theweleit, 1994). Females may have complete object love in one instance—when as mothers they give birth to a child they can love as a separate object. This satisfies their narcissistic feelings because the infant has been a part of their own body. Thomas Gould (1963) says Freud reduced love to a bodily function. I like to remember that he wrote 1,500 love letters (Theweleit, 1994) to his own object-choice, Martha Bernays.

Helen Fisher (1992) is an evolutionary anthropologist who is looking for biological and genetic roots of love. She associates human courtship with the mating rituals of other animals (e.g., foxes): Love is about survival of the species. Her postulation is that when humans came down from the trees and were forced to walk on two legs instead of four, caring for babies became a huge reproductive burden. Tools, weapons,[13] and help were needed for survival. Nomadic men could neither feed nor protect harems of females so pair bonding became the most successful way for both sexes to pass on their genes. Fisher has an evolutionary explanation for divorce. In the early hunting and gathering days, females likely nursed their infants for as long as four years. During that time mothers were dependent on males for some food and security. Once a child was weaned, however, that was less imperative. A new mate could be found. This, Fisher says, explains why divorce statistics tend to peak around the fourth year of marriage.

Contemporary sociobiologists are also arguing that the male propensity to view women as sex objects is rooted in biology and human nature. "It is a male sex-based trait just as aggression is" (Walsh, 1991, p. 233). Michael Liebowitz (1983) believes the emotions of love are neurochemical. He links such things as a new, hasty, "on the rebound" love following a failed relation-ship with the pharmacological phenomenon known as the *rebound effect*, and the possible biological basis for drug addiction with being addicted to ro-mance. The mysteries of love for these scientists reside in our biology and in the reproductive drives of our bodies.

Love Is God

The early Christians had a ceremony called the agapé in which devotions and fellowship were shared over a dinner, probably in a commemoration of the Last Supper (Love, 1991). This term, *agapé*, has come to stand for spir-itual (Hunt, 1959) or selfless love. Agapé is love as God loves: creatively, freely. As God loves even the most unworthy sinner, Christians believe we ought to love one another. This is love that creates value in its object, rather than love that is bestowed because the value of the object is recognized (Singer, 1984a). It does not strike us suddenly, but is an act of volition. It is not about desire but about fellowship and grace. Lust has no place in this conception of love. In fact, being lustful is considered the antithesis of love. Loving one another in this philosophy is a way of coming closer to God, of approaching the di-vine, for God is love; love is God.

In an attempt to be closer to God and to recapture paradise, early Chris-tians tried to demonstrate the strength of their spirit over their bodily desires. Ascetics tested the limits of human endurance by denying their bodies. They restricted and even tried to eliminate their human need for food, rest, sexual intimacy, and companionship. Elaine Pagels (1988) describes how early Chris-tians believed that they might triumph over death, not only in future resur-rections but here and now if they could break the power of natural impulses, above all, that of sexual desire. According to the doctrines of the Judeo-Chris-tian religions, death came to the human race when Adam and Eve gained carnal knowledge of one another. The story of their fall from grace can be interpreted to mean that love that includes physical desire or lust is sinful. Pagels quotes the Gospel of St. Luke (p. 128):

> The children of this age marry, and are given in marriage; but those who are ac-counted worthy of this age to come and the resurrection from the dead neither marry nor are given in marriage, nor can they die any more; for they are equal to the angels in heaven, and, being children of God, are children of the resurrection. (Luke 20:34–36)

Those inspired by this idea attempted to live the supernatural rather than the natural life. St. Jerome wrote of married love:

A wise man ought to love his wife with judgement, not with passion. Let a man govern his voluptuous impulses, and not rush headlong into intercourse.... He who too ardently loves his own wife is an adulterer. (quoted in Hunt, 1959, p. 115)

The *Confessions* of St. Augustine did much to perpetuate the belief that human pleasure was corrupt (Pagels, 1988). In the *Confessions*, Augustine describes his self-loathing at the pleasures of the flesh he enjoyed as a sinner and traces his movement away from them to finding God and unselfish love. Lust, as Augustine sees it, keeps humans from God. Augustine considers lust so powerful that Christian marriage has to impose restraints or people will have indiscriminate intercourse like dogs (Pagels, 1988). Within this philosophy, sexual love is equated with transgression against God (Hunt, 1959) and chastity and virginity are considered as divinely inspired. St. Thomas Aquinas extols the idea that it is by turning away from all adoration for women, through either matrimony or monastic celibacy, that sinful man may return to his creator. While love of a man for a woman is equated with sin, love of a man for a man is attacked with even greater ferocity (Hunt, 1959). The obstacle on this path to knowing God is primarily the risk of being seduced by a carnal, passionate love.

Loving too much is another risk. Though it may be difficult to comprehend in contemporary times, for people as late as the Victorians, love for a wife, mother, child, or friend was viewed as a possible rival to love of God (Lewis, 1960). "Love for God must come before all other" (Luke 14:26).

One of the greatest proponents of spiritual love is Dante. In his medieval writings of love, he casts it as a force that attracts us to a nobler life. He synthesizes love with religion: Love is a mode of transcendence. This belief is enacted in his imagination when he describes being guided in paradise by Beatrice, the girl-woman he idolizes as pure and angelic. In paradise those he meets demonstrate that human love finds its greatest fulfillment in the love of God. Dante does, however, understand desire and passion. He acknowledges, he emphasizes, the sufferings of lovers. For him, this is worthy suffering similar to that of the Christian martyrs. Though Dante places lustful lovers like Paolo and Francesca, Cleopatra, and Tristan among the damned, they are but in the second circle of Hell (the first being Limbo) and they are together, still moved by love. Dante saw love as a search for joy, and though these lovers transgressed, Dante is so moved by their fate, that he swoons (Bergin, 1968). Their fate is terrible to him, a denial of love's true happiness. True happiness lies in a spiritual union that culminates in the love of God alone.

John Donne (1994), a Christian theologian (the dean of London's St. Paul's Cathedral) and a metaphysical poet during the time of Shakespeare, reconciles love of God with passionate love. His poetry is about passion as well as the divine. Donne finds love is holy wherever it appears and sees it most obviously in sexual consummation. Donne does not see love as lust, but he sees the human soul as unable to experience love fully without the satisfactions of the body (Singer, 1984b). (Donne may be biased: He was a happily married man with 12 children.) His love poetry evokes an open sexuality:

> License my roving hands, and let them go,
> Before, behind, between, above, below.
> O my America, my newfoundland.
>
> *(Elegie XIX, "Going to Bed," Donne, 1994, p. 87)*

Donne's belief is in the goodness and ecstasy of sexual love. He finds nothing to prevent it embodying the spiritualness of love within it (Singer, 1984b).

The idea of love as a benevolent caring for others (that can and should be willed) appears in the writing of philosophers like Immanuel Kant and David Hume. What also appears is an acknowledgment of human sexual needs and a position regarding such needs as dangerous. Kant does not deny the possibility of sexual love, but sexuality for him is by its very nature bad. It is an appetite for enjoying another human being and thus is a degradation of human nature. Love, he finds, is goodwill, affection, promoting the happiness of others and finding joy in their happiness. He tries to determine the conditions under which love and sexuality can be combined and concludes that it is possible only in legal, monogamous matrimony (Singer, 1987). *Pathological* love is his name for non-will-governed, romantic love. *Practical* love is an attitude of concern for others that one can will. This latter love has moral worth, Kant believes, whereas pathological love can actually subvert virtue and morality (Nussbaum, 1990).

David Hume, the utilitarian, also advocates marriage and monogamy as a sensible and safer way of satisfying human needs. Marriage, however, must be based totally in friendship and not in passion. Passion can arise in a moment from nothing and fade in the same manner while friendship is based in affection, conducted by reason and cemented by habit (Singer, 1984b).

The idea that a spiritual love governed by reason and by the will is the only true love does not seem to be grounded in the selfless, Godlike nature of this love. What seems stronger is a fear and distrust of passion and bodily desire as lawless and irrational. It is Nietzsche's contention that Christianity gave Eros poison to drink; he did not die of it but rather degenerated to vice (Singer, 1987). Not only theology but moral philosophy is grounded in beliefs that do not allow for passionate love to be anything but subversive (Nussbaum, 1990). For many theologians and philosophers, women embodied this subversion. There was a correspondence with Platonic beliefs that loving a woman was ignoble, a denial of the possibility of transcendence. One theologian, St. Thomas Aquinas, argued that although woman was an inferior form of humanity (the result of a defective procreation since active male seed tends to produce a perfect likeness of itself), she was created by God and must serve some purpose. Women came to wonder if man thought that purpose was to serve (Valency, 1958).

Love Is Power

The authors of *Remaking Love* argue that eternal love, with its grand and magical meanings, is in reality about submission to male power (Ehrenreich, Hess, & Jacobs, 1986). Rather than being seductresses, women are actually the ones expected to surrender:

> Draped in mystery and mythic themes, sex itself was an act of sublimation for woman: not an immediate pleasure to be appropriated but a symbolic act to be undertaken for ulterior aims—motherhood, emotional and financial security, or simply vanity. (p. 195)

Distrust of love based in romantic feelings is fundamental to the women's movement. It is seen as predicated on a power relationship (Wollstonecraft, 1792/1975).[14]

In *A Vindication of the Rights of Woman*, Mary Wollstonecraft dramatically argues for the right of women to be educated as reasonable human beings, to be permitted to engage in healthy, active lives. She points out that in her society woman's only access to power is through charm and weakness. She uses Rousseau's prescription for the education of women to illustrate her point. Rousseau, she says, wants "woman" never to feel herself independent for a moment, but to be an alluring object of desire in the form of a coquettish slave. The ideal woman is expected to embody the soft playfulness of love whenever a man wants to relax himself with a "sweet" companion. Rousseau, she finds, only wants a meretricious slave to fondle. He would deny a woman knowledge and turn her aside from truth so that she is pleasing to him. Astonishingly, he does this in the name of love and devotion. Wollstonecraft wants a different approach to male–female relations, one not based in sentiment:

> To speak disrespectfully of love is, I know, high treason against sentiment and fine feelings; but I wish to speak the simple language of truth, and rather to address the head than the heart. (p. 27)

Her argument against love as a basis of the relationship between the sexes lies in the dangers of passion as a passing thing. "Love, considered as an animal appetite, cannot long feed on itself without expiring" (p. 73). Once love is devoured, the danger for the woman is that she is no longer a goddess but becomes more of an "upper servant." She is expected to accept this change in roles like a lady, without complaint. Young couples, Wollstonecraft warns, are wiser to check their passions and formulate a plan to regulate a friendship that only death ought to dissolve.

> When women are once sufficiently enlightened to discover their real interest, on a grand scale, they will, I am persuaded, be very ready to resign all the prerogatives of love, that are not mutual . . . for the calm satisfaction of friendship, and the tender confidence of habitual esteem. Before marriage they will not assume any insolent airs, or afterwards abjectly submit; but endeavoring to act like reasonable creatures, in both situations, they will not be tumbled from a throne to a stool. (p. 104)

Wollstonecraft's arguments were provocative and influential in her time. That her work has been reissued again and again suggests that society still has much to learn from it.

A contemporary feminist, Firestone (1971), goes beyond Wollstonecraft's position and determines that because of societies' inequalities between the sexes, love can never be fulfilled. Her position is that men, because of their insatiable lust for power, cannot know true love and that women, who can, get exploited whenever they try to love. She says it is because the social and economic oppression of women has failed to keep women in their inferior place that an ideology of romantic love has evolved. It has the same purpose: Romance is the modern means of female oppression.

Juliet Mitchell (1984), in *Women: The Longest Revolution*, summarizes Firestone's position that true erotic love is impossible in our society and compares it with Germaine Greer's position in *The Female Eunuch* (1971). Greer finds romance to be more about social class. For the rising middle class, romantic love came to replace parental coercion as that which forced one into marriage. Romance was no longer about adulterous courtly love but was embraced as leading to an establishment marriage. Rather than either Firestone's or Greer's works, it is Denis de Rougemont's *Love in the Western World* (1940/1956) that Mitchell identifies as the classical book on love. Rougemont's thesis that love and death, not love and marriage, go together—relates to her own. Romantic love is about searching for an ideal that cannot survive. Mitchell provides an analysis to suggest that romantic love was once, in the days of *amour courtois*, the male subject's search for his lost feminine self. It has become over time, however, a consolation prize for women. Romance is a woman's consolation for future confinement in domesticity—that is, if she has the luck and appeal to win a dark, handsome stranger as her lawfully wedded husband.

Madonna Kolbenschlag (1979), in *Kiss Sleeping Beauty Goodbye*, writes that women as keepers of the hearth and caregivers of the species have been condemned to the repetition of life rather than its transcendence. The romance fiction read by women perpetuates this as dreams of being rescued by Prince Charming. Rose (1985) finds in the fairy tale (the prototype for the romance script) manifest themes of unappreciated virtue, captivity, rescue, being, and waiting. The young woman waits to be validated and consumed by love. If the strong, loving stranger does not come to complete her life, she will be unfulfilled (Morgan, 1986; Nelson, 1983). "Woman has had an excuse for, and the luxury of, abdicating from responsibility for her own life, for remaining morally and existentially asleep" (Kolbenschlag, 1979, p. 20).[15]

The romance myth, on the whole, is seen as patriarchal and women's acceptance of it as self-destructive. At best, it sanctions drudgery and physical incompetence (Greer, 1971). At worst, it means that to accept a female destiny, a woman must renounce self-determination. Kathryn Morgan (1986) puts it forcefully: She finds romance immoral. It is the choice of an intrinsic evil (voluntary servility) and causes singular harm to both lovers and society.

Gloria Steinem (1992) in *Revolution from Within* discusses romance versus love. She believes that what characterizes romance is its separateness from other deep feelings—for a friend or a child, for the ocean or a sheltering tree. "What marks love is: It's all the same" (p. 282). Romance, not love, is about power. In real love you want the other person's good; in romantic love you want the other person. Steinem extols Charlotte Brontë's rendering of love in *Jane Eyre*. What she admires is Jane's refusal to be romantic. Unlike Emily Brontë's wildly passionate lovers in *Wuthering Heights*, who search for completion through one another, Jane Eyre successfully fights to keep her true self. Steinem holds up Jane's and Rochester's relationship at the end of the novel as an example of a sensitive, loving relationship. Here Jane tells Rochester that she loves him better now, because he is blind and injured and she can be of use to him, than she did when he was the giver and protector. (Steinem does not address the power issues inherent in *that* situation!) Steinem calls for a remything of love, one that will not involve power. She supports defining love as the refusal to think of another person in terms of power.

Luce Irigaray (1996) has a practical suggestion. She wants us to find a different way to say *I love you*. The dreams of adolescent girls, she says, are about sharing carnal and spiritual love with a male lover, of communication of body and spirit, of exchanging words and social activities. Girls dream about sharing love with another. Irigaray wants that to be possible for them. The phrase *I love you*, however, risks reducing the other to an object, even if an object of love. "In order to love there has to be two persons" (p. 131). Her suggested new words of love are *I love to you*. With this phrase one is saying "in you I love that which both is and becomes, that which is forever foreign to me" (p. 138). *To love to you* provides space for lovers to think about what brings them together and distances them, to think about the spacing that is necessary for their coming together. For Irigaray, loving and desiring in this way, with this phrase, would always be about questioning ("Who am *I*? Who are *you*?")[16] and about becoming.

Donna Laframboise (1996) offers a dissident feminist view of men, women, and sexual politics. She suggests that mainstream feminism is adopting an extremist view of the world in which men are the enemy. She refers to a 1991 article published in the Nov.-Dec. issue of *MS* magazine: "Orchid in the Arctic: The Predicament of Women Who Love Men" (pp. 31–33). Written by Kay Leigh Hagan, a former heterosexual who is now lesbian, the article seeks to give women who still sleep with men guidance about living life with "the oppressor." It tells women that by having sex with men they are being "intimately colonized." Women who think their fathers, husbands, or lovers are exceptional men are in denial. Hagan tells the readers of *MS* to keep one rule in mind: "if he can hurt you, he will." She advises them, also, to try to get a room of their own with a door that locks. Laframboise also reviews a 1992 book, *The War Against Women*, by the respected feminist author Marilyn French. French proposes in this work that men have been waging a centuries-long global attack on women. Laframboise paraphrases a list of 10 items French provides, which *"the vast majority of men in the world do one or more of."*[17] Four of these items are beating their spouse, murdering their spouse, raping women they know or women who are strangers, and sexually molesting female children. Laframboise sees these positions as extremist, as she does the view that all sex is rape. This latter doctrine she attributes to Catherine MacKinnon, author of a 1989 book, *Toward a Feminist Theory of the State*, who believes that consent by a female in a male dominated society is not a meaningful concept. Laframboise looks to a more balanced view of the relations between the sexes, one in which a woman can love a man without being a collaborationist.

Perhaps Simone de Beauvoir (1949/1989) captures most eloquently the position of those who conceive of love as a struggle for power. She writes: "On the day when it will be possible for woman to love not in her weakness but in her strength, not to escape herself but to find herself, not to abase herself but to assert herself—on that day love will become for her, as for man, a source of life and not of mortal danger" (p. 669).

Beyond Theory

Of the theories developed to explain love, and reviewed in this chapter, I find none to be particularly satisfying. Nussbaum (1990) claims that theories about love are too simple. "They want to find just one thing that love is in the soul, just one thing that its knowledge is, instead of looking to see what is there" (p. 283). How do we see what is there? How do we try to understand love without reducing its complexity? Saul (1995) in what he terms a *Dictionary of Aggressive Common Sense*, defines love as "a term which has no meaning if defined" (p. 194). How do we get closer to love without destroying its meaning? How do we get closer to the way it is lived?

One way might be through the love story. Stories have "a complexity, a manysidedness, a temporally evolving plurality" (Nussbaum, 1990, p. 283). Stories bring us closer to the richness, the confusion, the paradoxes of everyday life. In the next chapter some of the great love stories are briefly retold and considered.

Notes

1   "I'm On Fire."

2   "The love that moves the sun and the other stars."

3   They defined romantic love as "any intense attraction that involves the idealization of the other, within an erotic context, with the exception of enduring for some time into the future" (Jankowiak & Fisher, 1992, p. 150).

4   It is debated whether Diotima was a real woman or not. Mantineia was a city in the Peloponesus.

5   Irigaray (1989) contends that incompatible positions toward love are attributed to Diotima. One position is that love is a demonic intermediary between lovers through which they may discover what the gods have to offer; the other position is that love is a means to such offerings (immortality) through which the lovers lose each other. Irigaray favors the first.

6   "Plato resembles a tenacious mother who encourages her son to sleep with many women in the hope that he will never become attached to any of them" (Singer, 1984a, p. 68).

7   Plato's views do not support this evolution. Plato believed that those who loved women would not find their way to a soul and the only immortality for them would be in the existence of their children (Gould, 1963).

8   Pascal ends this thought (Pensée #688) with "Let us then stop scoffing at those who win honor through their appointments and offices, for we never love anyone except for borrowed qualities" (Pascal, 1966, p. 245).

9   Italics in original.

10   His later banishment from Rome to Tomis on the Black Sea was due, in part, to the "immorality" of this seduction poem (Green, 1982).

11   "Thus do old men love."

12   The possible exception to this, Freud wrote in *Civilization and Its Discontents* (1961), is the love of a mother for her male child. Freud, despite his theory, could not accept that Mama didn't really love him.

13   See Elizabeth Fisher's 1975 *Woman's Creation* for a broader version of this: The first tool was most likely a container, a carrier bag, rather than a stick or bone.

14   Although according to Sartre (1956/1994), *all* love is an attempt at domination of the other. Gender is beside the point.

15   Men's adventure script is one of independence and conquest. Their dependency needs are ignored (Rose, 1985).

16   Italics in original.

17   French's italics.

4
The Love Story

For when we read
how her fond smile was kissed
by such a lover,
he who is one with me alive and dead
breathed on my lips the tremor of his kiss.
That book, and he who wrote it, was a pander.
(Dante, 1307 A.D. quoted in Bergin, 1968)

These are Francesca's words to Dante when, in his descent into Hell, he asks her how she and her lover, Paolo, came to fall in love (and sin): They were reading a love story.[1] Love stories are powerful. They shape our beliefs and behavior (Bloom, 1993; Campbell, 1968; Christian-Smith, 1990; Fiedler, 1992; de Rougemont, 1940/1956; Highwater, 1990; Nussbaum, 1990; Rabine, 1985; Rose, 1985) and, in turn, derive their potency from our lived experiences (Bloom, 1993; Campbell, 1968; Highwater, 1990; Nussbaum, 1990). Longus, the third-century A.D. author of "Daphnis and Chloe," tells us in his prologue that he saw, while hunting in Lesbos, a painting of a love story. He is determined to tell the story he saw there. It is a tale that "will remedy disease, solace grief, bring fond recollections to him that has loved, and instruct him that has not loved" (Longus, 1953, p. 3). Such are the uses of stories of love.

Great stories not only give us a rich description of phenomena and words to use in talking about them, they shape our experience. Leslie Fiedler (1992), author of *Love and Death in the American Novel*, suggests that literature (as it expresses and defines societal conventions) tends to influence "real life" more than life influences it. In *Love and Friendship*, Allan Bloom (1993) writes: "Books about love inform and elevate the fantasy life of their readers and actually become part of the eros while teaching them about it" (pp. 30–31). Nussbaum (1990) in her collection of essays, *Love's Knowledge*, puts forward a similar belief:

So literature is an extension of life not only horizontally, bringing the reader into
contact with events or locations or persons or problems he or she has not otherwise
met, but also, so to speak, vertically, giving the reader experience that is deeper,
sharper, and more precise than much of what takes place in life. (p. 48)

Nussbaum makes the point that reading novels puts us in a position both
like and unlike real life. In reading we are active with the characters and emotionally connected with them, but we are freer from sources of distortions
that in our own lives may impede our thoughts and actions. This distance
from a situation—when coupled with the engagement a good story provides—
allows us to think more clearly about it.

This distance-engagement aspect of reading where love stories are involved is seen as a dangerous thing by Linda Christian-Smith (1990). The
author of a study of adolescent girls' experience of romance fiction, she is
alarmed that "The novels operated at a distance from girls' own lives and
provided a comfort zone where there were no consequences for risking all for
love" (p. 106). She suggests that reading romances can affect sexual orientation. "Romance-fiction reading positioned girls within heterosexuality through
their identification with heroines" (pp. 112–113). "Heterosexuality is 'legiti-
mated' and the girl readers don't question the relations between the sexes nor
dispute 'the desirability of heterosexual romance'" (p. 20). Christian-Smith
acknowledges the power of romantic tales but sees it as noxious.

So does Denis de Rougemont (1940/1956). In *Love in the Western World*
he argues that love stories cast a spell that wakens a desire for suffering and
death. Happy love is not told; it has no history, he says. "Romance only comes
into existence where love is fatal, frowned upon and doomed by life itself" (p.
15). For him, in the love story we are seduced to death.

Reik (1941) writes that "There is no such thing as a love story. Love is a
story within a story" (p. 32). He is saying, I think, that the overall tale is that
of a personal journey, circumscribed by the life of the individual. Love takes
place beyond the boundaries of any narrative. The love story, Barthes (1977/
1978) says, is the tribute the lover must pay to the world. It is others who
demand that the subject reduce the "great imaginary current, the orderless,
endless stream which is passing through him" (p. 7). Meaning is assigned; it
becomes possible to interpret, to assign causality or a finality. Barthes believes
that the lover's true discourse is an orderless stream of fragments. He tells us
that these fragments, what he calls *figures,* take shape insofar as we can recognize, in passing discourse, something that has been read, heard, felt. The figure is outlined (like a sign) and memorable (like an image or tale). A figure is
established if at least someone can say: "*That's so true! I recognize that scene of*

language" (p. 4).[2]

If we are to speak of love, we need common words. Stories, shared works that all of us can read and discuss together, give us those words (Bloom, 1993; Nussbaum, 1990). They may help us understand or open up for us the lover's discourse. Reading novels is practice for falling in love (Nussbaum, 1990). It depends on your beliefs about romantic love as to whether or not you believe this is a good thing.

In this chapter, I outline four celebrated love stories taken from different parts of the world. I've selected these particular stories because each has been identified by one or more scholars (Ackerman, 1994; Archer, 1957; Bloom, 1993; Kakar & Ross, 1986; Campbell, 1968; Wolkstein, 1991) as a proto-typical or paradigmatic tale of love. Each has endured over several centuries within the culture from which it arose. There is no space here to share the poetry and beauty of these romantic myths. I hope, however, that by includ-ing at least the framework of such primal love stories in this work, we may attend to the images, ideas, and dreams of love that shape our own. The chapter closes with a fifth story, *Romeo and Juliet*. For those in the West, it is Shakespeare's "star-crossed lovers" who come to mind whenever one thinks of young love.

The Stories

Tristan and Isolde

Joseph Campbell (1972) says of this story in *Myths to Live By:* "In the Occident the most impressive representation of love as *passion* is to be found undoubtedly in the legend of the love potion of Tristan and Isolt, where it is the paradoxology of the mystery that is celebrated: the agony of love's joy, and the lover's joy in that agony, which is by noble hearts experienced as the very ambrosia of life" (p. 160). Early versions of this story extend back into Celtic antiquity. *Tristan* by Gottfried von Straussberg (1210/1960) is the classic form of the romance. von Straussberg chose Thomas of Britain's *Tristran* of 1160 as his source (Hatto in the introduction to von Straussberg's work, 1210/1960). Richard Wagner's great opera, *Tristan und Isolde* (written while he was in love with his patron's wife), is the form in which the story is known to many.

Tristan (from *triste*, sorrow) was born to Rivalin and Blancheflor (the sister of King Mark of Cornwall). He is conceived when his father is at the brink of death—Gottfried tells us that Blancheflor "left the anguish of a love-lorn heart, but what she bore away was death" (p. 58)—and born to a mother dying of grief at his father's death in battle. He is raised in Brittany by his father's loyal friend, Rual Li Foitenant, as his own until destiny takes Tristan (he is abducted) via a Norwegian trader to Cornwall. Adventure brings him to the attention of Cornwall's King Mark, who makes the exceptional 14-year-old Tristan his royal huntsman. It is not until four years later, when Rual finds Tristan and reveals the truth, that King Mark learns the brave and handsome boy is his nephew. Tristan is recognized by Mark as his rightful heir and co-regent, and the king declares he will never marry so that this will always be so. Tristan, with 30 companions, is knighted. He returns to Brittany and, by battle with his father's enemies, retrieves his lands and properties. These he gives to his foster father and family. We see by all that he does that Tristan is a virtuous and noble youth, generous and mindful of his familial duties and obligations.

Crossing the water again to Cornwall, he finds great distress. The king of Ireland has demanded tribute: 60 of Cornwall's finest young men. Morholt, the king's brother-in-law, has arrived to collect them. Tristan, throwing a glove at Morholt's feet, challenges him to combat. Taking up the challenge, Morholt is killed by Tristan with such a mighty blow to the head that a fragment of Tristan's sword remains in Morholt's skull. The body is returned to Ireland, where the queen, Morholt's sister and a great healer, grieves deeply at his loss.

Tristan, wounded by Morholt's sword (coated with a deadly poison), is mortally ill. His only hope lies in the healing balms of the Irish queen, and with Mark's permission, he sets sail. Within sight of Dublin, his companions place him, with only his lyre, in a small skiff. Once again, Tristan's fate is connected with the sea.

Water is a significant image throughout this story. Water is the element associated with the flow of the life force, with life's underlying essence. All forms of life drink of it, yet it remains distinct from them; they come and go, it flows on. It is the mysterious force that sustains creation (Chetwynd, 1982, pp. 422–423). Water symbolizes the unconscious, with its hidden meanings and irrational wisdom. It will influence these lovers right until the end, showing us that they are moved by life's undercurrents, by its concealed, enigmatic powers. On this trip, Tristan has no compass to guide him; he goes where the sea and wind take him. He has only his lyre. This symbol of music also gives expression to the unconscious and to deep feelings and emotions (Chetwynd, 1982, pp. 274–275). It is music that will bring the lovers together.

As Tristan nears the shores of Ireland, fishermen find him and take him, believing him to be a dying minstrel, to their queen. The queen saves Tristan and, enamoured of his musical skills, asks that he teach her daughter, Isolde. For six months the minstrel "Tantris" teaches the beautiful princess music and song and reading and writing. Called by his duties in Cornwall, Tristan finally takes his leave. The ladies are saddened to see him go, this man whom they would kill if they but knew his true identity.

There is great rejoicing when Tristan arrives home, healthy and full of stories of the beauty and accomplishments of the young Irish princess. Soon, however, all is not well at Castle Tintangel. Mark is resisting pressure from his barons to take a wife, as he is determined that Tristan will be his heir. The anger and jealousy of the barons toward Tristan become so severe that the young man fears he will be murdered. By declaring that he will leave rather than live in such enmity, Tristan convinces his uncle that he (Mark) should take a wife—Isolde. Not only is she the most blessed of all maidens, but marriage to her will bring Mark Ireland, as she is sole heir to its throne.

So Tristan, accompanied by some frightened barons—for any Cornishman landing on Irish soil is to be killed by order of their king—sets sail once again. He has the ship anchor a bowshot from the harbor and goes ashore alone. With gold and a story he gains permission from the royal marshal to stay in port. At this time in Ireland a terrible dragon is causing such harm to the people that the king has sworn to give his daughter to the one who rids the kingdom of it. Tristan arms himself and goes off to fight the dragon. He kills the dragon with a sword and a spear to the heart, but is weakened by the fight and poisoned by fumes from the dragon's deadly tongue. He now lies senseless. A steward of the queen, who wants Isolde for himself, finds the dead dragon. He sees his opportunity and searches about for the dragon slayer, meaning to kill him. When he finds no one, he returns to the city and orders a wagon to fetch the dragon's head. When Isolde hears the news, she is in despair. She swears to her mother that she will kill herself before becoming wife to the steward. That night, the queen uses her secret arts to advise her. She dreams the truth, that it was a stranger, not the steward who did the deed. A search is made and Tristan is found. He is r.cognized as Tantris, and, exacting a promise from the royal ladies that he may remain in Ireland without fear for his safety, he is again taken to court and nursed back to health.

Subterfuge, disguise, and deception are prominent aspects of this story. Here the queen must resort to magic to uncover the truth, to go beneath the surface of things to discover what is truly happening. Later there will be other attempts—trials by fire, tests, tricks—to disclose what lies veiled and secret.

Isolde, in nursing Tristan, stumbles across a dark secret. She finds herself wishing that fate had given this noble-looking man the position and fortune commensurate with his looks and skill. She is falling in love. It is probably love that makes her caress his armor and remove his sword from its sheath. It is then that she notices a notch in its shaft. Suspicious and afraid of what she will find, she brings to the sword the splinter of steel found in her uncle. It fits. Tristan is revealed. Isolde, sword in hand, goes to where Tristan is immersed in water—he is in his bath—and tries to slay him; her mother stops her. The Irish court itself is prevented from vengeance by its promises, and Tristan is soon on his way to Cornwall with a reluctant Isolde as bride for his uncle.

On this sea voyage occurs an incident that marks them for the rest of their lives. Unknowingly, they share a drink that is, in truth, a love potion, made by the queen for Isolde's and Mark's wedding night. Through this mistake it is the hearts of Tristan and Isolde that turn to one another. Their doom is ensured from that moment. These two, both owing fealty to King Mark, will long only for each other.

> The two were one both in joy and in sorrow, yet they hid their feelings from each other. This was from doubt and shame. She was ashamed, as he was. She went in doubt of him, as he of her. However blindly the craving in their hearts was centered on one desire, their anxiety was now to begin. (von Straussberg, 1210/1960, p. 195)

Love's rapture and pain does begin for Tristan and Isolde. They discover— it is a major theme of their story—that one cannot have the joy of love without its sorrow. Paradoxically, they also learn that love's sorrow is not without its joy. When Brangane confesses her error with the love potion—"that flask and the draught it contained will be the death of you both!" (p. 205)—Tristan responds with these words:

> Whether it be life or death, it has poisoned me most sweetly! I have no idea what the other will be like, but this death suits me well! If my adorable Isolde were to go on being the death of me in this fashion I would woo death everlasting! (p. 206)

Joy and sorrow, life and death, honor and shame, revelation and secrecy: Such polarities are the fabric of this love story.

Isolde marries Mark and her destiny unfolds bittersweetly. She and Tristan revel in their love and yet fight it, owing fealty to the trusting king. Their lives become a struggle to keep their love hidden. But love is impossible to hide and soon all but Mark recognize that the two are lovers. Many adventures ensue in which Tristan and Isolde must use cunning and guile to keep the truth from Mark. In one, Isolde must take a test by fire to prove she has been faithful to Mark. She contrives on her way to the trial to fall into a river and to have Tristan, disguised as a poor pilgrim, carry her to shore. At her trial she swears: "That no man in the world had carnal knowledge of me or lay in my arms or beside me but you, always excepting that poor pilgrim whom, with your own eyes, you saw lying in my arms" (von Straussburg, 1210/1960, pp. 247–248). Isolde then takes a hot iron bar into her hand and is not burned. Eventually, however, the lovers are trapped. Tristan is sent on a long mission and cannot resist seeing the queen before he leaves. He notices flour sprinkled about the queen's bed, and so leaps over to her. In so doing he opens a hunting wound and the lovers are undone by a trail of his blood. Tristan manages to escape, but Isolde is to be put to death by fire. Then the king changes his mind, finding a sentence worse than death for Isolde: She is given to the lepers of the town for their enjoyment.

The transgression of love puts the lovers outside of society. Their passion for one another overcomes all loyalties, morality, duty. They become, these once blessed, admired personages, castoffs. We see Isolde put away, literally turned into an untouchable. Except to Tristan: It is from the lepers that he rescues her.

These lovers flee the society that shuns them: They find refuge in the wild. There they come across a cavern hewn into the mountainside by the giants that ruled there in heathen times. The cave is round, broad, high, smooth and snow-white, and at its center is a bed cut from a slab of crystal. It is said that the two nourish themselves with gazes of love; that they feed on nothing but love and desire. One day after they have spent many months in the wild, their refuge is discovered. Warned by the noise of an approaching hunting party, they lie apart on the crystal bed with Tristan's unsheathed sword between them. They are sleeping thus when found. Mark rejoices, believing that he was wrong about his wife, and insists that the lovers return to court. Never again in all their days are they to be so free and open, so close and familiar as they were in the wilderness.

Tristan eventually leaves the court to find relief from his sorrow, leaving Isolde in pain and torment. Without him, she feels neither dead nor alive. One day, lonely and wretched at the thought of Isolde and Mark, Tristan takes a bride, Isolde of the White Hands, but, still loving Isolde of Ireland, he never consummates the marriage. Tristan makes his way back to Cornwall and his true love.

The cycle of discovery and banishment begins again. Their story ends as Tristan, near death from a poisonous spear, waits for the only one with healing gifts strong enough to save him—his Isolde. He tells the friend sent to get the queen, if you bring her raise white sails when you enter harbor; if you do not, raise black sails so that I might prepare myself for death. As the ship enters harbor, Tristan's wife—now aware of the reason his love was lost to her—lies and tells him its sails are black. In sorrow Tristan dies, believing his love would not come to him. When Isolde reaches him, she puts her arms about him and joins him in death. They are buried side by side. Legend has it that a briar springs from the tomb of Tristan, climbs and falls to root in Isolde's tomb. Though it is cut many times, the briar always returns. Here is the ultimate message of the story: Love, stronger than will, reason, duty, honor, is also stronger than death.

Layla and Majnun

An ancient Persian tale, Nizami's (1966) version of the story was written down in the twelfth century when Sufism became one of the dominant forms of Islam. Majnun is the spokesman for the Sufi view that love is everything—we have no other task before us. I have used Gelpke's translation of Nizami here.

Qays, born in the desert of Arabia, is the son of a great chieftain. He is extraordinarily beautiful and gifted, and when old enough to study, he is sent to school where he amazes his classmates with his wisdom and skill. One day the daughter of another chieftain comes to the school. Because of her long black hair, she is known as Layla, meaning *night*. The moment Qays sees her enter the classroom, he is struck with wonder. He no longer reads nor writes, but sits and stares at this lovely girl. Layla may only respond by lowering her head, but she blushes with pleasure at his glance and smiles. Soon the two are spending their nights in dreams of one another and then rushing to school in the morning to be together. Qays tries to hide his love, knowing that he puts Layla in peril by it, but such love cannot be hidden. One day, he can stand it no longer, and rising up in the classroom, he shouts "Layla, Layla" and runs out into the streets. He runs through the bazaar shouting her name. The people watching him shake their heads and say, "a majnun" (a madman). Thus Qays becomes "Majnun."

Layla's father, learning of this young man who dares to call out his daughter's name in the streets, takes her home to her tribe. Majnun, in despair, follows her into the desert. Layla is watched and guarded by her people, but one night, restless, she looks from her tent, and there in the moonlight, Majnun appears. They do not speak, but share their fear and grief and love in one long, silent gaze. Majnun disappears back into the desert. The very names of these lovers, *night* and *madness*, express the dark, desperate, forbidden passion that they share. It is a passion beyond ordinary speech—Majnun will come to sing it.

Now, overwhelmed by sorrow at their separation, he becomes even wilder. He loses not only his heart, but his reason. His clothes in rags, he wanders, singing songs of Layla, listening to no one. His behavior brings shame and dishonor to his family and tribe, and in desperation his father decides to ask for Layla as a wife for his son. Despite the riches that are offered for Layla, her family refuses. She cannot marry a madman, even one of whose madness she is the source. Majnun's family find him other beauties, some even more beautiful than Layla, but he desires only his beloved. Refusing any consolation, Majnun leaves his people and becomes a desert nomad, solitary and demented.

In this story, too, the lover can not keep his place in society. Majnun now lives outside it in the great expanse of the desert. Layla, also, becomes an outsider, but within the tribe, separate, guarded, confined within the walls of her tent. Once the jewels of their community, except for their dreams of one another, both are now solitary.

Majnun's father, however, will not abandon his son to his madness; he tries to save his son by taking him on a pilgrimage to Mecca. Majnun, however, when in front of the holy Caaba, does not ask Allah to save him from his madness. Instead he prays:

> If I am drunk with the wine of love, let me drink even more deeply. They tell me: "Crush the desire for Layla in your heart!" But I implore thee, oh my God, let it grow even stronger. Take what is left of my life and add it to Layla's. Let me never demand from her as much as a single hair, even if my pain reduces me to the width of one! Let me love on, my God, love for love's sake, and make my love a hundred times as great as it was and is! (Nizami, 1966, p. 44)

His prayers are answered: He becomes even more inebriated with love. Like Tristan, he embraces the deadly ecstasy of his love. Layla, too, is filled with love, but she is captive and, kept in her woman's place, may speak to no one of her longing for Majnun. His voice, however, finds its way to her. His songs of love are heard by everyone, and soon they make their way to Layla's ears. She writes her answers to his words on sheets of paper and sends them out to him on the wind. Nature supports these lovers. The wilderness of the desert protects Majnun; the wind carries messages of love between them. Music forms their communication, though it is only Majnun who sings. Layla is permitted no real voice.

One day while out hunting, a Bedouin prince, Nawfal, comes across an emaciated recluse. It is Majnun. The prince is told Majnun's story by one of his men, and moved by pity, swears to bring the two lovers together. Nawfal's demands are refused by Layla's people and a great battle ensues. It is a battle Majnun will not join. "The heart of my beloved beats for the enemy, and where her heart beats, there is my home. I want to die for my beloved, not kill other men. How then could I be on your side, when I have given up my self"

(Nizami, 1966, pp. 80–81). Majnun does not exist except for Layla: He cannot be a warrior; he is only a lover now.

Though Nawfal wins the battle, Layla's father refuses to release her. It is a decision Nawfal respects. Layla is, instead, married to Ibn Salaam. He loves Layla deeply, and when she will not consummate the marriage, he continues to adore her from afar. Layla looks only for Majnun:

> Might not a breath of wind bring a speck of dust from his mountain cave? As if drunk, Layla would sometimes take two or three steps, stumbling to the entrance of the tent. There her soul, sadder than a thousand love-songs, would escape for a while, so that she could forget herself. She lived only in thoughts of Majnun, hoping for a message from him. (Nizami, 1966, p. 113)

Majnun continues to endure in the desert, and his father, dying, tries once more to bring his son to his senses. Majnun explains to his father that it is too late; he is already dead to the world. After his father's death Majnun grows more peaceful, more in touch with the desert world and the animals around him. It is as if nature now fathers him (Kakar & Ross, 1986). It seems that Majnun is totally freed from civilization with the death of his father. His being is fully within nature, which, like water in the story of Tristan and Isolde, represents unconscious forces (Chetwynd, 1982), the primal undercurrents of life itself. It will be in a garden—nature within civilization—that these lovers come as close together as they may in life.

Through an intermediary, Layla and Majnun are finally able to exchange letters of love, and to arrange a secret rendezvous. One night Layla is guided to a garden by an old man. She finds Majnun waiting for her. Immobilized by the sight of him, she seems enveloped by a magic circle she cannot break. She knows she can go no further:

> So far I am allowed to go, but no farther. Even now I am like a burning candle. If I approach the fire, I shall be consumed. Nearness brings disaster, lovers must shun it. Better to be ill, than afterwards to be ashamed of the cure…. Why ask for more? (Nizami, 1966, p. 187)

She tells the old man to approach Majnun and ask him to recite some of his verses to her. Majnun does, then suddenly falls silent. He jumps up and flees as a shadow from the garden into the desert. "Though drunk with the scent of wine, he still knew that we may taste it only in paradise" (Nizami, 1966, p. 189). Love so powerful cannot be realized on earth. This moment foreshadows the deaths of these lovers.

Ibn Salaam dies of a sickness brought on by his unrequited love, and now Layla is free. She must, however, mourn her husband for two years. Before the two years can pass, Layla dies, weakened by her own silent sorrow. Majnun learns of her death and leaves the desert to find his beloved's resting place. When he does, he embraces her gravestone and dies with the words, "You, my love..." on his lips. In this story too, it is only in death that the lovers may entwine.

Radha and Krishna

This is the story of the love of the Lord Krishna, the young incarnate god, and Radha his married and mortal mistress. For a Hindu, according to Sudhir Kakar and John Munder Ross (1986), this story is most likely remembered as a succession of episodes "seen and heard, sung and danced" (p. 76). Their story is portrayed in thousands of miniature paintings, in Indian classical songs and in the movements of an Indian dancer, depicting Radha. Episodes of the love story are sung in temples. This legend, then, is less told as a narrative than it is evoked as moments of passion, of the joy and pain of love. It is the Sanskrit poet, Jayadeva (1170 A.D.), who shaped the tale for the later poets and song writers like Vidyapati, Chandi Das, and Bihari Lal (Archer, 1957). "The story, aiming to fix the essence of youthful ardour, has an amorous rather than geographical landscape as its location; its setting is neither social nor historical but sensuous" (Kakar & Ross, 1986, p. 77). I have used William George Archer as a primary source for this story.

The young Krishna lives with Nanda, his foster father and the chief of a community of cowherds. One evening, the sky dark with clouds, Nanda asks Radha, loveliest of the married cowgirls, to escort the young Hari Krishna home through the forest. On this journey home, passion triumphs and they become lovers. For a while, Radha enjoys the love of the charming Krishna, but he is not true to her. He resumes his sexual dalliances with the other cowherd girls. Radha is full of anger and grief at his betrayal, to the point of madness:

> My eyes close languidly as I feel
> The flesh quiver on his cheek,
> My body is moist with sweat; he is
> Shaking from the wine of lust.
> Friend, bring Kesi's sublime tormentor
> to revel with me!
> I've gone mad waiting for his fickle love to change.
> (Kakar & Ross, 1986, p. 78)

Krishna, meanwhile, becomes filled with remorse. No beautiful woman any longer satisfies him; he wants Radha and goes in search of her. A friend of Radha tells him of her tormented state and he asks that she bring Radha to

him. Learning of Krishna's repentance and of his sincere love for her, Radha
dresses herself for love and waits for him at their special place in the forest.
When Krishna does not come, Radha imagines him making love to another
and is filled again with jealousy and fury. Krishna finally appears, but she
turns away from him. The separated lovers long for each other. Desolate,
Radha abandons her pride and allows her friend to look for Krishna. When
she is alone, Krishna appears and implores her to end her anger. He with-
draws and goes to wait for her in the forest. Radha, full of desire, decks herself
with ornaments and, escorted by her friends, goes to meet her ardent lover.
Left alone with Radha, Krishna sings:

> Throbbing breasts aching for love's
> embrace are hard to touch.
> Rest these vessels on my chest!
> Queen love's burning fire!
> Krishna is faithful now. Love me Radhika!
> (Kakar & Ross, 1986, p. 80)

After their lovemaking, Radha teases Krishna by asking him to help her
with her hair and clothes:

> Bind my masses of hair with a beautiful garland and place many bracelets upon my
> hands and jewelled anklets upon my feet. (Archer, 1957, p. 83)

It is said that Jayadeva, the poet, was hesitant to write that the god touched
Radha's feet—a sacrilege, as it is a sign of submission and lower status. Jayadeva
stopped writing his poem and went to bathe. When he returned he found the
verse completed (no doubt by Krishna):

> Her yellow-robed lover
> Did what Radha said.
> (Kakar & Ross, 1986, p. 81)

The love of Krishna and Radha must be shared in secret. Radha continually overcomes her terror of discovery and of the dangers (snakes, storms,
scratched and burning feet) that threaten on her way to her nighttime trysts
with the Lord Krishna. These lovers and their love, nevertheless, survive. Radha
is believed by some to have become a goddess herself.

The lovers in this tale must come together, like the others, outside of
their community. Their overpowering desire leads them away from society
and its rules and obligations. Full of passion, they meet and love in the forest.
Again love is secret, forbidden, to be hidden. Here again is a story set in the
shadows, in the night. Music does more than play a role in the love of Radha
and Krishna: The love itself is a song.

The Tale of Genji

Lady Murasaki Shikibu wrote this masterpiece probably in the first decade of the eleventh century in Japan. It is the story of the loves of Prince Genji, an emperor's son by a consort of inferior rank (Keene, 1955). In the story, which takes place when Genji is seventeen, Yūgao is revealed as his first great love. She is a girl of the lower classes, a type Genji and his friends have previously dismissed as unworthy of attention. Ironically, his love for her will haunt him throughout his life.

One day Genji, on his way to a secret tryst, stops to visit his foster mother who, having suffered through a long illness, has decided to become a nun. While he is waiting for his servant to get someone to open the gate, he looks about the street. At the house next door he sees a group of female faces, peeking through their blinds. He is certain no one can guess who he is as he has come in a plain coach with no outriders. The house is a poor dwelling but over its fence is an ivy-like creeper with white flowers among its leaves. The petals of the flowers "were half-unfolded like the lips of people smiling at their own thoughts" (Murasaki, 1955, p. 106). One of his servants informs Genji that they are called *Yūgao* (evening faces), and Genji sends him to pick some. As the servant begins to do so, a little girl comes out holding a heavily perfumed white fan. She asks, "Would you like something to put them on?" At that moment Koremitsu, the son of Genji's old nurse, comes to take Genji to the nurse. After a tearful reunion with the old woman, Genji returns to the street. He sees the fan upon which the white flowers have been laid and finds a poem elegantly written upon it: "The flower that puzzled you was but the *Yūgao*, strange beyond knowing in its dress of shining dew" (Murasaki, 1955, p. 109). The handwriting shows a breeding and distinction that pleasantly surprises him. Genji sends a reply to the poem on a piece of folded paper:

> Could I but get a closer view, no longer would they puzzle me—the flowers that all too dimly in the gathering dusk I saw. (Murasaki, 1955, p. 110)

Koremitsu is asked by Genji to discover the young woman's identity. She has lived in the house next door secretly for several months and her notes reveal that she must be a girl of good position. She is very pretty, and though she addresses the other girls as her equals, they sometimes slip and refer to her as "my lady." Koremitsu effects a secret meeting between Genji and the lady.[3]

They are not told one another's name, nor do they ask. Genji goes poorly dressed and with only one attendant. The lady is mystified by all the precautions and has someone follow him when he leaves her at daybreak. Genji throws his pursuer off. Disguise, deception, stealth: They are the conditions of this love.

Genji becomes very fond of the girl—too fond—and is miserable if anything interferes with his visits. Soon he is spending most of his time at her house. The hours when he is not with her are unendurable. "What is it in her that makes me behave like a madman?" he asks himself (Murasaki, 1955, p. 115). It is clear that he is not her first lover and that she is astonishingly gentle and unassuming to a fault. He asks himself again and again what is it that fascinates him, but he finds no answer. To her he seems like a demon lover, coming in disguise when everyone is asleep, always hiding his face. (He covers part of his face with a scarf, a practice usual with illicit lovers in medieval Japan.) His smallest gestures reveal that he is someone special, perhaps of high rank.

Genji recognizes that people are becoming suspicious and, afraid that the girl might disappear as swiftly as she came, he tells her he is taking her to a place where no one will disturb them (his own palace). She agrees in such a tone of submission that he is touched at her willingness to follow him, a stranger, in what must appear to be a bizarre adventure. When he tells her that he wants to spend entire nights with her rather than sneaking off before daybreak, she asks him why. It is then that he vows that she will be his love in this and in all future lives. She answers so passionately that she seems transformed. He takes her in his coach, not to his palace, but to an untenanted, rather desolate, mansion close by. She sees the deference with which Genji is served there and draws her own conclusions. He lets her see his face for the first time. His beauty "surpassed all loveliness that she had ever dreamed of or imagined" (Murasaki, 1955, p. 121). She will not tell him her name: "I am like the fisherman's daughter in the song, I have no name or home." But she is happy and bold; her merriment suits her. That night while she is lying beside him, Genji sees standing over him the figure of a majestic woman. She speaks to him, asking how he can think himself so fine when he brings such a common, worthless creature to toy with him. She makes to drag the girl away. Genji rouses himself and sits up. The lamp has gone out. He draws his sword and calls for the watchman to be brought. Then he notices the girl is trembling from head to foot. Nothing he does seems to relieve her. In a cold sweat, she is losing consciousness. Her servant tells him that her mistress has had nightmare fits all her life. This is surely one of these. The girl seems to sink further into unconsciousness and soon is as cold as death. Genji sends for Koremitsu who sees the girl and has her body taken to a temple. Genji tries to follow, but is persuaded to go home to the court.

The irrational, unconscious forces of life are personified in this tale by the images of demons. Genji appears to Yūgao as other than a mortal lover. A ghostly wraith arrives, outraged by the unfitness of their union. Ultimately, it is these dark forces that deny love. The lovers have been successful in keeping their love hidden, but in their revealing of themselves to one another (in Genji's literal unveiling), in their open acknowledgment of love, they call up the spirit world. Yūgao is taken from her prince.

Genji has been missed at the court and the Emperor has been looking for him. Back at the palace, Genji becomes ill with grief and his life is in jeopardy. He stares vacantly before him and bursts into weeping without warning. Many think he is possessed. (Ironically, he is dis-possessed.)

One night, speaking with Ukon, his love's former servant, he asks why the girl had never revealed her name to him.

You ask why she hid her name from you? Can you wonder at it? When could she have been expected to tell you her name…? For from the beginning you treated her with a strange mistrust, coming with such secrecy and mystery as might well make her doubt whether you were indeed a creature of the waking world. But though you never told her, she knew well enough who you were, and the thought that you would not be thus secret had you regarded her as more than a mere plaything or idle distraction was very painful to her. (Murasaki, 1955, p. 133)

Who am I to name in my prayers, Genji asks. The servant relents and tells him the girl's history. Her parents died when she was quite small and she came to the attention of a lieutenant, married to a daughter of a royal minister. Though happy with the lieutenant for three years, she began to receive disquieting letters from his wife and so went into hiding. Genji finds his love has a daughter, born the previous spring. He brings the child to his palace to be raised. It eases his misery to have some remembrance of his Yūgao near him.

Romeo and Juliet

This story, immortalized in a play by William Shakespeare (sometime between 1591 and 1597), originally appeared as *Storia di Verona* by Girolamo della Cortea and was told as a true story happening in 1303. The earliest English version is a 1562 poem by Arthur Brooke entitled *Romeus and Juliet*, founded upon a French novel, *Histoire de Deux Amans,* by Boisteau. Brooke's poem and a translation of Boisteau's novel were likely Shakespeare's sources. For his play Shakespeare reduced the period of the story from months to days (Rolfe, 1904). *Romeo and Juliet* has been transferred to film several times, including an American musical adaptation, *West Side Story.*

Romeo and Juliet, in this story of Renaissance Italy, are the children of two feuding families, the Capulets and the Montagues. They encounter one another at a Capulet feast and fall in love. Juliet meets Romeo again when he comes at night to the garden of her home. As she stands on the balcony outside her room, he overhears her sighing for him:

> O Romeo, Romeo! wherefore art thou Romeo?
> Deny thy father and refuse thy name:
> Or, if thou wilt not, be but sworn my love
> And I'll no longer be a Capulet. (Romeo and Juliet, 2. 2. 33–36)

Romeo makes his presence known, and when Juliet recognizes his voice, she asks how and why he came over the orchard walls: This place is death for a Montague. His answer: He loves, so nothing can stop him.

> With love's light wings did I o'er-perch these walls,
> For stony limits cannot hold love out,
> And what love can do that dares love attempt;
> Therefore thy kinsmen are no let to me. (Romeo and Juliet, 2. 2. 66–69)

In this moving balcony scene, the two avow their passion and love. Romeo leaves before he is discovered but the next day, with the help of Juliet's nurse and a friar, Laurence, to whom Romeo has turned, they are secretly wed. Their joy is short-lived as the family feud is heightened by the death of Mercutio, a comrade of Romeo, killed by Juliet's cousin, Tybalt. Romeo, angry and taunted at the fight, in turn kills Tybalt. He is banished from Verona.

Juliet, grief-stricken over the turn of events, is told she will be wed to one of her suitors, Paris. She turns to Friar Laurence for help. He conceives of a plan in which she will drink a vial of distilled liquor that will put her into a deep sleep for 42 hours. She will take it the next evening and thus seem dead when the members of her family come to awaken her for her wedding. As a corpse, she will be then taken to the ancient Capulet vault. Death and deception unite in this love story. Death is used as a device to deceive; death is the disguise. This love, as in the other stories, sets the lovers apart, against family and society. In fact, the lovers look for safety among the dead. The burial vault of the Capulets strangely calls up the image of the cave of Tristan and Isolde.

The friar reassures Juliet that he will write to Romeo, now in Mantua, and tell him of the plan. Romeo will surely come and, with the friar, be there for her waking. Juliet is afraid but, desperate, she does as the friar bids her. The lovers' ill fortune continues, however, when the friar with whom Laurence has sent his letter is quarantined en route. Instead of the letter, Romeo's servant Balthasar arrives with news of Juliet's death. Romeo rushes to the Capulet tomb. There, Paris finds him, and suspecting him of coming "to do some villainous shame" to the dead bodies, attacks Romeo. Romeo slays Paris, and dying, Paris asks to be placed in the tomb with Juliet. Romeo grants this wish and then turns to his still and silent bride. Wanting to join her in death, he takes a draft of poison and then kisses her. With his last breath he says, "Thus with a kiss I die." Friar Laurence and Balthasar arrive soon afterward at the tomb to find Romeo dead and Juliet awakening. They witness Juliet finding the body of her love, his lips still warm. She refuses to leave the tomb, and abandoned by the friar and alone, she snatches up Romeo's dagger. Juliet stabs herself and falls dying on her lover's body.

We are left with this terrible image of the lovers, forsaken by all, as triumphed over by death. Their innocent hopes for union seem to have been doomed from the start. And yet, this tragic ending can be seen in another light. These lovers chose death as a final act toward union. Their very dying is an expression of the belief that love cannot be denied. The friar is left to explain the deaths to the families. In shame and grief, they resolve their longtime feud: "For never was a story of more woe / Than this of Juliet and her Romeo" (Romeo and Juliet, 5. 5. 309–310).

The Course of True Love Never Did Run Smooth[4]

These stories reflect our mythical images of love: Love comes as a thunderbolt from the sky (*un coup de foudre*) or like a wind, shaking its victims. It strikes without warning as an arrow from the bow of a mischievous god: Not only Cupid, but Kama, the Hindu god of love, is so armed. It seizes us through a love potion, unwittingly ingested. Lovers are struck, smitten. In each of these stories the lovers are young, beautiful, talented. They are exceptional individuals—one, in fact, is an incarnate god—full of promise for their community and society. When love comes abruptly they respond impetuously, full of ardor. They love without reflection or calculation; love comes as an all-encompassing passion. Even if they try struggle against it, to fight it, to hide it, to overcome it, they cannot.

Once it enters the lives of our lovers, love rules over all other commandments.[5] Love moves lovers beyond petty prejudices, boundaries, the ties of family, of tribe. Love joins enemies, prince and commoner; god and mortal. Status loses its power over the lover: Lord Krishna touches Radha's feet! Passion and desire overcome rules and mores, reason and duty. The love story overturns society (Campbell, 1968). Love changes everything.

In each of these stories, love is a transgression. The loves are illicit. Secrecy is a leitmotiv in them all. Tristan and Isolde weave elaborate plots to trick the suspicious courtiers. Majnun hides his love for Layla until he can do so no longer and runs mad in the streets. Layla bears the burden of her love for him in silence. Nizami gives her eloquent words to describe a lover's secrecy:

> I have no one to whom I can talk, no one to whom I can open my heart: shame and dishonor would be my fate: Sweetness turns to poison in my mouth. Who knows my secret sufferings? I cover the abyss of my hell with dry grass to keep it hidden. (Nizami, 1966, p. 112)

Radha and Krishna meet furtively in the forest at night. Genji does not even know the name of his beloved; she sees his face for the first time the night of her death. Romeo risks death in his clandestine journey into the Capulet garden; their marriage is a covert act. The shroud of secrecy, which pervades these tales, is expressed in ways beyond the actual acts and thoughts of the lovers. Darkness is palpable in the stories.

No matter the country or culture, the place (the space) of our great love stories is the night. It is only then that it is safe for these lovers to come together: *I have night's cloak to hide me from their eyes* (Romeo and Juliet, 2. 2. 75–76). Yūgao's and Layla's very names call up the night. Night is the time of ghosts and dreams and magic. Its darkness envelops things in mystery. Juliet cries this aloud: *O blessed, blessed night! I am afeard, / Being in night, all this is but a dream, / Too flattering-sweet to be substantial* (Romeo and Juliet, 2. 2. 139–141). She is right to be afraid—the lovers' way through the dark is lit by moonlight, after all. It is the moon, a portent of love and bewitchment, that guides them.

Symbolically the moon is an image of magical transformations, unlike the sun, that never changes its shape. The moon is inconstant, ambiguous; its affinity is to the imagination not the intellect (Chetwynd, 1982, p. 269). The very word, *lunacy,* comes from the Latin, *luna,* meaning moon. *Love is merely a madness, and, I tell you, deserves as u·ll a dark house and a whip as madmen do.*[6] Madness is a part of these stories. Tristan, Majnun (madman), Genji, and Radha are all for a time *lunatics.* Madness is love's great danger, surpassing that of death. Michel Foucault (1961) says, "Madness is the déjà-là of death" (p. 16). This seems true in these tales—our lovers die.

Once the moon was believed to be the abode of the dead. The souls of the dying would leave their bodies and be silently drawn up to it. The moon also symbolized the pregnant womb, the giver of new life (Chetwynd, 1982). Our lovers, then, are guided by an orb that represents a cavern of death and a portal of life. Their lovers' journey seems ill-fated from the start, star-crossed.

Though others contribute to the suffering of the lovers by foiling their quests to come together, there are no real villains in the stories. Good people surround the lovers: King Mark, Ibn Saalam, Koremitsu, Paris. Even the characters whose actions speed the ensuing tragedies—the other Isolde, Layla's father, the friar—seem forced by their roles and by events to act as they do. In all the tales (except when one lover is a god) the quest for union is futile. The lovers' yearning to be as one fails; they are denied that ecstasy.

Kakar and Ross (1986) find that in most religious traditions of the world, the longings of passionate love are essentially a vain quest for a *unio mystica*. It is a quest that must flounder since the love is directed toward another mortal: Only in loving the Creator can a true oneness be realized. Love must transcend us and take us toward the sacred; profane love is doomed. Each of the stories ends, except for that of Krishna and Radha, in the death of the lovers. The story of Krishna and Radha may end in union because he is a god and she becomes one.

The lovers in these stories are reaching for the impossible. Passionate love in patriarchal societies—the setting for them all—can only be illicit, overturning one's dutiful life (Campbell, 1968; Kakar & Ross, 1986). "Tales of passionate love in patriarchal societies are thus also tales of sexual and social revolution" (Kakar & Ross, 1986, p. 60). Love versus honor, passion versus reason, nature versus convention: Such struggles must end in death. It is the only permissible solution. Lovers, nevertheless, feel transported beyond temporal laws and relationships. In loving, they have lost the distinction between flesh and spirit and time and eternity; they have a new sense of life in which such oppositions are one (Campbell, 1968, p. 159). In this, perhaps, lies their nemesis.

The power of these stories is that despite the hubris, the transgressions, the madness, we are on the side of the lovers. We sense that though the stories are over, the love is not. These tales seem to take us beyond the grave to an image of lovers finding a togetherness that eluded them in life. Sometimes we are given a clue, a symbol of this, like the briar that grows from Tristan's grave to Isolde's. When all is said and done, who (but the most cynical among us) can believe that these lovers have not found some eternal union of spirits? We picture them *together*—even if it be whirling in the winds of the inferno like Paulo and Francesca. There is a palpable hope in the telling of these tales that death is not the end: Love ultimately triumphs.

There is an irrationality to this, of course. Our mythical tales are meant to touch us in a way logical thought does not. They touch us emotionally, revealing dreams, phantoms of our collective imagination. Considering these love stories allows us to recognize some subconscious images of love, images that influence us unawares.

Amor

As I looked more closely at love with the help of psychological science, with that of scholarship and philosophy, and through stories of love, I recognized that I needed to express more clearly the kind of love I am trying to understand in the adolescent experience. It is not the love that exists between parent and child, nor friend and friend, but a love that has been called romantic, erotic, passionate. It involves a bodily quickening toward the other; it involves desire. It is not, however, primarily about lust. There are both spiritual (soulful) and lusty aspects to this love. I came across in Joseph Campbell's (1968) mythological work on love a way of addressing love that I find useful. He distinguishes, from agapé (charity, godly and spiritual love) and from eros (lust, sexual desire), amor:

> For amor is neither of the right-hand path (the sublimating spirit, the mind and the community of man), nor of the indiscriminate left (the spontaneity of nature, the mutual incitement of the phallus and the womb), but it is the path directly before one, of the eyes and their message to the heart. (p. 177)

Amor is Latin for love; an *amator* is a lover. The French call it *amour;* the Italians, *amore*. I will refer to the love that is the focus of interest in this study as *amorous love*. In the following chapter, I describe the way I have tried to gain a better understanding of the way in which the adolescent experiences amorous love.

Notes

1 It was ᴀhe story of Lancelot and the queen.

2 Italics in original.

3 Murasaki omits the details of this plan from her tale as they are "tedious."

4 *A Midsummer Night's Dream*, 1. 1. 134.

5 In the story of Tristan and Isolde, a love potion is assigned responsibility for this—it seems a necessary device to allow these Christian lovers to remain "good," if sinful, people.

6 *As You Like It*, 3. 2. 420.

5
A Way to Understand Adolescent Love

I wanted a way to research adolescent love that would allow me to get closer to its essential nature. Research is a word compounded of *re* (again) and *search* (to explore). *Search* has its roots in the Latin *circare*, to go around—as in the word circus, a ring (Skeat, 1993, p. 81). The re-searcher is one who is seeking (as in *rechercher*), attempting to come closer and closer to an answer to a question.

If such a quest arises from within the natural science perspective, this question will be one that addresses whether or not particular hypotheses can be confirmed or disconfirmed. The methods used will involve precise measurement; the scientist will aim for objectivity and "truth" and for an answer that will allow prediction and control of the object of inquiry. For instance, studies of love within this paradigm involve scales that rate or measure love; their results may be used to predict success in a love relationship or to identify potential problems. If the quest arises from a human science perspective, however, what the researcher hopes to capture is a greater understanding of the essence of some human phenomenon. The question is "What is this particular experience like?" Sought is a richer, deeper description of human experience. The efforts of the researcher are directed at uncovering the essence of a phenomenon. Research of this type may be used to bring us closer to *the things themselves*, to enlighten our encounters with the phenomenon in question, to promote a greater sensitivity to one another in our shared experiences.

Because my intent was to enrich my (and my readers') understanding of the experience of the adolescent in love, I chose a hermeneutical phenomenological approach to inquiry. My search was not for explanations, for abstract conceptualizations, or for a way to measure adolescent love. I wanted to know how the adolescent lives love: What is it like for the teenager in the midst of everyday life to encounter another and fall in love? What is love like when it is felt, thought about, and acted upon for the first time?

What is the meaning and significance of this experience to an adolescent? I wanted to develop a description of this experience "as it is" and, through interpretation, to come closer to adolescent love. Throughout this work, I have found the image of the researcher as one who encircles particularly apt.

Researching Lived Experience

Phenomenology is grounded in the writings of philosophers like Edmund Husserl, Martin Heidegger, Maurice Merleau-Ponty, Paul Ricoeur, and Hans-Georg Gadamer. To take a phenomenological approach to a research question is to reach toward the *eidos* (essence) of a phenomenon by studying its concrete particulars. It is the study of the world as we immediately experience it, pre-reflectively, rather than as we conceptualize, categorize, or reflect on it (van Manen, 1990). In a sense, it is making a phenomenon more visible by describing it, by using specific examples of it as it is constituted in everyday life.

There is no actual method (i.e., technique or procedural requirements) to this type of research. One attempts to look at some part of life in a way that gets beyond all the expectations and assumptions one has about it. Our commonsense certainties about the world mean we come to take things for granted, to let them go by unnoticed. To arouse them and bring them to view we need to suspend our recognition of them (Merleau-Ponty, 1962).

What is it about a particular thing that makes it *this thing* and not something else? The investigator considers personal experience and converses with others who have experienced the phenomenon of interest; reads what others have written about it; examines the words that are used to speak of it; and follows other clues found in poetry, painting, or music a means of discovery. Then one tries to put what is uncovered about the phenomenon into words. The results are a text, a written description that evokes the phenomenon, elicits it through words.

There is a *methodology* to human science research in the sense of a philosophic framework or theory that guides the work. van Manen (1990) offers a methodological structure for pursuing hermeneutic phenomenological studies that provides a meaningful guide to the process. This structure is conceived as a *dynamic interplay* among six research activities or themes (p. 30):

- turning with *commitment* to an abiding concern;
- *investigating* the experience as it is lived;
- *reflecting* on essential themes;
- describing the phenomenon through *writing and rewriting;*

- maintaining a strong, oriented relation to the question;
- balancing the research context by considering parts and whole.

I have used these activities as the framework for my investigation of adolescent love.

Commitment

Commitment in phenomenological research involves the recognition that it is a personal undertaking: The researcher cannot be placed outside the problem he or she formulates (Bergum, 1991). In the first chapter, "A Question Arises," I describe the evolution of the research question in my personal and professional life. It has also been necessary to develop a consciousness of my own presuppositions, thoughtfulness and a self-questioning attitude (Bergum, 1991). Objectivity, in the usual sense of the word, is not considered a possibility from the human science perspective. Knowledge of the life world is physically, socially, and historically embedded. Like everyone else, the researcher may only know the world—reality—from within an intentional consciousness. In the early days of phenomenology, Husserl proposed that we bracket out our preconceptions and place them aside. This would allow us to break with our familiar acceptance of the things of the world and allow us to grasp them in a new way.

The metaphor of *bracketing* as a device of *phenomenological reduction* no doubt arose from Husserl's background as a mathematician. Husserl struggled with the problematic of reduction: We are in the world always so we can never truly break with our way of seeing it. This may be the most important lesson we gain from bracketing: its final impossibility (Merleau-Ponty, 1962).

Heidegger argued that this forestructure of understandings is integral to our interpretation of a phenomenon and that, rather than bracket it, we make it explicit and acknowledge its influence (Plager, 1994). Our subjectivity is a strength if we recognize and use it in our rendering of the phenomenon. Unlike Stendhal writing of love, the phenomenologist studying love does not struggle to be dry, but rather endeavors to be strongly oriented to love as the object of study. The task for such researchers is to recognize the vantage point from which they perceive an experience and the lens through which they are seeing. "It's not that we know too little about the phenomenon we wish to investigate, but that we know too much" (van Manen, 1990, p. 4). A verse by T. S. Eliot (1987) in his poem "Little Gidding" captures for me the intent of a phenomenological investigation:

We shall not cease from exploration
And the end of all our exploring
Will be to arrive where we started
And know the place for the first time. (p. 2535)

In studying adolescent love, I have had to consider my beliefs about it. This has included the common sense preunderstandings about love that I share with others in my society, as well as the theories and suppositions of my academic disciplines. I attend to these perspectives in the chapters, "Love and Psychology," "What Love Is," and "The Love Story." Consideration of beliefs has demanded very personal reflection, as well: This work is shaped by the fact that I have experienced amorous love, as an adolescent and as an adult. In a true sense, phenomenological research involves a quest for the self. Francine Hultgren (1995) proposes that a central goal of phenomenology is to become more fully who we are. In using a research methodology that requires the personal, the novice human science researcher may experience a struggle to stay in the angst that evolves. A *letting go* is required—first of the idea of objectivity, and then that of distance—that can make us feel at risk. We are more vulnerable as we go closer and more openly toward our own and others' experience. I hesitated to write—I *resisted* writing—my own adolescent love experience. It was revisiting that experience in a deeper way that I resisted. Once I had done so, sharing it with others was not difficult and I begin this text with it. To do phenomenological research is always to question the way we experience the world (van Manen, 1990). Commitment means a willingness to stay within the unease created by that questioning.

The focus of this study, love, demanded the personal as well. Nussbaum (1990) has written: "How clear it is to me that there is no neutral posture of reflection from which one can survey and catalogue the intuitions of one's heart on the subject of love..." (p. 329). Soble (1990) prefaces his work, *The Structure of Love*, with the acknowledgment that, because of the nature of his topic, the difficulties he encountered in writing it were personal ones. José Ortega y Gasset (1941/1957;1971) believes that love is the most revealing of human acts. I agree with these philosophers that to make explicit one's intuitions about love is to self-disclose (self to self and self to other) in a very real way.

Investigating

I explored adolescent love through anecdotal accounts from persons who have experienced it. For the most part these accounts were gathered through conversations. Individuals who were willing to reflect upon their teenage loves were recruited, primarily by an article in a local newspaper, *The Edmonton Journal* (Faulder, 1994). In the article, my adolescent love experience was mentioned, along with that of the journalist. There was a description of the proposed study and a request for male and female volunteers between the ages of 18 and 24 years who were "willing to talk about adolescent love." I wanted participants who were not in the midst of an adolescent love experience, because I believed that to consider a phenomenon intently in a dialogue with a researcher could change the experience of it. This seems obvious if we imagine asking individuals in the throes of anger to describe it. The very act of pausing and reflecting moves and changes what is happening. As participants came forward, I had cause to change the stipulated age range. Some individuals over 24 years of age asked to be included in the study, saying that they thought I should hear their story. A written anecdote from a 15-year-old is also used in this work.

The desired atmosphere of the conversations was one that enabled the participant and myself to become engrossed in the description of the phenomenon freely and in as rich and deep a way as possible (Becker, 1986). Initially participants were asked to recall and describe a personal experience of love that occurred during their adolescence. They were asked to recapture this experience in such a way that essential aspects could be recognized or uncovered. It was *concrete, specific* descriptions that were encouraged—that is, personal anecdotes about being in love.

Conversation connotes better than *interview* the process that occurred. Gadamer (1960/1990) describes conversation as "a process of coming to an understanding" (p. 385). "To conduct a conversation means to allow oneself to be conducted by the subject matter to which the partners in the dialogue are oriented" (Gadamer, 1960/1990, p. 367).

All conversations were audio-taped and later transcribed. I did the transcriptions myself. I found this to be a useful strategy as it allowed a reliving of the conversation and an opportunity to make notations of such things as silences, poignant pauses, laughter. I assigned a pseudonym to each of the participants: Allan, Céline, Derek, Hari, Jocelyn, Joe, Nicole, and Veronica. I obtained confirmation from most participants on the accuracy and completeness of the conversations as transcribed, and I obtained feedback from them on my initial written interpretations. One participant did not want to view the transcripts and another was travelling in the Far East and unavailable.

Not all the "quotes" used in this work can be considered as direct quotations. Though no substantial change was made in cited dialogue and exact quotes are primarily used, some have been changed to protect anonymity. Others have been altered for the sake of brevity (e.g., omission of the inevitable "uhs" and "ehs" that occur during conversations) or to make an excerpt more concise or clearer. Two of the female participants generously shared their adolescent diaries with me and allowed me to photocopy any entries I chose. I found the diaries to be wonderful sources of the immediate feelings and reactions of adolescents in love.

"No matter how far back my love memories go, I find it difficult to talk about them" (Kristeva, 1983/1987, p. 1). Love can be a difficult subject to bring to speech. Kristeva says that the "ordeal of love puts the univocity of language and its referential and communicative power to the test" and that the "language of love is impossible, inadequate, immediately allusive when one would like it to be most straightforward; it is a flight of metaphors—it's literature" (p. 3). Alberoni (1983), a sociologist, finds that the language we have available to speak of falling in love is shaped and muted by societal institutions that wish to control it. For Barthes (1977/1978), too, the language of love is forsaken, ignored, disparaged by surrounding languages: "the lover's discourse is today of an *extreme solitude*" (p. 1).[1] Barthes also suggests that "the lover speaks in bundles of sentences but does not integrate these sentences on a higher level, in a work" (p. 7). Perhaps because the language of love is a subverted one, the lover feels stupid. ["What is stupider than a lover?" Barthes asks (p. 177).] Lovers are afraid to offer their discourses publicly without mediation. They offer a novel, a play, or an analysis (Barthes, 1977/1978). Susan Synder (1992), studying college students' constructions of love, found participants expressed concern about her reaction to their responses: It was not uncommon for some of them to preface their remarks with phrases like "You're gonna think this is stupid." Alcibiades in *Symposium* (Plato, 1956b) says that lovers, like those bitten by an adder, are unwilling to speak to anyone except another victim—as only another victim will not judge harshly what one has said and done in one's agony.

The fact that the newspaper article (Faulder, 1994) describing this study alluded to my own adolescent love story may have been significant in opening up the dialogue with participants. That I was involved in a quest to understand adolescent love as a real and meaningful phenomenon was made explicit by the article's author, Liane Faulder. This may have lessened any hesitation to speak. No one, however, shared with me an anecdote of a gay adolescent love relationship. The climate in our society is such that gay individuals may not feel safe or welcome to discuss their adolescent love experiences with a researcher who does not specifically ask for them. Where the description of my own experience, a heterosexual one, possibly encouraged others to share, it did not have that effect for gay lovers.

The *Edmonton Journal* article included a suggestion that, for those who didn't want to be interviewed, a letter describing their experience with adolescent love would be appreciated. Also, following a "First Love Contest" for Valentine's Day sponsored by the paper, the *Edmonton Journal* staff forwarded to me entries that were about adolescent love. They had previously contacted the contestants for permission to do this. When texts of letters were used in the study, I again assigned pseudonyms: Carmen, Brent, Leah, Naomi, Penny, Kate, Gerri, and Jasmine.

Literature, movies, songs, and poetry were other sources of information about adolescent love. I also explored the etymological sources of words of love and the everyday sayings about being in love. I tried to get closer to the commonsense meaning of love. Commonsense ideas are felt to be somehow true by most people and reflect custom and common consent. *Puppy love, crush,* and *falling in love* are phrases that I examined within this text. I considered metaphors, too, as conveyers of meaning (Kristeva, 1983/1987). They help define our reality, affecting thought and action (Lakoff & Johnson, 1980). Love as *madness*, love as *sickness* are examples.

During the process of this research, friends and acquaintances sent me articles, poems, and newspaper clippings; they referred me to books, movies, and songs. Many anecdotes of young love came to me in a serendipitous way. At times strangers approached me after learning about my research, wanting to tell me a friend's or their own love story. (I have named them as "informants" when I have included their words.) Once at the public library a book entitled *A Love Story from Nineteenth Century Québec* (Ward, 1986) literally fell off the shelf at me. It was the edited journal of George Jones, an anglophone adolescent who fell in love with Franoise Perreau, a francophone girl in the late 1840s in Québec City. Such readings and impromptu discussions were a great source of pleasure throughout this work.

Reflecting

"As soon as we have the thing before our eyes, and in our hearts an ear for the word, thinking prospers" (Heidegger, 1971, p. 84). A process of reflection and explication was used to gain insight into the essence of adolescent love. The existentials *of spatiality, corporality, temporality,* and *relationality* guided this reflection. This is evident in the textual structure of the resulting themes.

I determined essential themes by coming to the descriptions of the phenomenon again and again. And *again* and *again*. Herbert Spiegelberg (1972) describes this process of going from the particulars to the general as looking through the examples to the general essence. I had to keep before me constantly the question: Am I being true to their and my experience (Bergum, 1991)? I kept a journal and recorded reflections on my readings, my personal experiences, the conversations, and the anecdotes. I wrote as freely and openly as possible, trying to catch initial impressions and insights without the vigilance of an internal editor. These journal entries were useful as triggers for further, deeper reflection.

I discovered that one truly becomes immersed in the subject when taking a phenomenological approach. My awareness of teenagers, teenage couples, and lovers of all ages has been heightened. My attention is drawn to them; I see love everywhere. The idea of dwelling in a phenomenon is no longer a concept for me; it has quickened into reality. This has been so true for me that I confess I would hesitate to study a less life-enhancing phenomenon.

The Writing

When I first decided to use a human science approach in this research, I read van Manen's (1990) book, *Researching Lived Experience*. He eloquently describes in his chapter, "Hermeneutic Phenomenological Writing," the experience of creating a text. Writing a phenomenological text is seeking to make external something that is internal; it is creating a space in which meaning can be captured; it is putting into language the things of the world. Phenomenological text should reflect the fullness and the ambiguity of experience, capture what is seen and spoken, and be attentive to the silences that fill the spaces around the words we use. The reader of phenomenology faces challenges as well. The reader must bring an attentiveness and thoughtfulness to the text and "to what is said *in* and *through* the words" (van Manen, 1990, pp. 130–131).[2]

I once came across an explanation—I cannot remember where I came across it—by an artist that her sculpture was more than the work the public saw. It was also all the clay that had been shaped and formed and thrown away, all the efforts that had been expended and discarded. It would not be this work without all that. I respond to that idea. It seems to have much relevance to phenomenological work.

Reliability and Validity

Reliability and validity, being the common indices of the quality of measurement in quantitative research, cannot be similarly applied to studies using qualitative methods. They can, however, be conceptualized in a way suitable to an evaluation of the credibility of a phenomenological study. Attention to them in phenomenological research begins with disciplined self-awareness, an awareness of one's values, biases, and assumptions about the phenomenon in question. A study of this type is valid to the extent that the description of the phenomenon that emerges resonates with the experience of others who have lived through it. It lies in its power to evoke recognition of the experience: "Yes, that's it. It was like that for me."

Reliability in this kind of research relates to a sameness of meaning that emerges from a multiple view of the phenomenon. This sameness of meaning is present even though context and details within descriptions of the experience may vary. It is dependent on the degree to which the researcher is able to promote and maintain a conversational relationship to each participant and thus keep a strong stance toward the phenomenon (van Manen, 1990). This type of study requires that the researcher be visibly grounded in the place from which the phenomenon is viewed and that understandings are derived from strong and genuine involvement. The resulting text is to be vivid with concrete description, examples, and anecdotes. The inherent ambiguity and mystery of life is not to be denied.

There can be no expectation that the results of this study will be generalizable or that they will be found again if the study is replicated—in the way that is meant in the natural science paradigm. It is hoped, however, that the description of adolescent love presented here will resonate with those who have experienced it, but who were not participants in the study.

The greatest limitations of this work are situated in my abilities as a phenomenological investigator. The work is limited by the extent of my skill at uncovering the experience of adolescent love through the conversations, texts, and other sources. It is further limited by my ability to evoke, through written language, the phenomenon of amorous love as teenagers live it.

Ethical Considerations

The study was reviewed and received ethical approval by the appropriate university committee. Participants signed a consent form that delineated the activities of the research process and in which issues of confidentiality, anonymity, and the right to withdraw were addressed.

The Themes

In the following four chapters I present the description of adolescent love that evolved from this research study. I attempt to capture the essence of this lived experience through the themes of awakening, falling, being possessed, and becoming. The existential conditions of body, space, time, and relation underlie the development of these major themes.

Notes

1 Italics in original.
2 Italics in original.

6
Awakening

I'll always remember my first date. I took her to a Saturday matinee and after, I don't know how long, maybe I'd done it three or four times and I finally, maybe it was the third date, I finally got enough courage right at the beginning of the show to put my arm around her. I had no idea what to do once I got my arm around, so I left it there for an hour and a half. The pain—they could cut my arm off before I would take it from around her shoulder, but I was dying. The tears were coming up, it hurt so badly—but it took a lot of courage to get that arm around her, boy— I never even kissed her.[1]

This moment between two young people reveals some of the excitement and bewilderment—the tumult—that arises at the brink of sexual maturity. In the placing of that young male arm around a waiting shoulder, we catch a glimpse of an awakening. There is an innocence that makes us smile, but a subtle terror is evident as well.

The maturing child is opening to new possibilities, to something quite momentous, if not yet tangible. To *awaken* means "to be aroused, to be excited from a torpid or inactive state, to come to life" (Thatcher, 1984). An awakening involves hesitant movements, slowly becoming more purposeful; a vague awareness growing into an effort to be fully present. What was dormant is finding its way to existence.

This boy and girl are on a date, or what the dictionary refers to as a "courtship appointment" (Morehead & Morehead, 1981). The date likely began with a question: "Would you like to go to a movie Saturday afternoon?" and an answer: "Yes. I'm sure I can go. What time?" These simple sentences belie their meaning. Boy and girl recognize that this excursion is not really about viewing a film. It is about coming together. Within that realization lies the tentativeness and excitement that envelops such an "appointment."

The setting of their date is one favored for courtship. A movie theatre allows for a kind of public intimacy: A couple sits, side by side, facing the screen and not each other, comfortably surrounded by strangers. As the lights go down for the show to begin, they are wrapped in darkness, the sense of intimacy rising. It is at this moment, when darkness descends, that the boy reaches out. His gesture has been coming for three matinees, an *almost-motion*, tarrying in his mind. Perhaps he is following an older brother's advice: "Reach your arm out like you're stretching...." He tells himself, "Do it; do it," and with courage at last he puts his arm about her—and she doesn't move away. He savors the moment and will remember it years later.

As the minutes pass, however, the blood begins to drain from the proud arm. The arm begins to tingle, a gentle but thrilling sensation that seems rather fitting until it turns to numbness. Numb, the arm deadens. Once the embodiment of his entire movement toward her, it becomes disembodied. He cannot remove his arm; that would sever the connection he has boldly made. He realizes that he doesn't know what is to follow. He knows only that he will not go back, not give this up. *They* can't make him do that. The pain continues; he sits in agony. The moment for which he has waited, planned, has come. It is precious and now each second is felt, paid for in a manner he had not expected. Here for him, perhaps, is a foreshadowing of the cost of this new kind of attachment, of the pain that will accompany the joy of reaching out.

We know that this contact of arm and shoulder in a movie theater is not simple contact, it is a *shaping* (Sartre, 1956/1994). The boy is not taking hold of the girl's shoulder, nor just bringing his hand to that part; he is placing himself against her. Her shoulder is a means for him to discover his own body. As he feels new and different sensations in the presence of this girl (and, no doubt, others), he is beginning to experience his body in a new way. An arm about a friend, a buddy, is a different arm. This one—the arm that hugs a date—he is just learning to move. And he feels inept and clumsy. This encircling arm is the embodiment of his desire; her acceptance, a reception of connection. This touch makes their nearness different. They have achieved a tentati,e togetherness with daring, and even a sense of defiance. These youngsters are on the threshold of discovery. I picture them sitting there, expectantly facing the future as well as the screen.

Awakening of the Body

The body begins to ripen to sexual maturity in adolescence with a growth spurt around the eleventh and twelfth years. Significant changes in weight and height take place. Body hair begins to appear, muscles and breasts develop, voices deepen, menstruation and nocturnal emissions occur. There is the rounding of hips in girls and the broadening of shoulders in boys. The adolescent becomes awkward in a body literally thrown off balance by longer arms and legs. Awaiting the changes, the young teen is expectant, wondering and imagining when and how they will happen. Older siblings and friends are observed; information is gathered at school, in sex education class and outside of it; rumors are heard and considered (Flaming & Morse, 1991):

> When am I going to change? Is the book telling the truth? Are my friends telling the truth? Just wondering about the changes. About if what you hear is correct, or whether it's different. Just generally is what I read the truth? When is it gonna happen? What's it gonna be like? Am I gonna be a different person? Am I gonna be say, be more of a jerk, a nicer guy? (p. 216)

These questions are not about curiosity. They are about anxious anticipation. Something so big is going to happen to me that I will never be the same. Will I like the new me? How much time does the old me have? Is anything being hidden from me? The waiting is fraught with excitement and doubt, fear and anger.

Peter Bertocci (1982) describes talking to the 12-year-old daughter of friends about menstruation (at the friends' request) after her "upsetting" first period. He wrote that he will never forget the look on her face when he answered her question about the number of years she would likely have her period: "I can still hear her 'I will not! I will not'!" (p. 379).

This young girl was likely readied, educated for the start of the menarche. She has the information, knows what the book says will happen. It is the blood for which she is unprepared. It has started this fundamental change in her body. She is told the blood will come again and again for years and years. She refuses it.[2] But it cannot be refused. It is inevitable.

Teens are apprehensive about the coming changes, but also worry that they won't happen or that they won't happen on time. The age of onset of the maturational cycle varies. A 14-year-old can look over at his or her same-age friend and see major disparities in body size and shape. Being "out of sync" with others is a cause of grave concern. Don Flaming and Jan Morse (1991) in a study of boys' experiences of pubertal changes found that "The threat of embarrassment was so great for one teen whose pubic hair was late in growing that he was truant from school so often that he failed a grade" (p. 217). One of the boys in their study told of "this one guy" that everyone was calling "Baldo": "They say he had no hair on his, you know" (p. 217). How painful this development can be; how exposed the child becomes. Unlike some other species, the young human entering his or her metamorphosis cannot hide away inside a cocoon. The teenager evolves in public.

The adolescent must determine how to be in a new body—and how to be with others—in a different way. The changing body cannot be overlooked, taken for granted. It demands a consciousness, an attentiveness. As our body image is enriched and recast, our perceptions of the world transmute. The self and, therefore, the world are in flux. We must learn new meanings. Because our bodies locate us in the world—"Our corporality situates us in the here and now, without any alibi or excuse" (Sarano, 1966, p. 127)—changes in the body mean changes in the way we are in the world. Merleau-Ponty (1945/ 1962) describes how, when in a foreign country, one begins to understand the meaning of words through their place in a context of action and through a communal life (p. 179). There is no way of knowing it other than that of living it, of being lost in the drama that is being played out. So it is, I believe, for the adolescent in a developing body.

The drama unfolds as the bodily response to others, and of them to you, is altered. For the adolescent there is significant uncertainty. Parents and others sometimes treat adolescents as if their general maturity equalled their physical maturation. The six-foot-tall 14-year-old may face expectations appropriate for a young man, while his still small friend is treated as a boy. When my son was in Grade 9, I went along as a chaperon when his class visited France. On the flight over, a steward—going by appearances—offered a children's puzzle game to one student and wine to another. The former was mortified; the latter looked elated.

Some parents physically pull away when their child begins to develop "secondary sex" characteristics. They no longer bestow hugs and kisses, particularly in public (Haas & Haas, 1990). This may be a function of a new, ambivalent reaction on the part of their adolescent to such gestures, the "ill at easeness" that parents sense. The teenager, despite such ambivalence, may feel distanced, isolated, and even rejected by this change in relationship with parents and others (Haas & Haas, 1990).

The adolescent's new sexualiz.d response to others creates more uncertainty. The reaction of a maturing body is a source of potential embarrassment. When the French class arrived at a beach at Nice, I was surprised to note that, though the girls ran about, most of the boys just stretched out on the rocks. I knew from their talk of the trip that this was the place they had been waiting to see, and here they were, just lying face down on their towels. Then it dawned on me. The French women at this beach could choose to go "topless," probably the very reason Nice was the most anticipated stop. Once here, however, the boys couldn't trust their pubescent bodies not to betray them. Several of the girls in the class covered their bathing suits with large T-shirts—perhaps because of the unspoken but heightened awareness of breasts within the group—and, with this gesture of concealment, made their young, developing bodies more apparent and visible. The image of these students on the beach captures for me the raw vulnerability of this time of life. Eager, full of promise, they hesitate, revealing and concealing themselves. They are in transition, and still unsure of what is unfolding within them.

The Time of Awakening

Situated in the ripening of the body that occurs at puberty, this unfolding permeates their existence. Of this time of life Rousseau (1762/1966) wrote: "Then it is that man really enters upon life; henceforth no human passion is a stranger to him" (p. 173). We see their stirrings in the way they are with one another. I recall a moment when I was caught in the hallway of a junior high school as the bell released the students from their classrooms. As they clamored past me, I noticed how self-conscious they seemed with one another. A boy was showing off with a football, ostensibly for the benefit of his buddies beside him, but his eyes kept straying to a girl nearby. Girls sauntered along, talking so loudly that I knew their conversation was meant for other ears. I watched small flirtations being enacted around several lockers, and a girl across the way who was closely following a smiling boy's progress down the hall. The adolescent's move away from childhood was strikingly visible up and down that hall.

Karen Labahn (1995), a music teacher, writes of her students in the "Voices" column of a local newspaper: "They are an interesting blend of mind and bodies, these Grade 8 band students." "I did find them frustrating last September, all these mouths, arms and legs unleashed from their real classes to produce copious amounts of noise in band class. They talked, they socialized. Just one big party every other day." As she examines her frustration, she notes that they are in love with music, even band music. "Their passion is almost sexual in nature, and I prefer innocence at this age. As do their parents." In her brief description, she captures something of the intensity of this time of life: The noise, the social tumult, the ardor by which music (or sports or dance or drama) may be embraced as the adolescent being-in-the-world becomes "sexualized." In her wisdom, she surmises that it is adolescents' move away from innocence that unsettles the adults about them, not their noise.

G. Stanley Hall (1920a, 1920b), in the first major work on adolescence, written in 1904, described teenagers as psychologically equivalent to Adam and Eve when they first knew they were naked. He said teenagers are opening their eyes to a special consciousness of sex. MerleauPonty (1945/1962) describes sexuality as an atmosphere that is at all times present. It is an ambiguous atmosphere, coexistent with life. Sexuality, without being the object of any intended, specific act of consciousness, underlies and guides our experience. The adolescent is becoming conscious of this, and discovering the sexual undercurrents that pervade our existence and touch us as human beings.

In Turgenev's (1950) *First Love*, Vladimir, the narrator, recalls of his 16-year-old self:

> I remember at the time the image of woman, the shadowy vision of feminine love, scarcely ever took definite shape in my mind: but in every thought, in every sensation, there lay hidden a half-conscious, shy, timid awareness of something new, inexpressibly sweet, feminine.... This presentiment, this sense of expectancy, penetrated my whole being: I breathed it, it was in every drop of blood that flowed through my veins. (p. 24)

Something—new, sweet, powerful—is awakening in Vladimir. He feels it, indefinite, subtle, yet so strong it seems in his blood, in his very breath. It is as if some secret aspect of life is being revealed. Max van Manen and Bas Levering (1996), in their book on children and secrecy, evoke the strangeness and mystery that surrounds this discovery. They use the story of a young girl, Hedwig, from a 1990 novel by the Dutch author Frederik van Eeden, to do so. In the following excerpt, Hedwig is at a party:

> She saw how the boys liked her and admired her looks. The dance had started, and a strange, but not painful, amazement widened her eyes when she saw the nasty gestures and angry eyes of two boys who both thought to have been first in asking her to dance.
>
> The adults had started to dance too, and they became noisy and gay. Hedwig observed them with enraptured attentiveness, because now there was something new in their behavior, something queer. There was a certain understanding in their eyes and in their smiles—as if they all knew a secret which the children did not understand, but that now needed to be hidden less carefully, since there was a party going ⌐n and everybody was happy.
>
> To see this was nice but also somewhat frightening. Hedwig thought the older women too old, and now less deserving of respect. Not less kind, but there was something like betrayal in the manner in which they spoke and behaved with the men with whom they danced; very different from the manner in which they somewhat artificially turned to the children. (cited in van Manen & Levering, 1996, pp. 194–195)

van Manen and Levering (1996) describe the child encountering the incomprehensible dimensions of sexuality as living a form of secrecy that does not require a solution. "Some secrets in life are not just obstacles in front of us, rather they dwell in us as mysteries that touch our entire being" (p. 195).

Hedwig and Vladimir know something is happening to them and around them. They are *on edge*. One of life's mysteries is beginning to open to them. The discovery that this mystery is never fully revealed will come later.

Thomas Gregory (1978) in *Adolescence in Literature* finds that the powerful role sex plays in puberty is apparent in many stories about adolescence. The overt sexual issues, however, remain on the edge or are bypassed altogether, with the primary theme of stories being the adolescent crush. The narration of such stories is typically done with humor as a way of defusing the tension of the experience. With humor, the potency of this time is made less frightening.[3]

An illustration of this is the fictional account of an English schoolboy, *The Secret Diary of Adrian Mole*. Written for teenagers, the book has been a great hit with its young readers. My children read it in junior high school and found it—in a comforting way, I think—hilarious. The author, Sue Townsend (1982), captures the anticipation and realization of a first sexual attraction like this:

> There is this new girl in our class. She sits next to me in Geography. She is all right. Her name is Pandora, but she likes being called "Box" Don't ask me why. I might fall in love with her It's time I fell in love, after all I'm 13 $3/4$ years old.
>
> Thursday, January 15.
>
> Pandora has got hair the colour of treacle, and it's long like girls' hair should be. She has quite a good figure. I saw her playing netball and her chest was wobbly. I felt a bit funny. I think this is it! (pp. 17–18)

The possibilities that Pandora opens up for Adrian fill his diary. The diary ends a day after his fifteenth birthday when he writes, upon discharge from the hospital where he has had a model airplane removed from his nose, "Love is the only thing that keeps me sane…" (p. 187).

Like Adrian, many adolescents are expectan. This could be it! They are not always certain that they are ready for *it*, nor how they will learn the new movements that will be required. (What's it going to be like? Am I gonna be a different person? A jerk? A nice guy?) Sometimes they feel ready, but life just isn't serving up the opportunities:

> January 17: Dear sweet good loving understanding God—hear me, please. I'd love to go on a date with someone SOON. (Myrna Kostash [1987], excerpt from her diary, age 16)

When the opportunities do come, the adolescent can vacillate, posed hesitatingly on the edge.

In a delightful 1976 movie by Truffaut, on growing up, *L'Argent de Poche,*[4] two boys, about 13 years old, convince girls whom they've just met to go to the movies with them. Bruno is bigger than Georgie, more confident; the date is his idea. Once in the theatre, Bruno has his arm around one girl and after only a few moments leans over and kisses her. Georgie and the girl beside him are watching. They look at one another and she mutters, "What idiots!" Nevertheless, she looks hopefully at Georgie. Georgie turns to stare intently at the screen. Soon the girls change places. The new girl beside Georgie finds him staring even more intently at the screen. There is a shuffling of seats so Bruno can place an arm about each girl. Georgie is left to the movie.

Georgie is sitting in a movie theater beside a strange girl because he wants to be like his bigger friend. Bruno knows how to act around girls. This is what Georgie wants to learn, knows he is expected to learn. Now, in the theater, he only has to follow his friend's lead. In fact, everyone is waiting for him to do so. The expectancy of the moment sits there in the air, palpable. Even Georgie is waiting to see what he does. He does nothing. He's not ready, even though he wants to be. The test over, he is free to watch the movie, somewhat disappointed, somewhat relieved.

James Joyce (1916/1992c) in *Portrait of the Artist as a Young Man* captures this vacillation in his character, Stephen Dedalus:

> She too wants me to catch hold of her, he thought. That's why she came with me to the tram. I could easily catch hold of her when she comes up to my step: nobody is looking. I could hold her and kiss her. (p. 70)

But he does neither and, when he is sitting alone in the deserted tram, he tears his ticket into shreds and stares gloomily at the corrugated footboard. The next day, Stephen sits in his room and tries to begin a poem he will dedicate to the girl. He doodles on the cover of his writing book instead. "Now it seemed as if he would fail again but, by dint of brooding on the incident, he thought himself into confidence" (p. 71). His verses tell of the moon and the night and the breeze and, when the farewell comes, the kiss "which had been withheld by one was given by both" (p. 71). Finished, Stephen hides his notebook and, going to his mother's room, stares for a long time at his face in her dressing table mirror.

Stephen has found a way to give the kiss, though he paused before this moment as well. On the tram with the girl, Stephen feels as a tranquil, listless watcher of this scene in his life. He yearns to enter the stage boldly and, looking for a clue to when and how that time will come, tries to read the answer in his own countenance.

The Space to Awaken

In *L'Argent de Poche,* one of the girls, kissed by Bruno, pulls open the top of her shirt and peers down. She smiles. We sense that she is pleased. The changes in her body are taking her into a new world, one she is discovering she likes. At the door of the theater, she had not been so certain but agreed with her girl friend that they could "try it." This "it" is learning to be with those who stimulate new sensations. It is moving toward a different kind of relationship, a new kind of intimacy. "It" at the moment is taking place in a movie theater, but it could be set at a school dance, in a park, at a skating rink, or during a party in a basement recreation room. There is a common factor among the settings: This new movement toward another is a movement away from the family and takes place in a space away from them. The adolescent must find this space.

In our society, we see adolescents pulling away, keeping more to themselves, psychologically and physically. They like to stay in their rooms; they leave the dinner table as soon as they are excused. They may grumble about visiting relatives, and have to be dragged along on the family vacation. Friends and peers are becoming the focus of their attention and interest (Mitchell, 1979, 1986; Sebald, 1992). Teens turn toward an intimate relationship outside their kinship group. In some societies, this separation is not supported; the space is unavailable. Jung Chang (1991) describes this in *Wild Swans: Three Daughters of China* when writing of pre-revolutionary China:

> In fact, falling in love was considered almost shameful, a family disgrace. Not because it was taboo—there was after all a venerable tradition of romantic love in China—but because young people were not to be exposed to situations where such a thing could happen, partly because it was immoral for them to meet, and partly because marriage was seen above all as a duty, an arrangement between two families. With luck one could fall in love after getting married. (pp. 22–23)

Members of such societies do experience romantic love but live it differently. For them, it is not an expectation that romantic love will occur and provide the basis for reproduction, for marriage. "Lover" is not a role to which they are expected to aspire. Our society is different: Amorous love is expected, at least as a prelude to marriage. The space to learn and explore is usually given or found. Still the learning is something of an underground event, sometimes literally occurring downstairs. As Céline recalls:

> Dances and parties in junior high—that's where you learned to kiss and stuff. We would go to this girl's house who lived near school. We'd go there and sit in the living room. It was so uncomfortable. I had trouble looking directly at any of the

boys; I'd keep looking down or around at anything in the room. Somebody, usually a guy, would take charge. Two people would be chosen: "All right, you and you. Go downstairs to the back room. You and you, go to the other room." When you were chosen you'd go and you'd have to kiss. That's how I got kissed for the first time. Everyone knew that I liked this one boy. We were chosen that day. We went down the stairs, acting reluctant. Neither of us really were. I wasn't, but I felt nervous. We went into the room and left the light off. He kissed me on the lips. It was nice. Then we went back upstairs. The others would sometimes play "spin the bottle," but I refused to do that. About a year later, there was a party where all the girls necked with all the guys. We were all good friends and it didn't seem like a dirty thing or anything. It was a big thing to me, actually—I felt like I really needed the practice.

Like Céline, my memories are of basement parties with a record player, drinks, snacks, and an edge of self-consciousness. Though we would occasionally catch a little brother or sister peeking down the stairs—and thus adding to the furtiveness of the gathering—parents, for the most part, stayed upstairs. Parents become chaperons in adolescence. This change in parental roles signals further to teens that they are coming of age, that they have entered new territory. Now, when they are together it seems "something" could happen. We want adolescents to learn what they must to assume healthy adult roles, but we are full of caution. For them to take their first steps, we know we have to let go. Our skill lies in finding ways to keep our arms close by, to steady them or stop them from falling.

The night I arrived to pick up my daughter from her first dance in junior high, I found out quickly that I had no place there. I was a few minutes early and went inside the school to wait. The mortification on her face at seeing me *inside* the school doors was enough to ensure that I waited in the car thereafter. I had to learn how to supervise and guide her as a parent, and yet not intrude. I can see, looking back, that my daughter and I made the necessary space for her together.

In the movie *Man in the Moon*, a father sees his 17-year-old daughter off on a date. He asks the boy if he has enough gas in his car, and tells him, "You're responsible for my daughter for the next 5 hours and 7 minutes." As the young couple drive off he says, "I remember his father at that age." Another day his younger daughter comes running home after swimming with a boy. The father smiles at her happiness and tells her to "invite him to the house. Bring him around once in a while where I can get a good look in his eyes." The boy does come by later, and the father, having to leave, trusts the two to be alone together to wait for the girl's sister. The subtleties of parenting a teen are expressed here, it seems to me. This father wants his daughters to grow and learn and take on life. He knows the joys this can bring—we see it in his smiling response to his youngest's excitement. He also knows the dangers. His protection is not broad-handed, however; he is attentive to the particulars. He judges carefully—taking each situation as it comes. He makes himself strongly present to one young couple as they drive off—for 5 hours and 7 minutes—but senses that he can more safely be absent from another couple. Real parents, who like this movie father know their teens need to explore—are *going* to explore—must discover for themselves (the movie father gets a script; we don't) the safest way to grant them the freedom to do so.

As adolescents begin this exploration, questions arise for them. Anticipating a new kind of encounter, teenagers, like Céline and her friends, wonder "What am I going to have to do?" "How am I to behave?" "How do I do that?" as in "How do I get my arm around a shoulder?" "How do I kiss someone?" Unlike friendship, which until now they have comfortably experienced with one another, an amorous relationship is going to require some bodily expression. Lovers do things like holding hands and kissing. Holding hands doesn't present too big a problem—even as children, they have gone hand in hand with another. It is the kissing part that concerns them. This amorous kiss won't be like previous kisses, given to parents, aunts, little brothers and sisters. Nor will it be like the stolen boy-girl kisses of the playground, done on a dare. There is a quality of intimacy possible with a lover's kiss that is unique. A first kiss is a symbolic move toward the other. Though they sense this significance, adolescents initially are concerned with getting the technique right. How mortifying, if when the time comes with that special person, they don't know where to put their nose!

Alone, adolescents try kisses on the backs of their hands, or against the bathroom mirror, or with a clutched pillow. But "In love-play one does not really give a kiss, but it is enacted by both together" (Linschoten, 1987, p. 167). Perhaps that is why the party games of young adolescents exist—to provide safe partners-in-training. The device of a game provides a boundary and limits are placed around the exploration. The physical contact is play. It is explicit that this is a game. (Implicitly, things may be different—everyone knows that Céline likes, wants to kiss, her partner.) Game players are "ordered" to go kiss; a spun bottle determines who will proffer the other mouth; everyone will neck with everyone else. Necking with every boy distances meaning—this is, after all, only practice.

Guides for this practice are found by teens. One source of instruction—as well as a practice setting—is the movies. A movie is a space to which the young go to learn about love. Allan Bloom (1993) argues that the young need to rediscover Eros and the language of love by returning to the great works of literature, but the movie theater is where they are going. (Fortunately, great love stories may sometimes be found there. Shakespeare's *Romeo and Juliet* is a hit at my local theatre right now; Jane Austen's stories are on screen as award-winning movies.[5]) Put on screen or in written text, the love story teaches teens about romantic love. One meaning of story is "a set of rooms" and a related Low Latin word, *instaurare*, means "to provide necessities" (Skeat, 1993, p. 473). We may think of the love story as a space where some of the necessary stuff of romance may be found. In that space, romance may be experienced vicariously. There, like Stephen Dedalus in his poem, we can in our imagination move toward the other with certainty. Lovers in our stories embrace each other and the possibilities that may elude the reader in real life. There has been concern about the power of this at least since Dante.[6]

Storied Space: Romance Movies, Fiction, and Song

One of my participants provided an illustration of how the movies influence the adolescent's conception of amorous love. Hari told me that he had "pulled a Harry." I didn't understand so he explained: "You know, the New Year's Eve scene in *When Harry Met Sally*. He realizes he loves her and starts running to where she is." I did remember it, and it brought to mind others—Woody Allen's run to his teenage lover in *Manhattan* (1979) and Ben's run to Elaine's wedding in *The Graduate* (1967). "Run to her"—literally—is an image the screen had provided this young man.

Whether one considers romantic love as a societal invention (*Some people would never have been in love, had they never heard love talked about*—La Rochefoucauld) or a phenomenon fundamental to the human experience (*Any time not spent on love is wasted*—Tasso), one recognizes that it is culturally conditioned. We are "bombarded with the pervasive concepts of romance on every side—in the songs we hear on the radio, in the novels, magazines and newspapers we read; in the television shows and movies we see" (Loudin, 1981, p. 3). Love is a favorite theme of all entertainment as it is the only subject that interests everyone (Singer, 1984a). Our mass media are a source of meaning, both reflecting and constructing our understanding of romantic love (Lowery & DeFleur, 1988). Stanley Cavell (1984), a philosopher who speaks and writes seriously about Hollywood films, says that, as movies are made to satisfy the tastes of a mass audience, a movie's success at the box office reflects mass sentiments. This, if nothing else, he believes, makes movies worthy of thought and interpretation.

It is a facile generalization that popular cinema portrays life (and love) only as simplistic and unproblematic. At their best, movies can call into question a culture's knowledge to itself, reflecting doubts and ambivalence concerning basic assumptions (Cavell, 1984). What do the movies of today express about love in our culture? Many of the most successful romance movies are about recognition: How do we know our true love?

Two exemplars of this theme are *When Harry Met Sally* (1989) and *Sleepless in Seattle* (1993). The latter is a story that suggests that we will know, as if by magic, our true love—even though he or she be a stranger:

> It was magic. I just knew we were supposed to be together. It was like coming home, only to no home Id ever known. I was just taking her hand to help her out of a car and I knew. It was like magic. (Sam)

The storyline of *Sleepless in Seattle* implies that if we are brave enough to act on an intuitive knowing, we can find our love. *When Harry Met Sally* has a related message: We can recognize our true love, but some of us may take quite a while to do so—even if the person is right before our eyes. (Without magic, this recognition takes Harry and Sally twelve years.) The audiences of both movies are comfortably omniscient—the characters are such that it is certain they belong together.

A variation on this theme of recognition is also popular. After determining someone is the beloved, the hero/heroine then discovers that he/she has made a terrible mistake. In *Moonstruck* (1987), a young Italian widow soberly agrees to marry an older man and then falls in love with his estranged younger brother (while the troubles in her parents' marriage and the sensual score of *La Bohème* run in the background). In *While You Were Sleeping* (1995), another out-of-hope woman gets matched with the wrong brother. In *The Truth About Cats and Dogs* (1996), a fellow falls in love over the phone (and later makes love via this bit of technology!) with a radio host, who considers herself plain and not the type men want. In this story, a modern, female version of the classic *Cyrano de Bergerac*, the heroine has her neighbor, a classic "dumb blonde," take her place. The question is raised, of course, with whom is the hero really in love?

In the cinema, recognition is only the first of many difficulties the lover encounters. We can find our love, know it is right in the marrow of our bones, and then be too afraid to act on it, or meet obstacles (as great as death) that keep us apart. Love thwarted by societal conventions is the theme of many favorite movie romances: by class in *An Officer and a Gentleman* (1982), by class and age difference in *White Palace* (1990), by status in *The Age of Innocence* (1993), by fame in *The Bodyguard* (1992), by religion in *Witness* (1985), by misconceived dignity in *The Remains of the Day* (1994), and by marriage and family in *The Bridges of Madison County* (1995). A movie that calls into question our most fundamental ideas of whom we may love is *The Crying Game* (1992). Here a British soldier, held hostage by the IRA, becomes friends with one of his captors before he is killed. The Irish friend seeks out the dead man's lover, falls in love himself, and makes, along with the audience, a very shocking discovery.[7]

Love's power over death underlies at least two contemporary cinema stories, *Ghost* (1993), in which a murdered man comes back to save his love, and *Truly, Madly, Deeply* (1991) in which a young woman, grieving at the death of her musician lover, is startled to find him in her apartment as a seemingly alive ghost. These ghostly lovers refuse to leave their beloveds, a different slant on the old classic, *The Ghost and Mrs. Muir* (1947), where the heroine meets and falls in love with the specter of a sea captain. Other screen romances—*Casablanca* (1942), *Roman Holiday* (1953), *An Affair to Remember* (1957), *Doctor Zhivago* (1965), *The Way We Were* (1973), *Annie Hall* (1977), *The Year of Living Dangerously* (1983), *The Unbearable Lightness of Being* (1988), *Untamed Heart* (1993), *Four Weddings and a Funeral* (1994), *Circle of Friends* (1995), *The English Patient* (1996), *The Mirror Has Two Faces* (1996), *My Best Friend's Wedding* (1997), *You've Got Mail* (1998), *Shakespeare in Love* (1998), and *High Fidelity* (2000)—illustrate the twists and turns, joys and sorrows that Eros may bring. A movie about romance stories is *Romancing the Stone* (1984). It is a new take on pulp fiction romance—the heroine is a repressed novelist who finally experiences her own romantic escapade.

Some examples of movies where adolescents are the heroines/heroes include the following:

Better Off Dead (1985): In this comedy and caricature of contemporary America, a high school boy falls to pieces when his girl friend ditches him because she "can do better." He figures he is better off dead With the support of a pretty French exchange student who moves in across the street, he ultimately channels his death wish into a ski contest with his ex's new jock boy friend.

The Crush (1993): A 14-year-old girl's unrequited love for a young journalist, Nick, turns into a search for vengeance. Befriending the girl turns into a nightmare for Nick as he becomes a romantic fixation for her. The film writer, Alan Shapiro, based the story on his own experience with a teenager.

Flirting (1992): Set in an Australian boarding school around 1965, this is a rich and witty story of first love. Two students, Danny and Thandiwe, are brilliant, independent, and ostracized by their classmates (mostly for their brilliance and independence). Their flirtation starts as they recognize one other as kindred spirits and evolves until they are separated: She's caught in a coup in her African home and he in the anomie of the outback.

Mad Love (1996): Falling in love at a "7 Year Bitch" concert, two teens end up on the run. The girl seems fun and flamboyant until she pulls a fire alarm during the boy's SAT exams. A suicide attempt follows and she ends up in a psychiatric unit. She flees with him until he realizes how ill she really is.

Man in the Moon (1991): The summer when Danielle becomes 14 years of age, she discovers love and death. The boy she loves falls in love with her older sister, Maureen. Neither wants to hurt Dani and they struggle with what to do. It is a tender but dark story. At a moment of joy—he is throwing his hat in the air—a terrible accident occurs.

My American Cousin (1985): This is a coming-of-age story set in 1959, based on the director's personal experience. A girl learns about love through her infatuation with her handsome American cousin.

Romeo and Juliet (1996): This is Shakespeare's play set in our time. The lovers are still caught up in and overcome by tragic circumstances and the tyranny of their elders but guns, in this version, take the place of swords.

The Summer of '42 (1971): An autobiographical account (by screenwriter Herman Raucher)[8] of a 15-year-old boy's infatuation with a 22-year-old war bride. Love, sexual discovery, and death combine in this story of young love.

Titanic (1997): Rose and Jack find one another on board the ill-fated Titanic, despite the fact that she resides in first class and he in steerage. Forbidden love, destiny, courage, and survival are the themes.

It seems that the dark side of love and life is a strong undercurrent in the movies specifically focused on adolescent love. There are madness, death, the terrors of being different. Even the teenage crush, normally dismissed as puppy love, becomes a deadly thing put on screen. It is different from adolescent literature where, according to Gregory (1978), lightness and humor predominate.

Music—the food of love[9]—also shapes our expectations. This seems such a truism that some believe the songwriters of twelfth-century France, the troubadours, invented romantic love. Cavell (1984) describes how the love songs performed by Fred Astaire and Ginger Rogers in their movies affected him as an adolescent. For instance:

> Heaven, I'm in heaven
> And the cares that hung around me through the week
> Seem to vanish like a gambler's lucky streak
> When we're out together dancing cheek to cheek.

was experienced by his adolescent self—"though I would have lacked as yet words of my own in which to say so" (Cavell, 1984, p. 5)—as if "there were a region of chance and risk within which alone the intimacy emblematized or mythologized in the dancing of Astaire and Rogers is realizable" (p. 6). Cavell found life wisdom in the lyrics and in the images of joyful dancing of these Hollywood musicals. He reminds us not to discount the power of popular cultural offerings.

Donald Horton (1957), a sociologist, suggests that popular songs provide us with words (a conversational language) for dating and courtship. He analyzed the songs of June 1955 as published in magazines of lyrics. He found romance was the dominant theme: 83.4% of the songs were conversations about love. The songs could be placed in a framework of courting phases (p. 575):

- prologue (wishing and dreaming);
- courtship (direct approach, sentimental appeal, desperation, questions and promises, impatience and surrender);
- honeymoon;
- the downward course of love (temporary separation, hostile forces, threat of leaving, final parting);
- all alone (pleading, hopeless love, new beginnings).

"The drama reflects the dialectical progression of a complex and difficult relationship, and this is undoubtedly the character of romantic love generally and of adolescent love in particular" (Horton, 1957, p. 577). The songs, Horton believes, help the young, inarticulate lover: They can be used as messengers to the beloved. Once love is experienced, the songs acquire personal meaning and are used to translate cultural patterns into personal expression and promote a sense of identity. Horton emphasizes the adolescent search for identity in relationship:

> The working out of a socially valid and personally satisfactory conception of himself and his role in relation to the opposite sex is one of his most urgent tasks, at least in contemporary America, where so much of the responsibility for this phase of development is left to the young people themselves, aided by their cynical and somewhat predatory allies of the mass media. (p. 578)

I explored Horton's idea of songs as a courtship dialogue by completing a content analysis of popular songs[10] (Austin Hurtig, 1992). I categorized the lyric samples and tested for significant difference (using a chi square equation) between the song themes of 1955 and those of 1991. Although the majority of the 1991 songs (66%) had love as their dominant theme, love was significantly more often a theme in 1955.[11] The love songs of 1991 did fit the framework generated by the 1955 analysis. There were no songs in the prologue phase but the songs were representative of the other phases. No significant differences between categories were found except for "all alone," which had significantly more representatives in 1955 than in 1991. This may be due to the inclusion of "country" songs (which Horton referred to as "mournful") in Horton's sample.

In the analysis, I found the songs provided metaphors for love. In nearly a fifth of the songs, being in love was described as a dream (e.g., Is there someone who can make me / wake up from this dream?—"Spending My Time"). Other metaphors included love as a storm, a guiding light, a silly game, a god. A belief expressed in many of the songs was that the lover will do anything for the beloved ("All 4 Love," "Do Anything") and does everything with the beloved in mind ("[Everything I Do] I Do It for You"). As I write this, in fact, the radio is playing a song with a chorus that goes "Anything at all / you got it, baby." Love songs, like movies, provide words, images, and potentials for action.

Scripts are also provided by popular romance fiction. A *romance* ("popular book" in Old French) originally meant a book written in the vernacular (Fallon, 1984).[12] Once fables of love, adventure, and war, romances are now novels in which the love story moves the plot. There are literally millions of regular romance novel readers—primarily female (Fallon, 1984; Nelson, 1983), making them a significant cultural influence. Rose (1985) explains how novels shape romance and desire and provide a blueprint for gender behaviors. It can be argued that this blueprint has disastrous effects on the lives of women, that romance novels are major contributors to the societal lesson that teaches men to dream big and women to dream of big men.

Despite their popularity, women often read these novels covertly or defiantly.[13] They hide them inside another book or beneath a plain book cover. There is an illicit aura about romance fiction. Other "escapist" genres— mysteries, science fiction, westerns—do not carry the same taboo. (One can read an Agatha Christie anywhere.) Perhaps Virginia Woolf was correct:

> Speaking crudely, football and sport are "important"; the worship of fashion, the buying of clothes "trivial." And these values are inevitably transferred to fiction. This is an important book the critic assumes, because it deals with war. This is an insignificant book because it deals with the feelings of women in a drawing room. (Woolf, 1929/1977, p. 81)

In romances, love and domesticity are treated as universal issues of human life, not peripheral concerns. It may be that romance novels are disparaged precisely because they are female fiction (Fallon, 1984).

Christian-Smith (1990) analyzed adolescent romance novels and identi-fied an implicit code of romance within these texts (p. 17). The code, she says, is as follows: Romance is a market relationship, a heterosexual practice, and a transforming experience, giving meaning and prestige to heroines' lives. Romances are about the dominance of men and the subordination of women and about women learning to relate to men. Romance is a personal and pri-vate experience. This code is at the center of the concerns and criticisms aimed at romance fiction. Christian-Smith's study indicated that teens read romances for the same reason as adults do (Ramsdell, 1987): As an escape from prob-lems at home and at school, as better reading than dreary textbooks, for en-joyment and pleasure, and to learn what romance and dating are about.

Christian-Smith (1990) finds that romance in teen novels is organized as an exchange relationship, where fair terms are established. These terms are coded as gender qualities. The female's are fidelity and devotion; the male's, status and special privileges. Heroines may give up their freedom to the male, but they expect to be cherished and protected in return. Teens, however, com-bine the romance texts and real-life experiences and are stimulated to think about themselves as females and about the gender tensions they face. The teens studied were clear that, though the world of romance was an enjoyable one, they recognized it as make-believe. They may like castles in the air, but they don't expect to live in them.

Since Samuel Richardson's time,[14] romance novels have provided instruc-tions for their readers regarding the nuances of romance.[15] Not unlike songs that provide courtship dialogue, these works teach ways to recognize the signs and symptoms of love. How do we know if someone is attracted to us? What are the clues? Who is worthy of love? Who may deceive us? How do we attract another? What to wear? What to say? A perspective on sexual desire is also to be found. Assiter (1988) claims romance fiction is as much a form of pornog-raphy ("the representation of the eroticisation of the relations of power be-tween the sexes" [p. 103]) as *Penthouse* or *Playboy*, though from a female perspective. The romance hero is always a consummate lover (Nelson, 1983). Heroines, however, respond; they do not initiate. Most fundamentally, their sexual passion is legitimized by an overwhelming love.

Teens are trying to determine how to assume the role of lover. When they look about the world for guidance, the messages of movies, music, and fiction are ready to hand. The media presence shapes the space in which ado-lescents explore, in which they struggle to understand the emotion, the desire that is awakening in them.

Awakening to the Other

> I am at a party and I meet this girl. I am very friendly and attentive—I act real interested in what she is saying. All the time there are two conversations going on—one with her and one with myself in my head. Every time I say something to her, I go over it, weighing its effect.
>
> "I saw you dancing. You looked good."
>
> Maybe I shouldn't have said that; she'll think I'm just interested in her body.
>
> Which you are.
>
> Don't let her know that, stupid.
>
> It's like a game and I have to figure out my moves as I go along. I know she is probably going to have to think I really like her a lot to let me get physical with her.

Joe, the boy at the party, doesn't believe that romantic love exists. For him, even if others refuse to admit it, love is really all about sex. Engulfed by his sexual urges, Joe figures that what he has to learn is how to "unleash" these urges safely. He wants to find a way to satisfy himself that will be socially permissible. After watching and listening to those around him, he decides that males must hide a quest for sex with the trappings of love. He must learn how to cover over what Céline refers to as a "dirty thing." The trappings of love, he figures, are necessary for a girl to acquiesce. Like other adolescents, Joe is trying to make sense of his physical experience. He struggles to integrate a new physical imperative within the context of his life. He feels pressured. Joe, too, is asking: "How should I act in relation to the other?"

> I felt such a drive for sex. It was there 24 hours a day. It seemed everything I thought and did was motivated by sex. It was like this power that you needed to unleash—and you just didn't know how to control it. You've got to do something to stabilize it, to fit it into your life.

Joe searches for what society expects him to say and do. As a pubescent boy in an all male Catholic high school, Joe struggles with his "urges" and worries about masturbation—a "sin" he seems unable to resist. He recalls a conversation when he was 14 with the priest who was his spiritual advisor at the school. He was asked, during this regular assessment of his religious life, if he masturbated:

> It was unbelievable to me that he would ask that. I was so worried that someone would find out my secret and here I was being asked directly. I was in shock. I looked down at the desk and then at the floor. I never said anything. Then he asked, "How many times do you do it? Once a month?" At that time I was doing it every night. I didn't say a word. "Once a week?" I was frozen. "Every day?" I didn't

want to admit anything. I felt really guilty. "Where are you doing it? If you're going to do it, do it in the shower." I just sat there. The priest spoke. "Okay, Joe, I think you might have a bit of a problem. I want you to go to confession." I was so scared. I thought I was going to die. I ran to the confessional line-up right away. I told the priest there everything. I ended up sitting in the church for a half hour doing "Our Fathers and Hail Marys." I went home just humiliated.

Joe is ashamed and afraid of his sexual urges. Yet denying them seems impossible; he can't. Secrecy seems impossible, too. One day his father takes Joe into the bathroom, pulls out his own penis, and explains to Joe how to clean himself after sexual intercourse. There, that's how to avoid "the clap." That was it. Joe doesn't quite understand what his father is telling him. His father assumes he is at risk for getting gonorrhea? It's okay, just protect yourself? His father, he knows, considers women as something less than men. There are good women like his mother, but other women—women who arouse a guy's sexual urges—are objects more than persons. With his father, as in his interview with the priest, Joe is silent, embarrassed, and confused. It is with relief that he finds some reassurance in the locker room joking and kidding of his hockey team:

> Everybody is suffering from the same thing you are without really talking about it. So you joke around—even about masturbation.

Joe's experiences tell him sex is a powerful thing. He comes to see it as sinful and illegitimate but as part of being a man. It is there every day and all the guys are having trouble with it.

The solution some boys find isn't for Joe. One of his close friends has a steady girl. Joe sees this friend as trapped, forced into an intimacy that he has to endure for the sake of a sexual partner. His friend has to do all that "guy stuff" like acting protective, plus he has to spend time with her when he could be hanging out with his buddies:

> I wasn't interested in bothering with going through the motions of seeing someone, of building up a friendship, of taking all this time.

Joe discounts the possibility that his friend and the girl are "in love." His idea of love echoes that of Freud: Love is lust combined with the ordeal of civility. Joe wants to find an acceptable solution for dealing with this. He wants to solve the mystery, discover the secret. How is he going to be able to get his needs met without getting into trouble? He looks for clues in the dry, dispassionate information of sex education class, in the coarse advice from his father, in the warnings and admonishments of his church, in the jokes and antics of the locker room. He tries on the surface behavior, learns the lines that are expected and schemes to "make it" with available girls. For Joe, sex seems to be something girls have that guys try to get.

Harry Stack Sullivan (1953), in his theory of human development, describes lust as a new dynamism in the self-system as a result of puberty. Sullivan asserts that at adolescence the genitals must be integrated into an approved and worthy social self. The body is becoming ready for reproduction and this new capacity must be accepted and incorporated into teenagers' understanding of themselves. Arousal and sexuality need to become an accepted component of the self-image.

The awakening desire for sexual satisfaction, however, collides with a pressing need for personal security. This security, encompassing self-esteem, feelings of personal worth, and an absence of anxiety, becomes threatened by the possibilities of embarrassment, confusion, humiliation, shame. Sartre (1956/1994) puts it this way: The Other reveals the world as a world of desire, and with that the world becomes "ensnaring" (p. 392). As Derek recalls,

> I'd get sick to my stomach; a deep ache in my gut, a dryness in my throat, a tightness—I couldn't swallow. It seemed kind of like guilt. I didn't have a very good self-image at the time and I remember thinking that everything—maybe because of my family was very religious and strict—that anything pleasurable must be sinful and so you should feel guilty about it. Christians weren't supposed to have fun, to have pleasure—not physical pleasure, anyway.[16]

Here Derek is describing how he feels around Amy. He senses something unlawful about his feelings. He attributes his queasy stomach, dry throat, and sense of choking to guilt—Amy's a "very curvy" 15-year-old. His awakening "instincts" affect his experience of her and he is lustful. *Lust*—dictionary definitions of lust read "longing desire; eagerness to possess or enjoy; but also allude to depravity, as in unlawful desire of sexual pleasure" (Thatcher, 1984, p. 505). For Derek, there is a sense of transgression associated with his response to Amy. *They* out there disapprove.

Like Derek, the young man who reached bravely for the shoulders of his date in a darkened movie theater was also aware of a *they* somewhere, out there. "They could cut my arm off before I would take it from around her shoulder." *They could cut off his arm!* How dangerous this bodily movement toward the Other seems.

Heidegger in *Being and Time* (1927/1962) says that in our existence, Being-with-one-another, we stand in subjection to Others. We situate ourselves in terms of them; they are a constant care. *They* are not definite individuals nor *some people*. Others are an anonymous *they*. "The they" (*das Man*) is everyone and no one:

The "they," which is nothing definite, and which all are, though not as the sum, prescribes the kind of Being of everydayness. The "they" has its own ways in which to be. (p. 164)

"They" maintains itself in everydayness, demands averageness and "keeps watch over everything exceptional that thrusts itself to the fore" (p. 165). It is not surprising that the adolescent, feeling the first stirrings of passion, becomes more conscious of this generalized Other. Love arouses us from the everyday. Desire heightens our bodily awareness of the world and of the Other's presence in it. What lover feels *average*?

Connie, a girl interviewed for Myrna Kostash's (1987) *No Kidding*, finds herself the object of four boys' attention. One has offered to take her to a movie Friday night; another has invited her to a party; two others are hanging around her at school, making each other jealous. "This is fun," she thinks. Her girl friends, however, pull her aside. Everyone is talking about her. She better choose one guy, and fast. "*Guys*[17] can fool around with a bunch of girls at once, but for a girl it's different" (p. 121). "She looks, you know, sluttish" (p. 121).

Connie is initially happy and excited by the admiration and attention she is receiving from the boys at school. Boys like her—she must be *desirable*. They want to be with her; they are even competing with one another to be with her. She feels special, exceptional. It feels good to be liked. Fun. Fun, until her spontaneous enjoyment of the boys and their movement toward her gets redefined. Her friends, girls who care about her, tell her "No." This is not permissible. Girls who have boys "after" them mustn't be seen as encouraging them. Girls can't openly enjoy being pursued, wooed. Not by a lot of boys, anyway. Girls who openly enjoy are suspect. People are talking about her. Teenage boys "chasing" a girl are interested in something more than friendship. They are aroused. Connie is the stimulus of that arousal and a potential source of that something. She could be giving the ı what they want: slut.

Hall's Adam and Eve analogy does seem apt. Along with the special consciousness of sex awakening in the pubescent child is the discovery of an undercurrent of forbiddenness. Grien (quoted in Linschoten, 1987) describes the vague sexual desire of a young girl in her puberty:

> I took off my nightgown and looked at my body.... I admired the whiteness of this flesh which I had never seen; my hand placed itself on it and received a sensation of delightful freshness, and I asked myself why this would be bad. (p. 153)

Teenagers may be admonished about the potency and dangers of passion and desire long before passion and desire are fully present to them. The forbiddenness may take an opposing form: Sex can be made to seem nothing special, just a biological act. Kostash's girls also told her about how guys get "their rocks off." Girls let them—and then get taken to the movies. Teens learning about love and sex may accept the dictates of "the they" and never venture for themselves.

Perhaps here lies the real danger: The adolescent awakening sexually may choose to keep within the everyday and, like Joe, find a way to gratify desire without the risk of a relationship. The capacity for reproduction is realized but not the possibility of love. In *A Circle of Friends*, a 1995 Irish movie about young love, a teenage girl is seated in a theater with a date. We see his arm reach out and move across her—but he doesn't embrace her—he grabs her breast. The difference between this movement and that of the other young man reaching for his date is one adolescents must come to discover, if they are to learn to integrate desire with intimacy.

Notes

1 This quote is from a study by a colleague, Roberta Hewat, who was interviewing couples about their experiences with a crying baby. The father recalled this first date when he was describing his reluctance to place his sleeping baby in the crib.

2 Her story reminds me of my childhood friend who began to menstruate at 11 years of age. She stamped her foot and shouted at her mother, "No! No! I won't have it! I won't have it!"

3 Flaming and Morse (1991) found that humor was a major coping strategy for boys dealing with the embarrassment of pubertal changes.

4 *Small Change.*

5 There is also a contemporary American interpretation of *Emma* in the movie, *Clueless*.

6 Dante's Paolo and Francesca succumbed to passion while reading the story of Lancelot and Guinivere.

7 I do not want to reveal here the surprise that awaits the lover. It is sufficient to say it changes nearly everything.

8 According to Infobusiness's 1993 *Mega Movie Guide*.

9 From the opening line of Shakespeare's *Twelfth Night*.

10 Identified weekly as "Canadian Top 10 Hit Picks" in the Entertainment Section of the *Edmonton Journal* from September 24, 1991, to December 26, 1991.

11 In 1991, 15% of the songs were about "life" (getting ahead or surviving); this was not a category in the 1955 analysis. This may indicate a change in the concerns of today's teens who, when compared with the youth of 1955, may feel their future is less assured.

12 De Rougemont (1940/1956) believes otherwise. He says it comes from the Romania of the troubadours.

13 Writing a paper on "the romance myth" in graduate school, I discovered that I didn't want to be seen reading these novels at the university. Several of the readers of romances

whom I interviewed for my paper began our discussion with a defensive statement: "Look, I don't smoke or drink, I'm entitled to this vice"; "It beats Valium"; "Feminists may hate them, but I enjoy Harlequins."

14 Richardson wrote *Pamela*, the first British romance novel, that is, a novel in which the love story moves the plot, in 1730. *Pamela's* storyline has evolved into a formula for modern romances (Modelski, 1982).

15 Germaine Greer (1971) in *The Female Eunuch* notes the emphasis on clothes, objects, and settings in modern romances and suggests that the essential character of the romances is the ritualization of sex.

16 For Derek, sexuality was fraught with confusion. In his strict, religious family he was being sexually abused by his stepfather—the only thing he kept from Amy. He hid his hurt with what he calls a "macho-stud-football player" image.

17 Italics in original.

7
Falling

> I was sitting at a table in the big open area of the school with my buddy, Louis, doing some homework. I looked up and saw this girl I'd never seen before. She was walking across the room and going up the stairs. I was totally blown away. I jumped up and said to Louis, "Come on. That's the girl I'm going to marry!" I ran after her up the stairs and followed her to a locker on the other side of the school. It was lucky Louis did come after me. He was in "band" with the girl at the next locker, and we struck up this conversation with both of them. I don't know how we started talking, but I remember saying something about hair. I said something about wanting to shave my head and she said, "I don't know about that!"

Derek and Louis have sat here on other mornings just like this, aware of fellow students going by. Sometimes there has been only a dim recognition of this ebb and flow of classmates. Other times, welcoming a distraction from homework, they've gazed appreciatively at the girls or watched out for friends. This particular morning, however, Derek is so struck by the sight of a girl that he leaps up and chases after her. Louis has noticed the girl too, but his eyes returned to his book unaffected. He is surprised and confused by his friend's reaction and it is only loyalty that brings him to the chase. It is Derek who has been blown off "the cliffs of the heart" (Rilke, 1989a, p. 143).

Derek, on this school morning, seems to have recognized a girl on sight. "That's the girl I'm going to marry," he says. Like Louis, we are confused at Derek's reaction, particularly his certainty. How can he know a strange girl to be *the* girl, the one he wants to marry? This does not seem possible. A glance and he knows he wants to spend his life with this person? Still in that moment, Derek has no hesitation, no doubt. We might wonder if the abandoned homework is a certain Shakespearean play. Romeo and Juliet love immediately, without reflection. Juliet, upon noticing Romeo, directs her nurse to "Go ask his name," claiming: "If he be married, my grave is like to be my wedding bed" (1.5.136–137). Allan Bloom (1993) in *Love and Friendship* calls *Romeo and Juliet* "the purest description of the phenomenon love" (p. 274), saying it reveals the charm and vulnerability of lovers, loving freely, impulsively, without calculation or constraint. Derek, like these other young lovers, impulsively acts on his feelings. Is Derek under the influence of a classic love story or has Shakespeare captured in this play a true possibility of young love?

Veronica:
I first saw him at a track meet. He was... I thought, "This guy is so neat." I had no idea that he was going to my school. And then, when I got to school a few days later I was walking down the hall and I saw him. I thought, "Wow. What a great guy." I got to meet him soon after because I was trying out for the track team and he came out to help with training. I started putting myself wherever I thought he might be. I even asked his advice about another boy. I guess you could say I went after him.

Allan:
I'll never forget when she walked in the room—it was kind of weird because—well, the first thing I noticed was her hair. And when she walked in the room—I don't know—I felt something for her. I thought, "I've just got to know this person." She was a foreign student, new to the class. The teacher gave her the desk in front of me. I stared at her hair the whole class. It just kind of went from there.

Nicole:
I was talking on the phone to a friend of a friend when her brother came on the line. That's when it began. We started talking on the phone for hours. We'd try to picture what one another were like. I'd say, "What are you wearing?" and he'd tell me and then ask me what I was wearing. "What music do you like?" We would go on and on trying to learn about each other. I fell in love with him without ever seeing him.

Carmen:
I was with a friend at an outdoor cafe when I noticed workmen climbing out of a nearby manhole. As I casually watched them, the last man appeared. He was the most beautiful man I'd ever seen. I said to my friend, "That man there. If he asked me to marry him right now, I'd say yes." We laughed as the men climbed into their truck and drove away. "Great," I thought, "My first sight of him will be my last." I returned to that table daily in the weeks that followed, eating my lunch while I stared at a manhole. The man of my dreams never came back.

Jasmine:
I was camping with my family when I met this boy. His eyes twinkled and he had this enormous smile. By the time he said "Hello," I was in love. We sat around the campfire, talked, played games, and walked the beach. Before the week was out, we pledged ourselves to one another.

Brent:
She just lived down the block but we really never met. One night I went to a party with friends and I saw her. Her radiance caused my heart to jump into my throat.

I had never believed in love at first sight, but this girl had a smile I will never forget. She was smart and laughed at my jokes, and I just knew she would be important to my life.

Naomi:
He had beautiful long blond hair and always wore a green plaid lumber jacket that matched his green eyes. He sat in the desk in front of me in English class. I loved his hair, loved his eyes, loved that jacket. He let me wear it one day in class because I was cold; I sat there, wrapped in his jacket, feeling as though I was wrapped in his love.

Kate:
We were both on the yearbook committee. That was all we had in common, but at the Christmas dance, we ended up dancing together a little longer and more often than most of the others. He started coming to watch my basketball games and I tutored him in French. One night I was talking to him on the phone and he said he was coming to school early the next day. I asked him if he had a test and needed quizzing on something. He said, "No, I'm coming to be with you." I felt so warm inside.

Derek and these other teens are describing what they call *falling in love*. This is a common phrase: We know what they mean. It is almost too common a phrase. "I fell in love with this dress in the store window." "I fell in love with golf the first time I played." "We fell in love with Bermuda last summer." Trite usage of the words has taken away some of the power behind them.[1] If they are spoken with care, however, when someone tells us that they have fallen in love, it is a momentous claim. In fact, it is so momentous a claim we may be tempted to reply to these teens that they have not *truly* fallen in love. Could Eros come to a 16-year-old, doing his homework?

What is it "to fall in love"? Literally, to fall means "to sink from a higher to a lower position"; "to die, to perish, be overthrown"; "to pass into a new state, especially with suddenness or through inadvertence or ignorance" (Thatcher, 1984, p. 316). Fal¹ing is a sudden motion. It implies an immediate, downward change. We drop, sink. It is an involuntary movement. We are over-*thrown*. If choice is involved, we seem to use a different verb. Parachutists dive; stuntmen leap; thrill-seekers bungee jump. The lover falls.

Falling from the Everyday

When we fall, the ground—solid and expected—is suddenly lost beneath our feet. We cry out in shock. Our equilibrium disturbed, our arms flail in an attempt to regain it. We move awkwardly, without grace. How foolish we must look! Falling, we are *off* balance, unstable, outside the ordinary flow of things. Our sense of the *everyday* and our movement through it is disrupted. Heidegger (1927/1962) writes of *everydayness* and the sense of stability it confers on how things are done and what will be; "that which will come tomorrow is eternally yesterday's" (p. 371). A fall changes the rhythm of this taken-for-granted movement in time. Falling takes us away from a sense of the everyday.

There can be no *clock time* to falling. "It's time to fall." "I'll fall at 3 o'clock." These are not sensible statements. Clock time is measured time and clocks are devices we've contrived to provide us with a sense, however illusory, that time is structured. Measured, time can be planned, saved, spent, lost. Clocks are referents for *public* time. We set the time, decide a time, synchronize our watches. We control our time. Falling takes us away from that possibility. The moment of falling is abrupt, precipitous. Lovers succumb suddenly, plunging, tumbling, toppling.

Veronica sees a boy who inspires thoughts like "neat" and "wow" and goes after him. A girl with beautiful hair comes in the door and Allan—"it was kind of weird," he says—is drawn to her. Jasmine looks up from a campfire and is in love with a boy with twinkling eyes before he can speak. A young man climbs out of a manhole; a brother takes over the phone; a girl runs up the stairs. It seems to happen so quickly, falling in love. Brent goes to a party and recognizes a girl who lives down the street. We know he has seen her other times—she lives on his street! Yet he tells us he has fallen in love at *first sight*. He has seen her, in some sense, for the first time and falls. It seems to him to have happened in a moment.

For some, the moment of falling may be extended, as if in slow motion. He's been sitting there in front of you, in a green plaid jacket, every school morning. You fall a little more each day. Or perhaps there is an impetus that speeds your fall. Studying French together, you are with him every Thursday for weeks. He calls one night and says he is coming early just to be with you. Now you tell your friends, "I'm falling in love."

Occurring in a time that lies outside of everydayness, falling in love is a time of adventure. Gadamer (1960/1990) describes the fascination of adventure as just that—a movement into the uncertain and away from the conditions and obligations of every day. Adventure, he says, interrupts the customary course of events and tears us out of the context of our lives. Like all adventure, falling in love "belongs to the realm of the extraordinary" (Alberoni, 1983, p. 9) and occurs in *extra*-ordinary time.

What brings us to this time, to this adventure? Some suggest we must be ripe and ready in order to fall. Reik (1941) argues that "No one falls in love

He or she rather jumps into it" (p. 32). Even in love at first sight, he says, all has been prepared. One allows oneself to fall. Like Alberoni, Reik believes a spirit of discontent renders a person especially susceptible to "falling in love." There is an internal disquiet within one that is different from the normal rhythm of life (oscillations between mild satisfaction and slight discomfort with oneself).[2] Alberoni (1983) identifies adolescence as such a time. Fischer and Alapack (1987), in a study of adolescent love, write, "A ripeness is required if one is to notice the epiphany of the other's entrance into one's world; a readiness is necessary if one is to respond to the appeal in the other's eyes" (p. 96). Does this movement out of the ordinary begin only if we are, in some way, ready for adventure? Many of the participants in this study described falling in love early in the school year, several during the first days of September. Others fell while off in new parts, on vacation. Has all been prepared? Are lovers actually leaping? Søren Kierkegaard (1959) says we must leap: To love truly we must make a leap of faith into the unknown. It is a leap made with fear and trembling. Not surprisingly, perhaps, *fall* is derived from the Sanskrit word *sphal*, meaning to tremble (Skeat, 1993).

Off the Cliffs of the Heart

> what I like about diving is the feeling of falling. Of the water rushing toward you and there is nothing to be done about it. (Otto, 1991, p. 59)

> It was November 2 when we first kissed. We were in my room at home. We were sitting like this [motions that they were perpendicular to one another]. We were quite far away—our lips, right. The conversation got intimate. We were talking about kissing and she—we had this moment of silence—we were kind of bracing or whatever [laughs]—and then I leaned over and she started leaning over and then we met halfway. (Allan)

Allan says of this first kiss: "It was like diving." His movement toward her reminds him of going to the edge, pausing, and then leaping into space. There is no turning back. He solemnly reflects, "I could have hit my head." Sarah and Allan are friends. His fear is that if he misjudges her feelings, if he moves too soon, he will lose her. Their talk of kissing is a preliminary test, not unlike reaching down and checking the temperature and depth of the water. The water may seem fine, but the danger of the dive is still there: "I could sacrifice our friendship and it meant everything to me." Allan goes to the edge, braces himself, and moves toward her. To his relief Sarah leans too, she joins him at the brink and they dive together.

Hari describes spending time with Christine:

I was close friends with a girl in junior high. There was no physical part, but I
would daydream about her. We'd be riding horses and stuff like that. I had these
romantic notions about her but I didn't want to jeopardize what I had. I didn't
want to throw that away, so I hid my feelings from her. We spent so much time
together at school and afterward. We talked all the time, about everything. I thought
we were going beyond friendship. One day when we were going for a video, and
walking toward the store, I took her hand. It stayed in mine; she didn't take it away
from me. I thought, "That's a good sign." That's all that happened but I felt great.
Until the next day and she called me. She told that she hadn't wanted to hold
hands, but she didn't know what to do. She didn't want to suddenly pull away from
me. Then she said that she didn't know if she could be around me knowing how I
felt. I cried after that call. We weren't friends again until high school.

Hari and Christine's time together is spent as friends, talking, laughing,
sharing homework, watching movies. In Hari's daydream-time, however, he
imagines them with one another in a different way, a romantic way. Ironically
it is when he is alone with his thoughts that he feels closer to her. In this time
they share moments in a way he imagines lovers do. Hari dreams and waits
for a time when he may begin to act toward Christine as he does in his imagination. One day as they walk down the street, he takes her hand in his. Though
a small movement ("That's all that happened...."), it is an attempt to change
the meaning of their togetherness. It does—it changes everything—and he
loses her. As Allan would put it, Hari dived and hit his head. The pain is so
great, he cries.

Veronica too experiences a pivotal moment:

In the moment before I told him [how she felt about him] I thought I was going to
die. It felt like I was jumping over a cliff, knowing that there was only a 50/50
chance my parachute would open.

Veronica has seen a boy at a track meet, has met him at school and,
wanting him, has been in pursuit. They are now friends. To move beyond
friendship, Veronica knows she must tell him how she really feels. This revelation will be a definitive one. She feels the danger. Though she is cautious—
metaphorically, a parachute is packed—this unequivocal movement toward
him feels like a death-defying jump.

To venture into love and go outside the everydayness of things takes courage. In loving another, we are opening ourselves to the possibility of both joy
and sorrow. As we gain experience of this, as we meet sorrow and pain, there
is a danger that we may become fearful. We may develop a fear of falling.
Hurt in a fall, we may come to prefer only solid ground. We may learn to

shun adventure, refuse to leap. I remember a young man in his late twenties, in therapy for depression, who had never dated as an adult. He recalled vividly the day in high school when he gathered his courage and asked a certain girl to go out with him. She laughed in his face. He never asked anyone again.

It is possible to keep the extraordinary at bay. We can learn how to remain safely in ordinary time, to maintain some sense of clock time—that regulated, structured time—even when we are coming to love. I find that a scene in the 1977 Woody Allen movie, *Annie Hall*, succinctly illustrates this. Annie and Alvy are walking down the sidewalk on a first date. He stops and turns to her:

> Hey, listen. Give me a kiss.
>
> Really?
>
> Yeah, why not? Because we're going just to go home later right. There's going to be all that tension. You know, we've never kissed before. I'll never know when to make the right move or anything. So we'll kiss now and get it over with and then we'll go eat. Okay? We'll digest our food better.

Alvy thinks he has found a way to bypass the indecision, the fear and trembling that surround the moment of a first kiss. He is saying to Annie: Let's take control of this time, kiss *now*. This way it won't be *a move;* we can relax; there will be no risk of indigestion. The audience recognizes that *this is* Alvy's move—to refrain from falling. Alvy is no diver. The moment he creates with Annie becomes an ordinary one, a safe time with both feet firmly on the sidewalk. Its image is in stark contrast to another given to us by the painter Chagall. In Chagall's paintings, like *The Birthday Party* (1915), the lover is literally in flight. His artist's eye captures the possibilities of the time when we let our feet leave the ground.[3]

The Stomach Tells

> Gregory: I'm in love
>
> Friend: Since when.
>
> Gregory: Half an hour ago. I feel restless and dizzy. Bet I don't get to sleep tonight.
>
> Friend: That sounds more like indigestion.
> —*Gregory's Girl*

When I ask, "How did you know you were falling in love?" Hari replies, "My stomach told me." Céline answers, "I think your body lets you know.

I'm a stomach person. There are guys who make my stomach turn and make me feel like throwing up. Other guys just don't get a response." A stomach in knots, the inability to eat, sweaty palms, syncope: These are given as informing signs. Hari describes literally trembling and shaking before a special girl. "My voice seems confident. The rest of me is quivering. When it is over, I'm shaking. Just thinking about it makes me shake."[4] When we fall our body responds. We don't have to look down to know we are falling; our body reveals that we are ungrounded.

"The body is our general medium for having a world," Merleau-Ponty (1945/1962, p. 146) reminds us. We experience our life through the sensations created in and by our bodies. In everyday situations where, on the whole, we may take most things for granted, we are not normally aware of our bodily functioning. Walking down the hall at school, greeting her friends, Céline is unmindful that she is placing one foot before the other. Even if she becomes aware by a glance at her watch that she is late for class and starts to hurry, the increased movements of her legs and feet will essentially go unnoticed. Céline's sense of her body is assumed, silent, passed over without concern. The world about her and her purpose—to get to class on time—are foremost in her awareness.

If, however, Céline has injured her ankle at yesterday's basketball practice, she will wince as her pace quickens and have to slow down. Limping in pain, she experiences her body as immediately present to her and her attention to the waiting classroom recedes. Another situation could also change Céline's normal taken-for-granted relation to her body. Hurrying down the hall, she suddenly notices that Brian is looking at her. Her thoughts go to her movements, her appearance—what is it he is seeing? In her mind she scrutinizes this object, herself, and wonders, "How do I look in these new jeans?" She slows, feels awkward. Céline has become *self*-conscious. She is responding to Brian. Her body—she's a stomach person, she says—express.s her reaction to him. If Brian is a guy whom Céline finds attractive, her stomach may "turn over" as she passes him in the hall.

> On the way home [from a movie date] I was struck by how much I love you. I just glance over at you and it becomes difficult to breathe. Happiness grows in my chest and I realize that I want to look at you forever. I can't explain how I feel but it is so irrational that when it happens & you aren't there, my eyes fill up with tears & I get all choked up. (from 14-year-old Veronica's diary).

> The moment I set eyes on her I felt an electric shock; in fact I had no wishes, no hopes, I had no idea what was the matter with me, but I suffered acutely and spent

my nights in sleepless anguish. In the daytime I crept away like a wounded bird and hid myself in the maize fields and the orchards. (13-year-old Hector Berlioz, quoted in Kiell, 1964, p. 144)

C'est comme si un camion me passait sur le corps à chaque fois;
Comme si un jet brisait le mur du son quand je te vois;
Comme si un batteur de "rock" jouait "nonstop" dans ma poitrine;
a me donne un choc et ça fait monter l'adrénaline.
(1986 Québec song by Mandeville: *Teenager en Amour*)[5]

Veronica looks at Jason and the sight of him takes her breath away. She chokes and is moved to tears by the intensity of her feelings. She is unable to explain it and admits to herself in her diary: "it is so irrational." Shocked, anguished, blasted past sound, the body tells the young lover: "I am struck by love." Sappho wrote many centuries ago: "When I glance at you even an instant, I can no longer utter a word: My tongue thickens to a lump, and beneath my skin breaks out a subtle fire: my eyes are blind; my ears are filled with humming; and sweat streams down my body, I am seized by a sudden shuddering; I turn greener than grass, and in a moment more, I feel I shall die" (quoted in Handley, 1986). Elvis Presley put it this way: "I'm in love, I'm all shook-up." He was right. When we fall, twisting, turning—our center lost, our body moving, we are all shook-up.

After Florentino Ariza saw her for the first time, his mother knew before he told her because he lost his voice and his appetite and spent the entire night tossing and turning in his bed. But when he began to wait for the answer to his first letter, his anguish was complicated by diarrhea and green vomit, he became disoriented and suffered from sudden fainting spells, and his mother was terrified because his condition did not resemble the turmoil of love so much as the devastation of cholera (Márquez, 1985/1988, p. 61).

When Florentino is examined by a homeopathic practitioner in Gabriel García Márquez's *Love in the Time of Cholera*, the old man finds that the boy has no fever, no pain anywhere, and that Florentinos only concrete feeling is an urgent desire to die. "All that was needed was shrewd questioning, first of the patient, then of his mother, to conclude once again that the symptoms of love were the same as those of cholera" (p. 62). Florentino's body reveals to those around him that something beyond the everyday flow of things has happened. When he loses voice, appetite, sleep, his mother recognizes love. Later, as the severe symptoms begin, after he sends his letter—after he has leapt—she becomes afraid for his life. But Florentino is not dying; he only wants to die. He is afraid. The body's reaction to falling in love resembles fear. Love is *la belle épouvante*.[6]

Fear of Falling

There's no chill and yet I shiver.
There's no flame and yet I burn.
I'm not sure what I'm afraid of
And yet I'm trembling....
I feel as though I'm falling every time I close my eyes
　　　　　　　　　　　　　　　　—Yentl

Robert Burton (1977) wrote in 1621 that fear and love are linked together. He used what he termed every poet's catalogue of love-symptoms as support for his argument. Lovers are pale, bloodless; they look ill with waking and want of appetite; the green-sickness happens to young women, cachexia[7] effects men. They are *ut nudis qui pressit calcibus anguem*—as one who has trodden with a naked foot upon a snake (p. 133).

We show this link between fear and love today using biology rather than poetry. The human body is able to initiate, monitor, and arrest activities that, for the most part, are inaccessible to our normal awareness.[8] For instance, we are not conscious of our blood vessels contracting and the resulting increase in our blood pressure. It is the autonomic nervous system (ANS) that carries out such functions. When we are afraid or anxious, the ANS adjusts our body without any conscious effort on our part. The ANS has two ways of doing this. One is called a sympathetic reaction, in which the body processes are activated and we are readied for an emergency (fight or flight) response. The other, a parasympathetic reaction, has a different effect in which bodily responses are conserved. The sympathetic response is the predominate stress reaction, but in some individuals the parasympathetic one takes over.

Florentino is experiencing the latter, parasympathetic, response: faintness, diarrhea, nausea, frequency of urination. The sympathetic reaction is not unlike the feeling that comes when we go to the edge of a great height and look down, or when we dream of falling and wake shaking, and in a sweat. Our heart is racing, our breath rapid, we are tremulous and, lying there with a lump in our throat, we cannot return to sleep.

Anthony Walsh (1991) in *The Science of Love* writes that falling in love is a discrete event not happening on a fully conscious level. Falling in love occurs, he says, when someone has an anabolic effect on our hypothalamic-pituitary-gonadal axis—an effect identical to the stress response (pp. 186–187). It is the chemistry of our bodies that enables us to react with excitement to another. Whether we understand the biochemistry of falling in love or not ("One look from him and the neurotransmitters poured into my limbic system!"), we can recognize that the sensation of falling in love has a physical impact on the individual. This is true of the teenage lover.

Adolescent romance is commonly referred to as "puppy love." *Puppy love.* It conjures up the light, playful, innocent curiosity and joy of a small pup; the tumbling head over heels of a young animal at play. It is an image that brings a smile to the onlooker. But there is another way of naming young love—as *a crush.* Crush is from *cruisir,* an Old French word that evolved from the Teutonic *cruschyn,* to crack or crash, to overwhelm (Skeat, 1993, p. 103). The Danish have a comparable word, *kryste,* meaning to squeeze. In the *New Webster Encyclopedic Dictionary* (Thatcher, 1984, pp. 206–207), to crush is defined as "to press and bruise between two hard bodies, to squeeze so as to force out of the natural shape, to press with violence, to break or force down, breaking and bruising." These are fierce images. In naming teenage romantic feeling as a crush, we acknowledge the bodily impact of falling in love.

Falling into a Mad World

> "We're all mad here. I'm mad. You're mad." The Cheshire Cat tells Alice. "How do you know I'm mad", she asks. "You must be or you wouldn't have come here."
> —Carroll, *Alice's Adventures in Wonderland*

Listening to Derek tell of the morning he ran after a strange girl who was passing by, I was reminded of another story. Wasn't Alice sitting one morning with her sister, bored by a book, when a white rabbit went hurrying by? Didn't she jump up and run after him? I went to Carroll's (1865/1971) book, *Alice's Adventures in Wonderland,* to pursue the similarity. Alice's adventures begin with a fall. She tumbles after the rabbit, "so suddenly that [she] had not a moment to think about stopping herself before she found herself falling down what seemed to be a very deep well" (p. 8). We know Alice enters upon a strange enchanted place, a place where everything becomes "curiouser and curiouser" (p. 14).

"It was kind of weird." "I don't know how to explain it." "It seems kind of crazy, I guess." "It sounds stupid, I know." "It seems so trivial—but it's not." "Maybe I'm just crazy but (shakes her head)." When we ask people, as I do in this study, to tell us how they fell in love, they seem, not at a loss for words— even rejected lovers like to relive this moment—but without the means to describe their experience. "She was walking across the room and going up these stairs. I was totally blown away." "His eyes twinkled and he had this enormous smile. By the time he said 'Hello,' I was in love." "Her radiance caused my heart to jump into my throat." "I thought, 'Wow. What a great guy.' " There is a perceptible gap between the question asked and the answers given. Are these not descriptions of the beloved rather than accounts of the experience? These replies are about *who*, but *what happened?* How, where, was there *falling* in love?

We describe our experience of coming to love someone in a romantic or passionate way with an action word, falling. From where does this sense of action arise in association with love? We know that to fall is to go from one place to another. According to *Webster* (Thatcher, 1984, p. 316), it involves "passing into a new state, through inadvertence or ignorance." In what way, by falling in love, have we left one place for another?

To consider this further, we need to reflect upon our sense of location in the world. We can situate ourselves objectively: I am in a room in a house numbered "8," on such and such a street in Edmonton, Alberta, Canada. I can go so far as to stipulate that I am at 53 degrees latitude and 113 degrees longitude. By this referent my location can be pinpointed on the globe. This knowledge of place is *geography*. But I am at *home*. This room, my study, is where I work. It is cluttered with papers and books, pictures and mementos, postcards from friends. I sit in an old chair—a castoff from a company's office renovations—in front of my computer (with its too few megabytes). I can see the trees of my backyard through a window. The phone rings; a friend calls. He is not in this room, but his voice brings him close. He teases me about my work and I return to it, smiling. This is the space I inhabit. I am *in* it, not merely *at* it. This sense of place may be called *landscape*. Landscape is mood-saturated; it is how one is with the things around one, affectively rather than cognitively or contemplatively. This space is lived. I do not simply occupy this room, this place. I *live in* it.

Lived spatiality is not an isolated point. It situates me in relation to other spaces. It is my orientation, a position in reference to other places. Distance from this lived space cannot be judged by objective measurement. My friend calls from kilometers away, and I am no longer alone in the room. I picture him calling from his office and I am there, too. Remoteness/closeness in my lived space is not about actual distance. The mail arrives with a letter from Nepal. Though the mail carrier is the person standing before me—he is less than a meter away—it is my Nepalese friend who is brought closer to me. Lived spatiality is not oriented to our body but toward the center of our everyday concern (Kockelmans, 1989, p. 133).

> The face of all the world is changed, I think,
> Since first I heard the footsteps of thy soul
> Move still, oh still, beside me. (Elizabeth Barrett Browning)[9]

Falling in love changes our landscape. We actually move into a different lived space. Perhaps this is the reason we use the metaphor of *falling* to describe our sensations. Though our body does not literally leave the ground, suddenly because of this person with the twinkling eyes (radiant smile, green jacket, beautiful hair), the space in which we normally live changes. *He moves me.* This person, now of intense concern to us, affects the shape of our world. It shifts. We have a new prime referent to the place in which we dwell: It is because this individual has entered our space (or exists in our space in a new way) that we fall. Citing the image of the beloved may be the only way to describe falling in love, after all.

> But enough of this for I am always thinking of her and every time I do so I ask myself these questions. "Why am I thinking of her, why am I so anxious to see her to speak to her,"… and my answer is "I do not know." I must take care lest I should be deceived. It is true I like to be in company with Ladies, particularly when they are pleasing, but so far, I have felt no real love for any. (from the diary of George Stephen Jones, *A Love Story from Nineteenth Century Québec,* [Ward, 1986])

> I ask myself why is this bird sitting on the tree, singing all day. I don't know this being so much so why can't it go out of my heart. (*Ianlin Huar*)-(Ianlin Flower), Song of "starting love" from Central Mongolia, 1921 [Tsagaan Sar, 1992])

> Her hair smelled like the orange groves we passed when we drove to my grandmother's when I was 8. But that was her shampoo or whatever. (from the television show, *My So Called Life,* 1994)

A change of landscape is unsettling. "How queer everything is to-day! And yesterday things went on just as usual. I wonder if I've changed in the night?" (Carroll, 1865/1971, p. 15) When we begin to fall in love and find our world, our consciousness, invaded by another, a sense of uneasiness prevails. "Why am I thinking about this person? Why does she affect me so; I hardly know her?" "The smell of her hair overwhelms me—Oh, come on, it's only shampoo!" The other's appearance, voice, gestures take on a fascination that is disturbing. ("I stared at her hair the whole class." "He was the most beautiful man I'd ever seen." "I realize I want to look at you forever.") Slight gestures, momentary contacts, fleeting expressions: Associated with the beloved, these become full of significance, pregnant with meaning.

> In social [studies] we went to the library to do some research and I was looking through the National Geographic index. R was looking for the index and came up to me and said, "Oh you have it." Since we were both looking for the same thing he read over my shoulder. Now, I don't know if he was just flirting or what but he started coming so close to me that our shoulders and arms were touching. And then! He put his finger on one of the article references in the book and as he did that he touched my hand. (Veronica's diary)

After Veronica recorded this tremendous moment when R touched her hand (deliberately?), she wrote: "Sometimes it seems so trivial—it sounds so trivial—if anyone were to read this. And it's not." "I love him. I love him so much it hurts. That probably sounds stupid and corny but it's true." "*Oh dear, what nonsense I'm talking!*" says Alice (Carroll, 1865/1971, p. 15). Veronica defends her joy at what may seem a rather trifling occurrence to others. She recognizes that she may appear foolish to an objective observer. Like Synder's (1992) college students, who began interviews about their romantic experiences with "You're going to think this is stupid," she feels she will be judged as foolish.

Alcibiades, when it is his turn to speak of love in *Symposium* (Plato, 1956b), compares the lover's situation to that of someone bitten by a viper:

> You know they say that one who felt it would not tell what it was like except to other people who had been bitten, since they alone would know it and would not be hard on him for what he allowed himself to do and say in his agony. (p. 112)

Alcibiades has been bitten in the most painful spot—the heart—by the discourses of Socrates. He claims he is not afraid of speaking of his love in his present company but asks the servants and "*any one who is common or boorish*" "to clap strong doors on their ears" (Plato, 1956b, p. 112). Here is a glimpse of the lover's defiance: I may seem mad to you, but it is because you are too boorish (insensitive, unfeeling, unfortunate) to understand.

Stendhal, in a preface to *Love* (1822/1957), says his book is "simply an exact and scientific description of a brand of madness" (p. 25). In a "Second Attempt at a Preface" he asks "anyone who wants to read this book," "Have six months of your life ever been made miserable by love?" If not, "this book will arouse your anger against its author, for it will make you suspect that there is a certain kind of happiness you do not know" (p. 31). It seems, like Alcibiades, Stendhal considers a lover's madness (and misery) as a matter of fortune and grace.

When we fall in love we feel disturbed, unstable, in turmoil. We feel also released from the ordinariness of life. We have moved into a space for adventure. There is a thrill to this, an excitement. Like Alice, the lover thinks: "It seemed quite dull and stupid for life to go on in a common way" (Carroll, 1865/1971, p. 13).

To have a world means to have an orientation toward it (Gadamer, 1990). In love, the other becomes the landmark that reorients us. Those who have not fallen in love, who have never experienced a precipitous shift in landscape, see a different horizon. It is not surprising that to them the lover seems quite mad.

I always felt I had a sixth sense, that I knew where he was at all times. I always knew what class he was in. Let's say I'm in class and he's in gym—I could see him. This one guy I liked was one grade higher than me, but I always knew what class he was in. In my spares I would walk by his class. I'd go to parties because of him. And to the mall because of him. And the arcades and stuff—I'd stand behind him and watch him play. (Céline)

Where he is changes where she is. This is true, literally as well as imaginatively: She goes where he is. The space of the school is experienced in terms of where he is likely to be. She uses a particular hallway because his locker is there, or because he is scheduled to be in Classroom 213 at 10:30. A table in the cafeteria is her table; from it she can watch him meet his friends at that table over there. The school gymnasium becomes a place of infinite possibilities: basketball games, team tryouts, school dances, assembly. She can be *with* him in the gymnasium. Beyond the school there is the mall. Paradoxically, as a public space, it provides her with greater intimacy. Here she is free to move closer to him, to stand as an audience behind him at the arcade.

Céline, an honor student and member of the student council, hangs around a video arcade. She is not interested in playing Zombie Attack. The flashing lights and loud music barely enter her awareness. She is watching *him*. Does he even know she is there? Her friends are having fun elsewhere, without her. Surely this is foolish. What can she be thinking? Nicole, in love with a boy she has never met, except on the telephone, astounds her friends: "But you never see him!" She replies, "But I know him. What do you need to see?" She tells me, "My girl friends didn't believe me—'Who is this guy?'—so once on a school field trip I had to phone him and they got to hear his voice. I was just so excited." It was her excitement rather than his existence that amazed them.

Nicole, though she shares a close, trusting relationship with her parents, begins to lie to them:

My parents limited my telephone calls. I got rather sneaky about it. Once they tried to call home and the phone was busy for four hours. I made up a lie about the phone being disconnected by accident.

As when Alice enters Wonderland, different rules apply. Young lovers told me consequences didn't matter. "If I had to sneak out to see her or break my curfew, so be it." "Mom would be mad [if she knew], but I like him too much to say no." Reik (1941) points out that "The sweet-natured Juliet, ready to obey her parents and fulfil all filial obligations, becomes a scheming, lying and deceitful woman overnight" (p. 157).

I had football practice with a very strict coach. Practice started at 3:45 and you had better be on the field, cleats on, ready to play. Amy's last class was physics and it always went over. School was supposed to be out at 3:30 but it would go to 3:33, 3:34. I would run and wait outside the door so I could talk to her. I ran so many laps for being late for practice; you wouldn't believe it. I remember spending an entire social studies class figuring out how I could get my shoulder pads on faster between the physics class at one end of the school and the gym. (Derek)

To talk to her, Derek risks the wrath of his coach and the teasing of his friends. But it cannot be otherwise. "I really needed those 30 seconds with her." For him, now, the only path to the gym lies across the school and by the physics class.

To those whose feet are planted firmly on a different ground, the lover appears irrational. Shakespeare noted the fraternity of the lunatic, the lover, and the poet: they are *of imagination all compact*.[10] Tennov (1979), psychologist and author of *Love and Limerence*, writes that falling in love is often seen as mental illness. She believes that this is so because the reactions of lovers are at variance with rationality and the conception of human behavior as based on logical thought.[11] Before describing a "limerent experience" (her term for falling in love) in her research, she carefully stipulates: "Fred and every other person whose situation and limerence was similar to Fred's were fully functioning, rational, emotionally stable, normal, non-neurotic, non-pathological members of society" (p. 89). She anticipates negative judgments of Fred and other study participants. No, she says, they are not needy, abnormal, neurotic, unstable people. They were like you and me before they fell in love. "Nonlimerents"—persons, such as Tennov's happily married colleague, who have never fallen in love—are particularly likely to find the behavior of those in love quite odd and immature. (Perhaps all lovers act *adolescent*?)

Barthes, in *A Lover's Discourse* (1977/1978), addresses the perception that *I am crazy*. "It frequently occurs to the amorous subject that he is or is going mad" (p. 120). He says, as a lover, he is insane in his own eyes. "I know my delirium." "Every lover is mad we are told." But Barthes asks: Can we imagine a madman in love? His answer: never. Lovers have only a *metaphorical* madness. When we fall in love, we are falling into a new space, one about which we can take nothing for granted. Falling in love is venturing out into the uncertain. Our everyday, background knowledge of how we are situated vanishes; our orientation to the world changes. As if tumbling into Wonderland, we are disoriented. Others see us as confused, strange: We have left what is safe, what is predictable, and must reorient ourselves. Falling in love is such a radical dislocation that, like Alice, we know: "After Such a Fall as This, I Shall Think Nothing of Tumbling Downstairs" (Carroll, 1865/1971, p. 8).

Falling for a True Love

> "It was love at first sight," said R.M., 71. "I looked at him and said to myself, 'That's the man I'm going to marry,'" said M., 69. Six weeks later, they wed. Since then they have parented seven children and enjoyed 28 grandchildren. In retirement they spend most of their time together. They go shopping and to the health club together. Every night they do crossword puzzles together. (*The Edmonton Journal*, November 19, 1995)

This "love at first sight" story is heartwarming, told in hindsight. This couple found true love and they knew it in an instant. All those happy years together: How did they know? Perhaps Derek truly knows the girl on the staircase is the one for him? True love. *True.* These synonyms for "true" are offered in *Roget's Thesaurus* (Morehead, 1978, p. 518): faithful, loyal, constant, sincere, certain. Yes, this is what we want in love. Other synonyms: correct, accurate, actual, genuine, legitimate, rightful, real. Yes, we want to fall for the *right* lover. Is there someone who is right for us? *The* one. This may seem a fanciful idea but it is an old one.

This idea is seen in *Symposium,* in the form of an ancient story told by Aristophanes, the comic poet. Aristophanes begins his turn to speak of love by explaining that the natural state of man is not what it was. Once there were three sexes, male, female, and hermaphrodite, and humans had a round shape with four legs, four arms, and two faces on a round neck. Humans had terrible strength and great ambitions in those times and it is said that they challenged the gods. Zeus decided, as an alternative to destroying humankind, to remove its hubris by making it weaker. He sliced humans in two as "hard-boiled eggs with a hair" (Plato, 1956b, p. 87). It was that act that gave birth to mutual love. Now, says Aristophanes, the halves seek one another, each desiring to grow back together in an embrace. It is this, the striving to be united with the other, that we call "love" (Plato, 1956b, pp. 86–88). We find true love when we find our other half.

It is evident that Plato intended this speech to be an amusing but unenlightened depiction of love set against that of the wise Socrates. It is Aristophanes' rendition, however, that has caught and held our attention across the ages (Bergmann, 1987, p. 43). It has power, this myth. Our great love stories are grounded in its implicit message, as are contemporary fiction, movies, and songs. Many of us want to believe in its promise.

But what happens if we never meet our love during life's journey? What if we do, but the moment passes without recognition? What if we make a mistake and succumb to a false love? In *Guys and Dolls*, the lovers, Sarah Brown and Sky Masterson, sing "I'll know when my love comes along." Sarah knows the characteristics she desires in the man who will be hers. She has "imagined every bit of him" and "won't take a chance for, oh, he'll be just what I need." Sky believes in chance and chemistry. Sky will know his love at the sight of her face, "long before we can speak." The irony of their song is that they have found their loves—one another—and they *don't* know it. Like Sarah and Sky, most of us would like to believe that we'll know instinctively when we meet the person who is right for us. We tend to forget that Romeo is at the Capulet feast because he is mad with love for Rosaline and hopes to see her there.

"How will we know if it's love?" adolescents wonder. What does it mean if your stomach reacts to Angelo *and* Raj *and* Steve?

> We had these ways of trying to confirm who your true love really was. You would write his first, middle and last name plus your first, middle, and last name and then "true love." You would count all the t's and l's. This was done with every boy's name that you liked. The highest number was supposed to indicate your true love. (Céline)

Over the ages there have been games, signs, portents to which lovers turn for some sign from the universe, a clue, a nod that they are on the right track. Sleep with a piece of wedding cake under your pillow and you will dream of your true love. Pick a daisy and "he loves me; he loves me not" is revealed by the dropping petals. Use astrology: He's a Leo; you're a Libra. (Yes, compatible signs!) Try the Eastern version: He's "Year of the Sheep"; you're "Year of the Tiger" (No, this love is not in the stars.) Write your name plus all the boys' names and see which one looks the best with yours. Are such portents to be taken seriously? Céline says, "Usually, you didn't get the answer you wanted, so you just discarded it." I remember reaching for another, more propitiously petaled, daisy.

Several of the girls who participated in this study confessed that they had lists of boys they loved—prioritized lists. The word *confessed* describes the way they revealed this fac because, I think, they felt there was something fickle or calculating in having a list.

> In my diary I had lists of people I was in love with. I could have sworn that I was in love with each one of them. (Veronica)

> I had a list—there were four boys. Listed in order. They would change every so often, except for the first guy. He was always number one. I can name ten guys in my junior high that I was in love with. I went out with J. C. but I was in love with someone else. The guy that was my favorite. (Céline)

> The girls had these rating charts—I was so proud that I made it to that rating chart. It didn't matter what the rating was—all guys got slammed at one time or the other. It was being on the chart. I was happy I made the chart. (Hari)

The girls are *en-listing* the boys around them. Individually (privately in diaries) and publicly as a collective, they are keeping ledgers of names—catalogues in a sense—of desirable boys. Boys they love; boys they might love. We see, in Hari's relief at making the registry, the importance of these lists. He doesn't care about his rating; being recognized as potentially lovable is what counts. In considering the meaning of such lists, I reach for an etymological dictionary on the off chance that it might provide a clue. Here it is. *List*, "to choose, have pleasure in; see Lust" (Skeat, 1993, p. 253). The girls seem to be on to something. The old meaning of lust is given here as pleasure. Under it is cited: *lust, to please; if thee lust = if it please thee* and *the Anglo-Saxon lystan to desire, used impersonally*. There are old roots, then, to this manner of choosing, deciding—if impersonally—who gives you pleasure. The dictionary also reminds me that *lists* mean fields for a tournament, where knights fought it out to impress their ladies fair. (Today's competition takes place on paper lists?) List is associated with *listen*, from the Middle English, *lust-en*. Though compiling a list may seem somewhat heartless, the girls are trying to listen to their hearts, to make sense of their feelings.

In a 1991 Norwegian film, *Frida: Straight from the Heart,* the 13-year-old heroine reads Eric Fromm's *Art of Loving* and tries to make sense of love. She constantly berates her close friend and neighbor, Kristian, for his lack of romantic feelings. (We suspect he has such feelings for Frida but doesn't dare reveal them.) Frida has other boys in her life—she keeps track of them on a chart where she assigns them points. There is Raymond, whom she met on holiday and to whom she now writes. He is a soccer player and she has begun to study the sport. Martin is a boy at school whose attention she is stealing from another girl. She catches glimpses of Andreas, an older boy, at her music lessons. Frida tells Kristian that she "longs for Andreas, sees Martin, dreams of Raymond." Frida's character expresses the desire of the adolescent to know whom and how to love. Her chart is an attempt to make sense of her feelings, to help her know whom to love.

Perhaps more than attempts to understand feelings, charts, lists, and rating scales are devices for grasping love with the intellect, to make it reasonable. Frida's chart is a suggestion that—like Plato—she believes love is finding good, desirable properties in the other. Weighing, comparing properties of potential lovers is a way of deciding where love should be bestowed.

Frida does not recognize it, but there is at least one serious flaw in this strategy. Our appraisal and bestowal of valued characteristics on another is not necessarily reasonable. Stendhal (1822/1957) says that lovers endow the Other with "a thousand perfections." They draw from everything that happens proofs of the perfection of the loved one. Stendhal called this mental process *crystallization*:

> At the salt mines of Salzburg, they throw a leafless wintry bough into one of the abandoned workings. Two or three months later they haul it out with a shining deposit of crystals. The smallest twig, no bigger than a tom-tit's claw, is studded with a galaxy of scintillating diamonds. The original branch is no longer recognizable. (p. 45)

This metaphor of the crystallized bough implies that our view of the beloved follows an underlying form that actually exists, but that we glorify it. Our beloved sparkles. Friends who have been privy to the admiration of the lover are often surprised, even startled, when they actually meet the loved person.

Falling in love with someone may be a leap of the imagination. Contemporary psychologists (using factor analyses of love measures) also find that *glorification of the other* is common to falling in love (Murstein, 1988). Nussbaum (1990) and Haule (1990) both make reference to lovers' experiences of the loved person as surrounded, in moments, by a golden aura. Nussbaum describes the aura as being "like Turner's Angel Standing in the Sun" (Nussbaum, 1990, p. 316). If in love we cannot trust ourselves to see the other clearly—and seeing in light cast by a golden glow may not be so illuminating—how may we judge if we should love him or her? It is tempting to cry with Medea:

> O God, you have given to mortals a sure method
> Of telling the gold that is pure from the counterfeit;
> Why is there no mark engraved upon men's bodies,
> By which we could know the true ones from the false ones?[12]
> (Euripides, *Medea*, 431 B.C.)

There is no mark, perhaps, because the value of loved persons may reside beyond the persons themselves. In philosophical discus ons of aesthetics, the question remains as to where the value, the beauty, of an object lies. Is it in the object? Is it in the perceiver? In the act of perceiving and what lies between? These questions seem open with regard to love, as well. For Plato, value is to be found in the qualities of the loved one, with the task of the lover being to become ever more discriminating of beauty and goodness. An alternative view is that the lover bestows value on the loved person: Love creates a new value not reducible to the objective value someone may have (Singer, 1984a). In a third perspective, love is considered as a value response to another where the intention toward union, the loving itself, is the actual bearer of value (Owens, 1970).

Is what we feel toward the other truly love? How do we know? What if it is not *loving* but *infatuation*? (*Fatuous*, silly, feeble; from the Latin *infatuare*, to make a fool of.) Are we deceiving ourselves? Stendhal (1822/1957) in a chapter entitled "Concerning Infatuation" wrote that schoolboys entering society for the first time were prey to infatuation. "In youth and age too many or too few sensibilities prevent one from perceiving things as they really are, and from experiencing the true sensations which they impart" (p. 73). He suggests that some people hurl themselves upon the experience instead of waiting for it to happen. "Before the nature of an object can produce its proper sensation in them, they have blindly invested it from afar with imaginary charm which they conjure up inexhaustibly within themselves" (p. 73). Sooner or later—as when they discover that the object of their adoration is "*not returning the ball*" (p. 73)[13]—their infatuation is dispelled. "Love is a series of tests," says Alberoni (1983, p. 74). Maybe love and infatuation may only be known in retrospect. "The case for love rests with the future, not the past" (Keen, 1983, p. 254).

How do we distinguish love from *friendship*? (*Friend* is from the Middle English *frend* and means love.) Is it only the bodily signs, the intestinal turmoil, that separate one from the other? Reik (1941) says, "It is certainly untrue that sexual desire differentiates love from friendship" (p. 167). For him, sex and love are quite distinct, so this discriminator is useless. Reik's solution is to find the features of friendship that are absent or not pronounced in love. He makes a list. Love has urgency and intensity; friendship does not. Love is ardent, like madness; it hits you like an earthquake. Friendship is otherwise. The idealization that occurs in love is unnecessary for friendship—you can be critical and tolerant of a friend in a way you are not with a lover. In love, you feel the object of your love is superior to you—such a feeling of inferiority is lacking in friendship, though you may feel your friend is superior in some ways. Love is more exclusive and takes possession of your whole heart. Friendship does not want to own you, only to have a place in your life.

For Bloom (1993), friendship, when compared to love, is "gentler, soberer, without frenzy" (p. 547). Though friendship seems an easier relationship, Bloom finds it a rarer one. Friendship is necessarily reciprocal: You may love someone who does not love you, but you cannot be the friend of someone who is not your friend. Friendship is demanding like love, but its pleasures are entirely spiritual, without bodily passions to stimulate and sustain it. "Friendship is beyond mere bodily need and can be thought to be more distinctively human" (p. 547). Friendship consists more in conversation; much of love consists in gazing at the beloved. Both, however, require freedom (you cannot require someone either to love or to befriend you) and trust. You must possess for both the grace of encompassing another's happiness within the pursuit of your own.

These considerations of the properties of love and friendship are useful in some respects. In the actual relation with the other person, in living the relationship, however, such discriminators may not be so helpful. Stendhal (1822/1957) quotes from a letter, written in English by a young German girl to an intimate friend. The girl describes meeting a man, and after being in his presence for two hours, finding others' company suddenly wearisome. "I could not speak, I could not play; I thought of nothing but Klopstock." She meets Klopstock the next day and feels that "we were very seriously friends." He must leave Hamburg on the fourth day and soon they begin a correspondence. Her friends find her speaking of nothing but him and tease her that she is in love. She is adamant in her response: "they must have a very friendshipless heart if they had no idea of friendship to a man as well as to a woman" (p. 248).

> At the last Klopstock said plainly that he loved; and I startled as for a wrong thing; I answered that it was no love, but friendship, as it was what I felt for him; we had not seen one another enough to love (as if love must have more time than friendship) [p. 248].

Klopstock returns to the city and after a short time the girl is able to tell him that she loves too. As her mother will not let her marry a stranger, they wait for two years. Her letter is written in the fourth year of their marriage: She says: "I am so happy" (p. 248).

Initially turning love away and insisting upon friendship, this girl's experience is an example of the difficulties we have in understanding our relation to another. She tells her friends, and even her would-be lover, that they are wrong. This is *not* love. Her reason seems to be based on the factor of time. There has not been enough. We can almost see her smile to herself as she remembers this. "How silly of me! As if friendship comes more quickly." There are those who question whether a man and a woman can have a true friendship. For them, the relations between the sexes can never be totally "spiritual," the body must always intervene.

Some of our difficulty, our skepticism concerning how to recognize love, may come from our modern mistrust of emotion. We have been taught not to trust it. Yet often love doesn't begin with values but rather with the "experience of being struck by a mysterious kind of beauty" (Nussbaum, 1990, p. 328). Nussbaum argues that we need a text that has a plot (a temporal sequence of events) in which the complexities may be developed. We need this to show the cataleptic view of falling in love—that is, the view in which love comes suddenly as opposed to the view that time and a pattern of interaction are necessary. For Nussbaum a list will not do. She does write of making a list of qualities she wants in a lover, but she admits that it will be revised to fit the man she loves.

Nussbaum uses a story, "Learning to Fall," by Ann Beattie, as an illustration. Woven into this story is a metaphor for falling in love: a class exercise that teaches trust. In this exercise one learns to fall slowly, not to plop—this falling is not an accident but a yielding. One aims for grace. This falling is about trusting, trusting oneself and the other. It has to be faced that there will always be doubts, that there are no certainties. For Nussbaum, loving is an intricate way of being, feeling, and interacting with another person. When one falls in love it is not independent of evidence (attention has been paid; powerful feelings have evidential value) but one goes beyond evidence. There are no necessary and sufficient conditions (Nussbaum, 1990, pp. 274–284).

Not everyone comes to love through a fall. At the beginning of the novel *First Love* (Turgenev, 1950), three middle-aged men sit around the dinner table after the rest of the guests have taken their leave. Over their cigars they agree, "Each of us is to tell the story of his first love" (p. 21). The first man confesses that though he has courted and flirted with women, he fell in love, for the first and last time, with his nurse when he was six. The second man acknowledges, "There was nothing very remarkable about my first love either: I didn't fall in love with anyone until I met Anna Ivanovna, my present wife, and then it all went perfectly smoothly. Our fathers arranged the whole thing. We grew fond of one another and married shortly after" (pp. 21–22). The third man, Vladimir Petrovich, at first hesitates, but then reveals that his first love was not at all ordinary. It is the story of Vladimir's love that comprises the novel. It is his love that is a love story. It may be that we not only need a story to explain the cataleptic experience of love, but that such a falling— a falling out of the ordinary—is the kind of love that *is* st ried.[14]

The loves described in this chapter came about through a fall. Where did the fall take them? Derek is married to the girl on the staircase and she can still make his heart pound. They have three children. Allan and Sarah became high school sweethearts. She returned to her country and he visited her there. They were waiting to enter their twenties before committing to one another, but have gone on to other relationships. Veronica went with the boy from the track meet in an on-again, off-again relationship for three years. She's now at university and considers him a friend. Jasmine's parents thought that at 13 years of age, she was too young for a relationship. The boy with the twinkling eyes came back for her five years later. When she shared this story, she was 21:

They had been married for several months. Brent did get a date with the girl at the party and, after some awkward times, she began to return his feelings. It's been a rocky relationship and they have parted, a decision made, ironically, at a party in the same house. Thirteen-year-old Nicole broke up with her unseen telephone lover, or rather he broke up with her. He used the impossibility of a long-distance relationship "as an excuse":

> After we broke up we'd talk sometimes on the phone and then we never talked for years and years. One day I answered the phone. I had to ask, "Who am I talking to?" He said, "You mean you don't remember me?" We had a long talk and he wrote to me. I didn't even write him back.

Naomi started to date the fellow with the green eyes and green jacket just in time for graduation. Amazingly, Carmen met the workman coming out of the manhole! Giving up hope of ever seeing him again and feeling rather silly, she stopped going to the restaurant. She decided to get out and meet people and, having bought a new dress, she went with some friends to a club. Sitting with her back to the dance floor, she felt a tap on her shoulder. There he was, asking her to dance. It felt like destiny. He called her a week later and they were together for "365 or so days." His work took him away and, though she wrote often, she received only one postcard in return. She met him again for a few hours when he stopped over on a flight through her city. He's in love with someone else. Carmen still loves him.

Falling is an adventure, full of excitement and risk. With the movement of falling, our bodies react with fear and elation, our world turns upside down. The glorious other who precipitates the fall may or may not leap with us. There seem to be no rules to falling. Certainly none are to be found here in this description of it—except, perhaps, to be brave and to aim for grace. And hope you don't hit your head.

Notes

1   We have done this with death too. "I was so embarrassed, I could have died!" "They're in sudden death overtime." "I told him to drop dead."

2   Love is only one way of arresting this discord within the self. Joining a political revolution is an example of another.

3   Kern (1992) puts Chagall's paintings among the happiest celebrations of love in modern art.

4   Hari doesn't know he is quoting Dante, who described exactly the same reaction accompanying his thoughts of Beatrice.

5   It's as if a truck is passing over my body every time
    It's as if a jet is breaking the sound barrier when I see you

It's as if a rock musician is drumming non-stop in my chest
It gives me a shock and makes my adrenaline peak.

6   This translates literally as "the beautiful terror." It is the title of an award-winning Canadian book by Robert Lalonde (1982), in which he describes a personal love experience. The English translation by David Homel, however, is entitled *Sweet Madness*.

7   General ill health and malnutrition.

8   Biofeedback devices allow us to view activities such as our brain's alpha waves, that are normally unknown (inaccessible) to us. This knowledge allows us to exert some control over what had been previously "involuntary" (Restak, 1979) .

9   From Sonnet VII, in *Sonnets from the Portuguese*, published in 1850.

10   *Midsummer Night's Dream*, 5.1.8–9.

11   "[Her] book," Tennov says, "is aimed at taming a madness (limerence) by learning its habits, identifying its various parts and forms, and hoping thereby to make some predictions about its course" (1979, p. 173).

12   In Mack, 1987, p. 372, lines 504–507.

13   Italics in original.

14   De Rougemont (1940/1956) believes that it is the specter of death that makes a love into a love story. He says happy love is not storied, has no history.

8
Possessed

I thought about him night and day. He consumed every thought. His name. Um, I carved it in a tree. I thought about him all the time. His voice, his name, just everything consumed me. I loved anything he did. It was this whirlwind of magic—you know—it was being in heaven, this floating. It was everything. It's like being on top of the world. I would have died for him. I would have.

Nicole is *consumed*. Literally this means she is taken, wholly, completely (Thatcher, 1984, p. 183). He fills her thoughts, *night and day*. Imagine this filling of the mind. Nicole wakes and thinks of him. She combs her hair and wonders if he would like it this way, pulled back, or this way, off to the side. At breakfast, she pushes her food around her plate and wonders what he is eating. Later, at school, she sits in class, writing his name over and over again in the margins of her notebook. The page before her is filled with words she is copying from the blackboard, but it is the stuff of the margins that grasps her. It is the time between classes, too, that matters. It is then that she may speak of him to her friends. "He said the funniest thing last night." Volleyball practice (she pretends he is there, watching), supper, homework are got out of the way. Lived through. All thought is fixed on that moment of the day for which she has been waiting since opening her eyes that morning—the phone ringing; his voice saying, "hello." Paradise. He is her last thought before she sleeps.

Nicole is *obsessed*. From *obsideo* (Latin: *ob* before, *sedo* to sit), to obsess means to beset or besiege; to vex, to harass, as an evil spirit (Thatcher, 1984, p. 575). But Nicole's obsession is not a reluctant one, a surrender to harassing spirits. She feels captured, whirled about by a magical force, but it is taking her to the top of the world. She meets a boy over the telephone and now he is *everything*. This boy, the idea of him, has seized her.

Nicole is *possessed*. By love possessed. This phrase, though poetic, seems to fit this 13-year-old girl's first love experience. A boy is in possession of her *every thought, day and night, everything*. Possessed is from the Latin, *possideo, possessum,* to occupy (*pos* from *por*, before, near, and *sedeo*, to sit, as in reside, preside) (Thatcher, 1984, p. 647). The original sense of possess was "to remain near" (Skeat, 1993, p. 422), but it has come to mean to have and to hold, to pervade, to fill or take up entirely; to have full power or mastery over (Thatcher 1984, p. 647). The boy is before Nicole all the time. The thought of him engulfs her. Love, said Andreas Cappellanus in his twelfth-century *Art of Courtly Love*, is a kind of agony due to extreme meditation upon another person (Singer, 1984b).

Every Heartbeat Bears Your Name

> Early in the morning till late at night, I really do hardly anything else but think of Peter. I sleep with his image before my eyes, dream about him and he is still looking at me when I awake ... I don't know quite how long my common sense will keep this longing under control. (Anne Frank, 1952, p. 144)

For over a year and a half, Anne has been living in hiding with her family during the Nazi occupation of her country. Peter Van Daan and his parents share a secret "annexe" with the Franks. When they first came to this place Anne was 13, and she wrote in her diary:

> At nine-thirty in the morning (we were still having breakfast) Peter arrived, the Van Daans' son, not sixteen yet, a rather soft, shy, gawky youth; can't expect much from his company. (p. 20)

Now when she is past her fourteenth year, she longs to share her thoughts with someone and wants it to be Peter Van Daan. She awakes one morning from a dream about another Peter, a childhood sweetheart. In the dream she and this other Peter, whom she calls "Petel," are sitting together looking at a book of drawings. He looks into her eyes and says, "If I had only known I would have come to you long before!" She then feels "a soft and oh, such a cool kind cheek against mine and it felt good, so good." This dream affects her strongly:

> When Daddy kissed me this morning, I could have cried out: "Oh, if only you were Peter!" I think of him all the time and I keep repeating to myself the whole day, "Oh Petel, darling, darling Petel!"
>
> Oh Petel, Petel, how will I ever free myself of your image? Wouldn't any other in your place be a miserable substitute? ... A week ago, even yesterday, if anyone had asked me, "Which of your friends do you consider would be the most suitable to marry?" I would have answered, "I don't know;" but now I would cry, "Petel, because I love him with all my heart and soul. I give myself completely!" (p. 122)

For Anne the two Peters become as one. Her old feelings for Petel, reawakened in the dream, merge with her current preoccupation with Peter Van Daan. She finds now that "there is someone who governs all my moods and that is … Peter." "I am happy if I see him and if the sun shines when I'm with him. I was very excited yesterday; while washing my hair. I knew that he was sitting in the room next to ours" (p. 151). She lives from one meeting with him to the next. The company of the shy gawky boy now determines her happiness. Though just the idea of him nearby excites her, he is, in some sense, with her all the time. Waking, sleeping, he is there in her thoughts.

When one's thoughts are constantly focused on another, the rhythm of everyday life changes. Daily activities and responsibilities become secondary. Our attention is removed from them. We are essentially somewhere else, waiting, wondering, dreaming. What was once routine is now intrusive. Unless, of course, the beloved is part of that routine. Anne's assigned chore of retrieving potatoes from the barrel on the roof takes on great significance. She must pass through Peter's room to do it. The chore becomes an opportunity to be alone with him, the highlight of her day.

When Derek and Amy fall in love, it is their times together at school that are all important, not attending classes. Their grades, previously excellent, plummet. Céline, an honor student, maintains her grades but says,

> I was obsessed. My classes would be sort of secondary—in the breaks I had in between I'd try to find out where he'd be and purposely go to a class by a different route to pass his locker and see if he was there.

Finding *him*, seeing *him*, that's what going to school is really all about. One participant in this study told me that she convinced her parents to let her attend a particular school because she wanted so much to be a part of its music program. She really did—there was this certain boy enrolled in it. The disruption this loving focus on another can produce is illustrated in Dr. Buxton's (1987) description of teens in psychiatric care. The focus on another can invalidate professional psychological assessments and interfere with therapy. Kasi's erratic score on a personality inventory has more to do with the fact that she took the test sitting beside Brad than anything else. Jeff's distraught reaction in group therapy is no indication that he is relating to the discussion: Jose isn't there today and he is picturing her with Carl. The routine and expectations of the psychiatric treatment unit are not what is paramount in the lives of the teens. Their responses and behaviors are centered on what is most crucial to them, realizing their love.

In our experience of the world there is more than the physical and geometrical distance that stands between all other things and ourselves. There is a *lived* distance that connects us to that which matters to us most. Within that lived space or landscape some things exist for us more than others. Merleau-Ponty (1945/1962) says that the scope of our life (not just in the broadest sense, but in every moment) is measured by this distance. There is often a degree of latitude in our relation to events—they do not cease to concern us but we feel some freedom from them.

> Sometimes, on the other hand, the lived distance is both too small and too great: the majority of events cease to count for me while the nearest ones obsess me. They enshroud me like night and rob me of my individuality and freedom. I can literally no longer breathe; I am possessed. (Merleau-Ponty, 1945/1962, p. 286)

The lover goes through all the motions of everyday life, gets through all the *non*-sense, if impatiently. But what makes sense now, what counts is love. Love *possesses*. Rollo May (1969) says love is *daimonic*. He defines daimonic as any natural function that has the power to take over the whole person (p. 123). One is possessed, as if by magic. A spell has been cast; an arrow has struck; a potion has been swallowed. One is taken. Julius Evola (1983) says that anyone who, whether lacking in willpower or energetic, lazy or busy, knowledgeable or ignorant, poor or rich, falls in love feels that at a certain moment his thoughts are literally chained to a given person without any possibility of escape (p. 26). Just the name of that individual can call up the spell, like some potent incantation.

David, David, David. For Nicole the name David, which once had such an ordinary sound, now has the power to charm, to raise her spirits. She chants it, names him, at every opportunity. On the bus to school: "Going to the museum isn't such a great field trip. David's class is going to." At lunch: "David hates ham sandwiches." In class: "Michelangelo's David is the greatest sculpture ever, I think." She writes "David" on her hand, whispers it to herself. She carves "David" on a backyard tree. Her father finds the carved name and asks, "What's this?" She blushes. She cannot say "the name of the one for whom I would die."

> You like to talk about him. You work his name into the conversation whenever you can. You're careful about it, but it's probably obvious to everyone. (Casual Informant)

> I just read this entry [diary entry about wanting to ask a certain boy to dance] out loud to myself and just the sound of his name sends chills down my spine, nice chills, of course. (Veronica)

Emily Dickinson (1890/1960) describes her reaction to a beloved's name as "That Stop-sensation—on my Soul— / and Thunder—in the Room" (p. 136). The other's name is wondrous, powerful, spellbinding. *Maria: say it loud and there's music playing, say it soft and it's almost like praying.*[1]

> I went out of my way to find occasions for my parents to pronounce Swann's name. In my own mind, of course, I never ceased to murmur it; but I needed also to hear

its exquisite sound, to have others play to me that music the voiceless rendering of which did not suffice me…. The pleasure I derived from the sound of it I felt to be so sinful that it seemed to me as though the others read my thoughts and changed the conversation if I tried to guide it in that direction. (Proust, 1954, p. 447)

Name is from the Anglo-Saxon *nama*, evolving from the Aryan root *GNA*, meaning to know (Skeat, 1993, p. 301). When we act in the name of something, someone—as "in the name of God, what are you doing?"—we are invoking them, calling them to witness. David is present to Nicole all the time. Reciting his name at every opportunity, she brings him there—his name conjures him up. She breathes his name and he comes to life before her. Céline, too, tells me:

> Even now if I say his name, my breath will catch in my throat. Now that is love when you can't breathe.

If we imagine Nicole as she engraves "David" on a tree, we likely picture her enclosing it within the shape of a heart. The literal interpretation of the ancient form of the Chinese character for love is *breathing into the heart* (Pann & Stearns, 1992). It evokes the image of a heart coming to life. The breath in both the East and West is closely related to the spirit, the consciousness, the soul. *Psyche*, originally meaning breath in Greek (Skeat, 1993, p. 375), stands for soul or life. The Greek *pneuma*, the Latin *anima,* and the Hebrew *ruach* have the same associations. *Spiritus*, Latin for wind, breath, soul, is the root from which *inspire* is derived (Skeat, 1993, p. 458–459). Love inspires us, enlivens us, brings us to life.

The heart itself has become a symbol for the life principle, for the vital force that distinguishes a live body from a corpse (Chetwynd, 1982, p. 58). *Heart* evolved from the Sanskrit root *hrid, hridaya,* meaning that which quivers (Skeat, 1993, p. 198). Our hearts do quiver. A dark red, chambered muscle nestled for protection beneath the rib cage and small enough to be held in the hand, the heart pumps life-essential blood to the lungs and throughout the body. We are most often unaware of the contracting movements of this organ as it beats out the seconds of our life. We must feel for the pulse in our veins to count them. Sometimes, however, our heart seems to tremble or pound within us. Our heart skips a beat or even seems to stop momentarily, as if shocked. We say, "My heart is breaking." "I stood before a diagram of the heart in the bookstore wondering, 'Where would the crack in mine be?'" We say too, "I have a heavy heart." "As he drove off, my heart was heavy within me." In ancient Egypt the hieroglyph for the heart (*Ab*) was a dancing figure. The heart was seen as the seat of love, quickening at the sight or thought of a loved one (Ackerman, 1994, p. 145).

Love has been situated elsewhere. It has been thought of as a function of the liver (*cogit amare jecur* / the liver compels to love), an infection of the blood ("you are in my blood;"), and a passion of the brain, "by reason of corrupt imagination" (Burton, 1621/1977, III, pp. 57–58). Today the sophisticated understanding of the human body provided by science means few of us think that love or any other "emotion" resides in a particular place in the body. We know the heart is a hollow muscular organ divided into four chambers and enclosed in a membranous sac. Yet we understand the words of the French philosopher Pascal (1966) when he says: "We know the truth not only through our reason but also through our heart" (p. 58). We understand the words of the Sufi poet Rumi (written in about 1260):

> Your gaze has enchanted my heart
> with a poem
> no one could ever write. (1992, p. 12)

We understand those addressed to a lover in the diary of Lady Nijo (written between 1271 and 1306):

> Our pledge may end,
> But the stream of tears
> My heart calls forth
> Will never cease to flow. (1973, p. 129)

The heart does seem to be the landscape of action in love. Derek, telling of his love for Amy, places his hand over his heart. "I thought if I don't see her, my heart is going to break." In our bodily experience of love, it is the heart where love resides. "In my heart I know he loves me."

> We could define "heart" as that "part" of us where we are most tender and open to the world around us, where we can let others in and feel moved by them, as well as reach outside ourselves to contact them more fully. (Welwood, 1985, p. 61)

Lovers are *sweet-hearts*. On Saint Valentine's Day, the day of the year dedicated to sweethearts, "valentines" are exchanged. This custom is a very old one, evolving from an early Roman festival, Lupercalia, held on February 14. It was thought that upon this day birds began mating and Cupid aimed his arrows at soon-to-be lovers. During Lupercalia, men wore the names of the girls who were to be their partners pinned to their sleeves. We still say: "He wears his heart upon his sleeve." When Lupercalia became a saint's day—the Christian martyr was executed in Rome on February 14, 240 AD—couples exchanged gifts, and later handmade cards, sometimes paper hearts trimmed with lace.[2] Valentines became heart-shaped, symbolic of a gift of love (Valentines, 1968, p. 25).

Within the figure of the heart, lovers join their names—or in keeping with the mystery of love, their initials. We find these announcements everywhere: carved on a tree, drawn in sand on a beach, scribbled in chalk on a sidewalk, spray painted on a highway overpass, and even penned on public washroom walls. Barthes (1977/1978) says the heart is the organ of desire. "The heart is what I imagine I give" (p. 52).

> We were quickly climbing a steep hillside. He was a few steps ahead of me when he stopped, turned, and smiling asked, "How's your heart?" I could only smile back in response, but the words came suddenly to mind, "I don't know. You have it." I knew then; I loved him. (Informant)

It is what the other will do with the lover's heart, the lover's desire, that constitutes all the heart's problems (Barthes, 1977/1978).

Searching for Clues

Discovering the feelings of the person who now has one's heart in his/her possession becomes of great importance. We must discern if our heart is safe with them; prepare for grief or joy; find evidence on which to base even a fragment of hope. "The answer the lover tirelessly seeks is: *What am I worth?*" (Barthes, 1977/1978, p. 214).[3]

> I was totally obsessed the whole time—trying to know if he liked me. I was always reading things into the little conversations that we had—we'd have these three minute conversations that I'd be playing over and over in my head. (Veronica)

> I think you are always looking for clues in everything. Like in the way he looks at you and in how many times a day you see this person and what they say to you and how they say it to you. Everything. So you are totally analysing every single moment you're in that person's company, so you can find out if there are any clues that will tell you if they're interested in you. (Céline)

The other's every gesture becomes filled with meaning. A festival of meaning (Barthes, 1977/1978):

> A squeeze of the hand—enormous documentation, a knee which doesn't move away, an arm extended, as if quite naturally, along the back of a sofa and against which the other's head gradually comes to rest—this is the paradisiac realm of subtle and clandestine signs: a kind of festival not of the senses but of meaning. (p. 67)

Everything is significant; nothing is trivial. Movements, sighs, gestures: They are all clues to his/her feelings or intentions: *tout est signe en amour* (Stendhal, 1822/1957, p. 19).[4]

> Perhaps she does not give you her arm when at the theater you escort her to her

box; a trifle like this, taken in tragic earnest by a passionate heart, by joining a humiliation to every judgment which crystallisation makes, poisons the very source of love and may destroy it. (Stendhal, 1822/1957, p. 131)

To my great joy—I will be quite honest about it—already this morning I noticed that Peter kept looking at me all the time. Not in the ordinary way, I don't know how, I just can't explain. (Frank, 1952, p. 136)

[Six days later] Who knows, perhaps he doesn't care about me at all and looks at the others in just the same way. Perhaps I only imagined that it was especially for me. (p. 142)

Movements *not* there, withheld or forgotten: The expression of their absence can cause the vigilant lover much despair. Paradoxically, the absence of polite, everyday behavior can be also interpreted as a sign of love, of caring too much.

June 29: I know he is shy around girls he likes. Before the movie we kept glancing and smiling at each other. Then what was really funny is that after the movie when we were all outside it was like a first date; we all just stood there smiling and looking at the ground but *not saying anything.* (Veronica's diary).[5]

Rather than be despairing, the hopeful lover may read only the signs that suggest his/her love will be returned. Fundamentally, until love is openly declared, he/she must always be suspended in doubt. There is an essential ambiguity of meaning in language that is always there. Even after a declaration of love, there can be confusion. "Yes, I did say I loved you. But I meant I loved you as a friend." And always there is the realization that signs are not true proofs: Anyone can produce false signs and deceive us (Barthes, 1977/1978).

The following are excerpts from Veronica's diary:

March 21: Tom is really nice, but he sure knows how to confuse girls. From all that Katy tells me and from what I've seen of the way he acts around her, I think he likes her. But now that he and I talk a bit more and have become better friends, when we do talk he treats me the same way he treats Katy. So I don't know.

April 9: I've made up my mind that I would not let Tom confuse me. The boys were watching us in gym. Tom didn't come to talk to Katy but he was just looking at me a lot. I caught his eye a couple of times and held his gaze long enough to smile. In Math, he was throwing paper airplanes and one hit me. That could have been an accident, but another one came right under my nose. No one can tell me *that* wasn't deliberate.

April 18: Tom is confusing me and making me depressed and everything. Jan says he was looking at me all day, it was so obvious. I nearly screamed with delight. More confusion, but it was true. I caught his eye more today than I have all year. Dani and Rae both say he likes me considering he picked me *first* for baseball yesterday. Well, out of the girls, not including Brenda or Nicki. But out of *all* the rest of the girls even Katy.

May 11: I feel devastated. Tom is going out with Katy. I can't believe it. Especially after the dance—he held me closer than ever before and *it wasn't just me* who thought so.

Veronica is trying to decode Tom's actions. Tom seems to like Katy, but he has begun of late to behave in a similar way with Veronica. He looks at her pretty often now. Veronica's hope is situated in the truism that you can't keep your eyes off the one you love. If he wasn't looking at her, Veronica might choose to be guided by the truism that lovers avoid the other's eyes so he/she cannot see the love revealed there. She has enormous evidence in the choice of *her* nose as the crash site for his paper plane (he's trying to get her attention). Corroborating this is the fact that he picked her first for his baseball team—as good as first, anyway (he wants to be with her). Others' opinions are solicited. Veronica checks out her observations with Dani and Rae. Her judgment alone cannot be trusted; she wants too much to believe he cares for her. Careful though she has been—listening to others, admitting to confusion, attempting not to raise her hopes too high—when Tom chooses Katy she is devastated. It is unbelievable. It overturns the meaning of his tight embrace. Others think so too.

Veronica has tried to read Tom. Reading meaning into a person's actions is not unlike trying to read a text. We always approach a text with what may be termed as *foremeaning* (Gadamer, 1960/1990, p. 267): A person who is trying to understand a text is always projecting. As soon as some initial meaning emerges, a meaning for the text as a whole is projected. This initial meaning emerges only because we come to the text with particular expectations in regard to a certain meaning. Working this out is a constant process: We continue to revise on the basis of what emerges as we penetrate further into the meaning revealed to us by the text. This is essentially what we do whenever we try to understand anything.

A girl's thoughts may go like this: "He's wearing cologne? Maybe he's trying to impress me. I think he has put on cologne. He's made a special effort. He's trying to be attractive to me. That's why people wear cologne, right? Could he have done this for me? To impress me?" The boy in question may be wearing cologne because his grandmother gave some to him for his birthday and she's visiting today. His sister may have splashed some on him in fun as he ran out the door to school. He may have tried a cigarette during class break and has borrowed cologne to cover up the smell of smoke he is certain has permeated his shirt. He may not be wearing cologne at all; his family is using a new brand of fabric softener for their wash. But what if he is, and what if it *is* for her? Such a good sign.

The difficulties of determining if you are loved, of determining the chances of receiving the heart of the one who possesses yours, is captured engagingly in Jane Austen's *Emma* (1816/1976). Emma—handsome, clever, rich—is certain that she is deducing the truth about everyone's secret attachments, that she knows the secrets of everyone's feelings. A helpful girl, she proposes to give destiny a hand. The humor of Austen's story lies in the fact that Emma gets everything wrong. She doesn't even know her own heart.

Emma, for instance, decides that Mr. Elton is in love with her friend Harriet: "She had taken up the idea, she supposed, and made everything bend to it" (p. 678). Mr. Elton, on the other hand, feels encouraged by Emma. His attention is to Emma:

> The speech was more to Emma than to Harriet, which Emma could understand.
> There was a deep consciousness about him, and he found it easier to meet her eye
> than her friend's. (p. 646)

Mr. Elton reads to them while Emma sketches Harriet's likeness. His compliments on her drawing she takes as references to Harriet's beauty, and his eagerness to have the portrait framed, at some inconvenience to himself, she thinks has to do with the picture being of Harriet. When Mr. Elton confidently proposes marriage to Emma—his actions based on the obvious signs of approbation she has been sending him—she is most surprised. When she informs him where she believes his heart truly lies, he is most offended.

Though *Emma* is a satire on common beliefs about romance, all Austen's novels, like other romances, serve to teach their readers about love's informing signs. Romances are usually written in the third person, so the reader may know the inner thoughts and motivations of all the characters. The reader of the romance knows what to pay attention to, knows what is really going on. Real life, unfortunately, doesn't work that way. Gergen (1991) tells us:

> Any action, from the utterance of a single syllable to the movement of an index
> finger, becomes language when others grant it significance in a pattern of interchange, and even the most elegant prose can be reduced to nonsense if others do
> not grant it the right of meaning. (p. 157)

The lover's situation discloses, in a powerful way, our everyday challenge of making meaning in our world. In our communication with one another the possibility of misunderstanding is always there. We cannot know exactly if what we are signifying is what we wish to signify, nor even if we are signifying anything (Sartre, 1956/1994). The Other must grant significance to our expression. Meaning is created between us—and so much can go wrong.

> He was talking to me on the phone and said, "How's my baby?" and I just melted. I said, "Fine." and he said, "What are you talking about?" He had been speaking to his dog. But I thought it was to me and it made my world go round. At the moment when he said it, I absolutely melted. (Nicole)

His baby. Her world began to spin. Recalling those words makes Nicole relive the excitement of that moment, how she dissolved into it, into the bliss of being his. But then came more information and all was changed. Those earth-shaking words were for his dog.

Though they weigh and measure each syllable uttered by the person they love, turning it this way and that to drain out any nuance of meaning, lovers freely admit that *their* own speech is often incoherent. "What a stupid thing to say!" "Why did I say that? He'll think I'm an idiot!" "Where did that come from?"

> You talk a lot without noticing what you say, and what you say is often the opposite of what you think…. The strain is so great that you give no sign of warmth and love is concealed with its own abundance. (Stendhal, 1822/1957, p. 79)

It may be that Tom chose to ask Katy to go out with him because he believed he had a better chance of success with her than with Veronica. Though he can tell Veronica likes him, she doesn't seem very interested in him *that way.* She treats him pretty much the way she treats most of the guys in class. She doesn't even look at him when he talks to her sometimes. He tried at the dance to show her he cared, but she didn't seem to respond. It seems miraculous, all considered, that we are able to understand one another at all. For lovers, where touching, moving, knowing one another is everything, our essential distance from one another seems particularly poignant.

Sacredness

Eros turns life into a sort of religion (Evola, 1969/1983; Lewis, 1960). Norman Kiell (1964), writing about the authors of autobiographies as they recall their adolescent crushes and first loves, says, "There is a tendency on the part of nearly all of them to use spiritual phraseology in describing this phase of their lives" (p. 126).

> In the depths of her heart she keeps note of the number of times she has seen him; … twice they have met at dinner, and he has greeted her three times when she was out walking. One evening at a party he kissed her hands, and you will observe that since then she has been careful, even at the risk of appearing odd, to allow no one else to kiss her hand. (Stendhal, 1822/1957, p. 56)

The times they are together form a litany she recites to herself. The touch of his lips on her hand—she will not let others erase it. The memory of it lasts on her skin longer than any ordinary touch ever could. There is the thrill of connection in a touch, but there is something more. The touch of a loved person leaves something behind for the obsessed lover. It is as if a trace of the person has been bestowed. Sometimes the beloved's touch transforms an everyday object into a kind of relic, a sacred relic. *Sacred* comes from the Latin *sacrare*, meaning to consecrate (Skeat, 1993, p. 411). Something sacred is set apart from all other things.

> I slept with his glove beneath my pillow. I loved knowing that he had touched it, worn it. (Informant)

> I kept a gum wrapper that he discarded. (Informant)

> My mother once told me how, when she was a teenager, she was so in love with a certain boy that she picked up the Popsicle sticks he tossed away and kept them under her pillow, kissing them at night. (Ackerman, 1994, pp. 336–337)

> When we were nursing students, Jenny was mad about this intern. The day I assisted him with a surgical dressing change, I quietly put the disposable mask he had worn into my pocket. Jenny still has it, pasted into a scrapbook. (Author's journal entry)

> I normally find tooth marks on a pencil disgusting, but hers were sacred; her wonderful mouth had been there. (Tennov, 1979, p. 31)

It is as if an object can become endowed with the other's essence and thus turned into an object of reverence. It becomes a talisman, a magical influence. The transformation lies in its power to conjure up the presence of the beloved. In *Emma*, Austen acknowledges (with amusement) this tendency for lovers to create holy relics:

> I am now going to destroy—what I ought to have destroyed long ago—what I ought never to have kept: I know that very well (blushing as she spoke). However, now I will destroy it all; and it is my particular wish to do it in your presence, that you may see how rational I am grown. (Austen, 1816/1976, p. 779)

Emma cannot guess what is in Harriet's parcel labeled "Most precious treasures." "Did he ever give you anything?" The treasure turns out to be a small piece of court plaster. Mr. Elton cut his finger one day and needed a court-plaster. Harriet cut him a piece that was too large and he cut it smaller and played with what was left before he gave it back to her:

> And so then, in my nonsense, I could not help making a treasure of it; so I put it by, never to be used, and looked at it now and then as a great treat. (Austen, 1816/ 1976, p. 779)

Emma is divided between wonder and amusement. She asks Harriet: "And so you actually put this piece of court-plaster by for his sake!" She cannot imagine putting by a piece of court-plaster that Frank Churchill had pulled about. "I never was equal to this" (p. 779).

These objects of the beloved, kept secretly, looked at, felt—caressed—are kept in private. It is as if one secretly owns a piece of the beloved.

> When he got some new false teeth (he had two on a bridge) she made him give her the old set. She carried them around for ages, then put them in a drawer by her bed with his letters. (Drabble, 1975, p. 28)

This character in Margaret Drabble's *Realms of Gold* is an archaeologist and so might be expected to cherish fragments and relics. Later, however, having ended the affair with her lover, she takes to putting his teeth down the front of her brassiere, liking the feel of them. She finds that they keep her company. In this gesture she finds a way of keeping some part of him—even if it is false—close to her heart.[6]

There are other objects that are public symbols, tokens given openly to represent the love. They announce the love to others, and also serve to remind and reassure the lovers of the avowal of love that lies between them.

> I gave Amy the key to my car. It was my most valuable possession. She couldn't drive, it was more of a symbol. She gave me the key to her diary. (Derek)

> He gave me a perfect, red rose. I have it pressed between the pages of my diary. (Informant)

> He sold his bike and bought me a black Alaskan diamond ring in the shape of a heart. I still have it. (Gerri)

> He gave me a ring with interlocking hearts. We bought it at a hair salon in our town where they sold jewelry, too. The small fake diamond fell out within days. We went to the store right away and demanded a replacement. It was really important to us that I wore his ring. (Penny)

> We each had a key ring that was the shape of half a heart. The pieces fit together making one heart. (Informant)

These are symbols of love: keys (*Here is the key to my heart. I trust you.*) and hearts (*I give my heart to you*); roses (an attribute of Venus, the goddess of love) and rings (a circle signifying the cycle of time, a lifetime). The real significance of the love token may be that it has the power to transport the lover out of any ordinary space to that other holy land.

> I always had within reach a plan of Paris which, because I could see on it the street in which M. and Mme. Swann lived, seemed to me to contain a secret treasure. And for pure pleasure, as well as from a sort of chivalrous loyalty, on no matter

what pretext I would utter the name of that street, until my father, not being, like my mother and grandmother, apprised of my love, would ask me: "But why are you always talking about that street?" (Proust, 1954, p. 447)

As a youth, the narrator in Proust's *Swann's Way* is in love with Gilberte Swann. Everything that surrounds her, including her family, is impregnated with a special charm and excites in him a passion as she herself does. This seems to happen for other young lovers, as well. A participant in my study described her experience:

> There was this place he took me to. X is a big huge school with lots of nooks and crannies. There was this doorway, like an entry way. This is the very first place he took me to talk. To talk about each other and our interests. When he broke up with me, I'd go there and feel sorry for myself. I'd play over and over the song I associated with him. It was a song on a tape he had given me and it was playing the first time he kissed me. It was the first passionate kiss that I had ever had in my life. That place stayed special—if I even went past the doorway, even after he wasn't at that school anymore and when I had a new boyfriend that place had special meaning. (Veronica)

Associated with the beloved, the meaning of any space can change. It takes on a different essence. This change is "at once mystical and absurd" (Proust, 1954, p. 323). A space that can evoke the beloved is different from all other spaces. It becomes sanctified. A gravel pit, a doorway, a street: Each can become an exceptional place.

A place may become special to a lover because within it something of significance has occurred. It stands for something now, symbolizes a happening, like a first passionate kiss. Juliet's balcony was never the same after she found Romeo standing beneath it. A place may acquire meaning merely because it was introduced to one by the beloved. It may be a restaurant, a video store, a favorite seat in a movie theater.

> There was this place behind the school, kind of a park where we used to go at lunch or whenever we had a break from class. We always sat under this one tree on a picnic bench. It was really special. Magical. (Derek)

A place may acquire meaning because it is a place of refuge. It is in this place that the two may go to get away from the rest of the world. They find *sanctuary* here and in so doing transform it. Sanctuary is from the Latin *sanctuarium*, meaning a shrine (Skeat, 1993, p. 411).

Places where one goes to see the beloved become distinct, distinguished. Such places may be the hallway by his locker, the spot where she chains her bike, the shopping center where he works part-time, the street where she lives:

I have often walked down this street before,
But the pavement's always stayed beneath my feet before.
Does enchantment flow out of every door?
No, it's just on the street where she lives.[7]

A place may acquire significance simply because it once held him or her. A simple room can be transformed. A certain room is no longer just a room, but a place the beloved has been—right there, on that spot. "He/she sat there; I stood here." Being in such places can fill the lover with delight or torment. Though the beloved is the referent for the landscape—its source of meaning—his or her actual presence there is not required.

I got so I could walk across
That Angle in the floor,
Where he turned so, I turned—how—
And all our Sinew tore—(Dickinson, 1890/1960, p. 136)

A place can acquire meaning because it comes to symbolize the relationship itself. It is the place that in its entirety is summoned before the lover whenever the love comes to mind. A summer camp, a farm, a city. There are those marvelous lines in the movie *Casablanca* (1943):

We'll always have Paris. We didn't have it. We'd lost it until you came to Casablanca. We got it back last night.

Paris—*their* Paris—becomes sacred space once more. As the setting for their love, it altered radically for him when he thought that she had abandoned him, that she had never really loved him. With those tormented thoughts, Paris became a place of pain in his memory to which he struggled not to return. The discovery that she did love him, loves him still, gives him back Paris—Paris as seen through lovers' eyes.

A sacred space can be created in a deeper sense. It can be shaped out of air, as a mystical place, conceived in the mind of the lover. It may be the stars, the sky, the moon, or the night that become the "place" that evokes the beloved:

I look up at the moon,
And my heart feels you,
Although a thousand miles away,
Watching this same moon. (Su Tung Po, ca.\ 1075A.D.\1989)

In love seems a place in which the world is reduced, concentrated (Ortega y Gasset, 1971). Space becomes either *of the beloved*—and thus experienced as consecrated ground—or *not*.

Possessing Forever

> You touch so blissfully
> Because the caress preserves
> because the place you so tenderly cover
> does not vanish; because beneath
> you feel pure duration. So you promise eternity, almost from the embrace.
> *(Rilke, 1989b, p. 159)*

There is forever in a lover's touch. Rilke (1989b) wrote that he meant this verse quite literally: The place where the lover puts his hand is thereby withheld from passing away, from aging, from the near-disintegration that is always occurring in our integral nature—that simply beneath this hand, this place *lasts, is*. The beloved possesses not only the power to determine the lover's experience of space but that of time as well. "I think of these lines with a special joy in having been able to write them" (p. 321). In love, he has experienced the sensation that time is transcended. *L'amour, c'est l'espace et le temps rendus sensibles au coeur*—Proust, 1954.[8]

> I was aware of the sounds and the smells and the angle that a light was shining and aware of what he was wearing and how he looked and what he said. Everything.
> (Veronica)

All the things of this moment—the U2 song playing in the background, the pepperoni aroma rising from the pizza, the way the street light strikes the window next to the booth, the way the blue of his sweater matches his eyes, his laughter when she nearly spills her drink—are strongly present to her.[9] How keen her senses are when she's with him like this. Times with him, times that must seem ordinary to anyone else, are filled with a kind of excitement, tension. There is an energy present that enlivens everything.

Much of the time, the things of life are taken for granted. We are so in the world that we rarely think about it. Heidegger (1927/1962) refers to this as *fallenness*. In love (which involves a very different kind of falling) this natural attitude is altered. We experience—not all the time but often when we are with the one we love—a heightened awareness of the world. Objects, surroundings, our own and the other's physical presence are disclosed to us in an immediate way. In such moments we are fully conscious. Heidegger, though he does not pursue this idea in his work, believes that in love there is a revelation of being (cited in Halliburton, 1981, p. 215).

In James Joyce's (1914/1992b) story "The Dead," Gretta Conroy hears the notes of a song as she is leaving a family party with her husband, Gabriel. The music reminds her of a boy she once knew, Michael Furey, who used to sing the song. Hearing it now, decades later, she is moved. Gabriel sees a sudden grace and mystery about his wife that stirs him. Her cheeks color, her eyes shine, and he notices how richly bronzed her hair looks in the gaslight. "A sudden tide of joy went leaping out of his heart" (p. 213). He thinks of the tenderness they have shared, of loving words, glances, caresses. Back in their hotel room, however, he finds her distant from him. When he discovers the reason for her mood, he feels jealous. "I suppose you were in love with this Michael Furey, Gretta," he says. She answers: "I was great with him at that time." Gretta reveals that Michael died, shortly after she moved to Dublin. He was 17. "And what did he die of so young, Gretta?" "I think he died for me" (p. 221). Later that night, watching his wife sleep, Gabriel thinks of the boy who died for the girl she was then. He knows that he has never felt anything like that for any woman. He knows, nevertheless, that such a feeling must be love.

Gretta, moved to a time of love, becomes suddenly alive. She is transformed before her husband. Looking at her, he too quickens and this evening really *sees* her. It is as if, after all their years of being together, she is in some way unveiled to him. In the disclosure of Michael Furey's love for her, she is disclosed. Gabriel is *with* her on this night. In her sharing of this tragedy with him, their world achieves an openness that was not there before. Gabriel perceives his relation with Gretta more clearly in the light cast by Michael Furey's love. To die for her; that must be love.

Death is used as a measure of love. "I'd die for you," the love song goes.[10] Love makes the thought of death frequent, easy, without terrors; it becomes merely a standard of comparison, the price one would pay for many things (Stendhal, 1822/1957, p. 225). Nicole, in love with a boy she knows only as a voice on the telephone, says she would die for him. She claims this forcefully, spontaneously. She means it as the gauge of her love. Risking death is love's yardstick.

> I was like a knight in shining armor—very quick to jump to her defense. I got into a fight with another guy on the football team because he made some comment about her in the locker room. I wanted to protect her from the moment I saw her. (Derek)

> I look back to the age of Romanticism and stuff.... Girls were impressed if you dueled for their love. I'd like to be a knight in shining armor. I like to imagine if she was being attacked, I'd show up and save her—even die to save her. I'd rather not die, but I'd like to be the protector. (Hari)

Derek and Hari see themselves as fighters for and protectors of the one they love. Hari would rather not die, but he would die—for her. In fact, he seems disappointed that the opportunity is unlikely to arise for him. How wonderful if he could demonstrate to her his daring and bravery. She would see how much he loves her. "Lovers show a grandiose neglect of danger, a carelessness for one's own security, an absence of death fear" (Reik, 1941, p. 142). In the *Phaedo* (Plato, 1956a), it is argued that eros is motivation for facing death. An army composed of lovers and their beloveds would be an unbeatable fighting force. This is so not only because a lover is ashamed to be seen by his beloved doing cowardly things, but because, above all, a lover is willing to die for the beloved.

In our myths and stories of love, death does play a prominent role. Lovers brave the threat of death to be together. They risk all willingly. Some scholars suggest death is a kind of aphrodisiac. De Rougemont (1940/1956) says because confronting death makes us feel more alive, death is a goad for desire. He accuses lovers of seeking peril for its own sake and finds in romantic love a *dark desire*. He says of lovers: "In the innermost recesses of their breasts they have been obeying the fatal dictates of a wish for death; they have been in the throes of *the active passion of Darkness*" (p. 46).[11] Ackerman (1994), too, believes passion and death are linked "because we become most alive, most aware, on the brink of death—and we find that erotic" (p. 111).

Death, or rather our grasping the fact of it, does retrieve us from fallenness (Heidegger, 1962). Its anticipation puts us face to face with our existence. Death, like love, wakes us up to a more authentic experience of life. Perhaps this is one reason love and death seem so entwined in the human consciousness.

Another reason may be that death and the act of love are related. We see this link in the creation story of Adam and Eve. When they gain sexual knowledge of one another, Adam and Eve bring death to the human race. This is true biologically: Death came with our sexuality. The asexual reproduction of very primitive organisms occurs by cell division. The original cell divides and divides again, and lives on. Organisms that reproduce sexually, on the other hand, combine their genetic material, create a new organism, and die. Schopenhauer (1818/1966) says love is nature's lure to this act that ensures the survival of the species. But though death is inherent in it, "forever" lies in the sexual act as well. A part of ourselves, literally, as DNA, lives on in our offspring. *And nothing 'gainst Time's scythe can make defence / Save breed, to brave him when he takes thee hence.*[12] In this way love, death, and eternity are joined.

> When he left, he gave me a small, sealed glass tube with a note inside it. He had made it in the chemistry lab. He told me to break it open and read it on the day we were married or the day he died.

Kate knows the note reads that he will love her always. Their separation is a forced one. Tom must leave high school and move out of province with his parents. Both Kate and Tom are certain that they will be apart only temporarily. "The lover will find his way to his sweetheart, come hell or high water," says Reik (1941, p. 142). The only options lovers recognize are being together or death. For young lovers, death does not hold terror; losing the beloved does.

Rousseau (1762/1966) as the wise tutor in Émile recognizes that love creates great vulnerability in the lover. For Émile, Sophie has become his vulnerable spot. "What would you do if you were informed that Sophie is dead?" the tutor asks Émile. A responsible teacher, he feels he must prepare the young man for what can happen if his love is to leave or be taken from him. The tutor's strategy is to make Émile go away for a time and discover that he can endure. Though such a maneuver is hardly sufficient to vaccinate a young lover against despair at the loss of love, Émile's tutor's concern is legitimate.

> Come away, come away, death,
> And in sad cypress let me be laid;
> Fly away, fly away, breath;
> I am slain by a fair, cruel maid.
> (*Twelfth Night*, 2.4. 50–53)

Shakespeare, through Viola, says this song "gives a very echo to the seat / where Love is throned" (*Twelfth Night*, 2.4. 20).

> It is so well known in every village, how many have either died for love, or voluntarily made away themselves, that I need not much labour to prove it. *Nec modus aut requies nisi mors reperitur amoris* [love knows no limit or escape save death]; death is the common catastrophe to such persons. (Burton, 1621/1977, p. 187)

Burton, writing about love-melancholy, gives examples of "gentle ends," as when a lover departs and the wounded and distressed soul left behind falls sick and dies. Then there are those who offer violence to themselves and others because of love. Burton recounts that in 1615 at Neuburg,

> a young man because he could not get her parents' consent, killed his sweetheart and afterward himself, desiring this of the magistrate, as he gave up the ghost, that they might be buried in one grave. (p. 188)

Death is present in our love stories, not only as a measure of the power of love, but as an outcome. In these stories, lovers, when denied union, die. There is also the message, if often obscure, that love survives death—*for love is as strong as death*.[13] In the stories a thread of hope is woven that love overcomes mortality. Lovers denied union in life may find it afterward.

Two eighth-grade sweethearts, forbidden by the girl's mother to see each other, apparently drowned themselves in a canal, leaving suicide notes that told of their undying love, their desperation and their hope of being together in another world. (Wells, 1995, p. A12)

In this newspaper account of the death of two young lovers, the events preceding the tragedy were described as follows. Maryling's father found an autographed school picture of Christian in her room. He told her she had to be 16 to date. "You're still just a baby. What you have to do now is study." Both 14-year-olds were excellent students and had perfect school attendance records. Friends and parents wondered if Maryling was pregnant: An autopsy showed she was not.

Christian's note said, "I can't go on living. I've lost Maryling. I'm escaping from the realm of reality into the darkness of the unknown. Because reality is, I can't be with Maryling." He used a quotation from Beethoven that is included in an Italian opera, *The Players*, by Leoncavallo: "Applaud, friends, the comedy is over," and ended, "I love you all." Maryling in a note addressed to "Mom and Dad" said, "You'll never be able to understand the love between me and Christian. You don't let me see him in this world, so we're going to another place. Please don't cry for me, this is what I want. I want to feel happy, because I'm going to a place where I can be with Christian." These two young lovers acted upon a faith that holds love goes beyond the grave.

Lovers do vow eternity. "I will love you forever." Such eternal promises are made in good faith. They are meant; they are heart-felt. "Our love is for always." No experience cures us of this.

I was in love with a boy whose name I etched with permanent ink into my designer blue jeans. Unfortunately, the jeans outlived the relationship. (Leah)

But she fell in love again and, once again, assumed forever. Despite the collapse of previous relationships, despite the facing of betrayal or the coming of indifference, if love arrives again, it feels endless. This time it is the real thing (Lewis, 1960). "Eros has a right to make this promise. The event of falling in love is of such a nature that we are right to reject as intolerable the idea that it should be transitory" (Person, 1988, p. 39).

"Love is a life-and-death question" (Bloom, 1993, p. 238). It may be that love does transcend death. The transcendence may be simply that when you love, love becomes a part of you. That love, all your loves, are with you when you die (Haule, 1990). Young lovers, like Maryling and Christian, are perhaps too young in life to understand this. They conceive of love as possessing each other in a literal way. They have not attended to the words of Dylan

Thomas: Though lovers be lost love shall not; / And death shall have no dominion.[14]

Notes

1 Lyrics from "Maria," a song in the 1961 movie *West Side Story*.

2 The Duke of Orleans is thought to have made the first—while imprisoned in the Tower of London in 1415, he wrote love poems (valentines) to his wife (Valentines, 1968, p. 266).

3 Italics in original.

4 *In love everything is significant.* Original italics

5 Underlining in original.

6 A harmless enough comfort until, out at a party, she notices a man glancing at her cleavage and then staring in horror—the teeth are glaring back at him.

7 From the 1964 movie *My Fair Lady*. Screenplay by J. Lerner (1956).

8 "Love is space and time made perceptible to the heart."

9 The details of this scene are imagined by the author.

10 "(Everything I Do) I Do It for You" by Bryan Adams. By number of records sold, it was the international hit song of 1990.

11 Italics in original.

12 From Shakespeare's "Sonnet 12."

13 Song of Solomon, 8:6 (King James Version).

14 From his poem "Do Not Go Gentle Into That Good Night," written in 1952 (Thomas, 1971).

9
Becoming

Every time I am in Miss Tanswell's company I feel a pleasant sensation, which I never felt before. I sometimes become melancholy & speak very little. They perhaps say I have no sense. It is true I have not much sense. Still when I am in company with Ladies I generally talk & amuse them pretty much, but when in Miss Tanswell's company I am thoughtful. I speak very little but think a great deal. … And when I am with her, why I am afraid as it were to speak with her. (George Jones, in his diary, 1840s Québec, in Ward, 1986, pp. 35–36)

I found myself shy and tongue-tied in her presence. I wanted to talk with her, but every time I came near I felt oppressed and unfree and wanted to run away. (A young San Kim, the Korean revolutionary, written in 1905, quoted in Kiell, 1964, p. 162)

When I would think of saying anything to her my heart would begin to flutter like a duck in a puddle, and if I tried to outdo it and speak, it would get right smack up in my throat and choke me like a cold potato. (Davy Crockett, American frontiersman on his first love at 15, quoted in Kiell, 1964, p. 142)

When I was 13 years old and speechless before a boy named Sean, I never imagined that others—particularly those as brave as San Kim and Davy Crockett—experienced the same struggle. Before this certain person (with other ladies, George talks and amuses them pretty much) one's voice "sounds hoarse and strange and words don't come out as they used to do" (Carroll, 1865/1971, p. 17). In the presence of this particular individual, though one wants to speak, one cannot. One is struck *dumb*. In the dictionary, *to strike dumb* is to confound; to astonish; to render silent by astonishment (Thatcher, 1984, p. 269). To confound is from the Latin, *confundo*, *con* for together and *fundo*, *fusson*, to pour out, whence fuse, confuse, refuse. To confound is to throw into disorder.

How disordered I felt before Sean! Once, when I was standing with my girl friends in the hallway at school, waiting for the class bell to ring, Sean strolled up and joined us. "Hi," was all he said. The moment before I had been laughing, but I was silent now. One of the other girls chatted easily with him and then he continued down the hall. "What's the matter with you?" my best friend asked. "You should have said something!" She knew I liked him. I shrugged—no big deal, as we said then. But it was a big deal. The sight of him had astonished me. I froze the moment he appeared.

I liked it best when I saw him from afar, when I could see him without him seeing me: at a safe distance. Why? I dreamed of being with him, of talking easily with him as the other girl had done. Why was I so scared in front of him? What happened to me in his company? What tied my tongue?

Speechless

> I remember in religion class—I would see him right after, at lunch—I would write down a list of questions or things to say to him because I was always tongue-tied. So I had this whole list. Things like, "So, have you got a volleyball team yet?" I'd have these all written up. I'd have my friends help me during religion class. Of course, I couldn't have the list right in front of me—it would be in my books. Then, the minute I see him my mind goes blank. I have no idea what I'm doing. I felt this small (indicates a tiny size with her fingers). I felt exposed.

Céline, quoted here, gets tongue-tied, too. Our tongues make speech possible; tongues are the instruments of speech. A *tongue twister* is a phrase that is difficult to say; *tongue in cheek* means to speak with irony. We say *it is on the tip of my tongue* when we are on the point of uttering a word; *I held my tongue* when we choose to keep silent. To be *tongue-tied* is to be unable to speak freely. Due to shyness, it says in the dictionary (Thatcher, 1984, p. 880). There is no choice involved. To claim a *tied* tongue, as reason for a speechless moment, is to suggest that the words are in the mind, but the tongue can't be moved to speak them. The body, not the mind, seems the source of difficulty. Davy Crockett blames a fluttering heart for choking his words. To have the heart in the mouth is to be terrified (Thatcher, 1984, p. 395). Before a particular girl, this boy who, legend has it, "killed a bear when he was only three" was terribly frightened.

Céline tries to get beyond her fear and over her shyness. She has a plan to trick her tongue. She brings the words with her on a piece of paper. She pictures how it will be when she is with him. She will talk casually about innocuous things, safe things like volleyball. In her imagination the scene with him unfolds: she is standing there, unconcerned. Witty, casual remarks roll off her tongue, capturing his attention. Supported by her scribbled list of interesting things to say, she speaks; he answers, impressed. He wants to hear more of her. But when the time comes "at lunch" and she is actually before him, she freezes. When she approaches him at a table in the cafeteria, he looks up at her and her mind goes blank. She suddenly has no words.

If we could see Céline in this moment, when *he* gazes at her, we would likely see her cheeks redden. She is blushing. Blushing happens when we experience emotions like guilt, shame, modesty, or diffidence (Thatcher, 1984, p. 88). The word *blush* means to glow and is allied to blaze (flame), but also means to proclaim, noise abroad, as in to blow a trumpet, sound an alarm— hence the words blast, blare (Skeat, 1993, p. 44). Céline's body announces her emotion to herself and others. She feels exposed.

Exposed. Is that what stops the words in the throat, exposure? Derived from *pose*, a position, an attitude (Skeat, 1993, pp. 364–365), *expose* means to lay out, to make bare, to uncover, to disclose, to put in danger, to lay open to examination, to put forward in a position to be seen (Thatcher, 1984, p. 310). Is that it? We feel revealed, open, bare before this person? Is that why Céline, face to face with the boy she wants, is suddenly wordless?

> Exposed on the cliffs of the heart. Look, how tiny down there,
> Look: the last village of words and higher,
> (but how tiny) still one last farmhouse of feeling.
> Can you see it? (Rilke, 1989a, p. 143)

The tension of these moments, when suddenly a special person is before you, is reminiscent of a game we played as children. In *hide and seek*, to be seen by the other is to know you have been caught. Though you have hidden carefully, the moment comes when you see yourself being seen and the game is up. I remember playing hide and seek, crouched in the tall grass growing between a neighbor's fence and garage. I stayed so still that I could hear my heart pounding. The pulse of it filled my ears so that I couldn't hear anything else—a problem, as I needed to be alert to the sound of someone approaching. The way we played the game, the seeker had to call out your name and run back and touch "home" before you did. If I were found, I would have that last wild chance to run and make 'r to safety. In hiding, you could never just fade quietly into a spot. Muscles were tense in readiness; senses were keen. My body was present to me in a very real way. It seemed so large suddenly; the grass wasn't high enough to cover it. As I tried to make myself disappear, the opposite occurred: I was big as life and noisy with it; my breath, my pulse, and my trembling muscles would not be still. It was my body that would give me away. But it was an exciting game, hide and seek. And there was always the chance to run to safety.

In hide and seek, eye contact is a tension-filled event (Barritt, Beekman, Bleeker, and Mulderij, 1983). Mutual looking is transformed. The seeker and the sought become unaware of others, everyone else slips to the periphery of concern (p. 144). Seeker and sought are concentrated on the presence of one for the other. The tension in hide and seek is released with laughter and joy. This terrifying moment is make-believe. When children play hide and seek, a study has shown, the real anxiety of the game lies in the implicit question: Am I important enough in your eyes to be sought? To hide and to have no one look for you hurts. "It is very painful when they won't come to find you; a dirty trick; then you are alone *and* deserted. They would rather *not* see you. You are ignored" (Barritt, Beekman, Bleeker, and Mulderij, 1983, p. 155)." [1]

> [If] you like someone and they don't like you back, you don't want everyone to know. Every time you look at him you think, "Am I looking too long?" Or you can't meet their eyes because you don't want them to see the love in your eyes. He absolutely cannot know.

Here, Céline is worried that, in front of this boy, her body gives her away—her eyes seek him and look too long; love is present for all to see. If he is not seeking her in return, the very act of hiding exposes her to ridicule. "Everyone" will know that she wants him but that he is *not* looking for her. She is playing alone.

Like Céline, I felt terribly transparent and vulnerable before the boy who made my heart flutter. I wanted to hide the emotion that swept over me, but I knew that my body was betraying me. I was giving myself away. I recognize now that this was my first experience of desire. In front of him, this new attitude of mine, this new position toward another—that of desiring—was "put forward to be seen." I wanted him and it showed. My body revealed it to me.

In desire one is revealed. Sartre (1956/1994) says that in desire one is made incarnate: "The being which desires is consciousness making itself body. I incarnate myself in order to realize the incarnation of the other" (p. 389). The body of the other reveals my own body to me. I become *self*-conscious.

> There is such embarrassment around being transparent. One uses up a lot of energy hiding how one feels. It feels like shame. Shame is what can overcome you when you are with him. The scary thing is if I stopped liking him, I would have no shame in going up to him and saying, "Did you know that last month, boy, I had the hots for you. I thought you were the most gorgeous guy in the world." Then I could say to him, "I still think you're a gorgeous guy, but last month—holy cow!— I wanted you." I could actually say this. (Céline)

"I wanted you." Is the wanting where the danger lies? Freed of it—he's still desirable, but *she* does not desire him anymore—she is no longer at risk. In fact, a blatant confession of "I had the hots for you" is not even embarrassing. There is no mortification in such a confession. There is nothing to hide.

All the trouble, the tension, lies in the desire itself. Desire is trouble (Sartre, 1956/1994).

Sartre uses the metaphor of *troubled water* to elucidate his idea of desire. Compared with transparent water, troubled water remains fluid, but its translucency is troubled by an inapprehensible presence that is one with it. There is an invisible something present. In the other's presence the world becomes the world of desire. The world is troubled; the world is made ensnaring (Sartre, 1956/1994). This wanting of the other is not simply sexual. If desire was sexual, Sartre tells us, it would be distinct and clear like eating and drinking. It is not. Desire takes hold of us, overwhelms us. Only if we resist it will the desire, as it disappears, become untroubled like hunger. In desiring, what we actually want, according to Sartre, is to reduce the other to an object. We can touch, feel, possess an object.

When we desire, we want, also, to become an object of desire to the other. As desire must be an invitation to desire, to speak with desire is to speak with a new intention. "Desire is an attitude aiming at enchantment" (Sartre, 1956/1994, p. 394). Here, for Sartre, is the shame. We are reduced to an object in our desire for the other. Sartre denies the very possibility of a subject to subject relation.

Gabriel Marcel (1950), in *The Mystery of Being,* says the act by which we incline ourselves toward the other is essentially different from that through which we grasp an object. The very possibility of grasping at or seizing another is excluded in principle.[2] When we are together, before one another, we can be truly present as ourselves. Our way of being present to one another, however, is such a mysterious thing that it is incomprehensible. We cannot explain it. It may only be evoked, "the evocation being fundamentally and essentially magical" (p. 256). Consider, Marcel says, how a rose in a poem is present to us in a way that, in most cases, a rose in a seed catalogue is not. How is this so?

He gives this example. If I think of sitting across from a stranger, I recognize that this person is not really *present* to me, even though he is close enough to reach out and touch me. Communication between us is possible, but only in the sense of passing messages from a reception to an emission point. Something essential is lacking. "He understands what I say to him, but he does not understand *me*; I may even have the extremely disagreeable feeling that my own words, as he repeats them to me, as he reflects them back to me, have become unrecognizable" (p. 252).[3] In a fundamental way, I am not myself with him. When someone's presence is really felt by me, however, the opposite can happen. I can be revealed to myself; I am "more fully myself than I should be if I were not exposed to its impact" (pp. 252–253).

Céline, before the boy she desires, whose presence she feels so strongly, is revealed to herself as well as to him. It is the essence of such an encounter that the body is the medium through which the person reveals and conceals himself (Linschoten, 1987, p. 161). The silence of the one in love can be experienced as a blast of noisy revelation. In desire, our sense of self coincides with our bodily, carnal existence (Carotenuto, 1987/1989). In wanting the other, one becomes fully conscious of one's own embodiment.

To speak to another is to attempt to transcend what von Hildebrand has termed one's *world-for-oneself* (cited in Owens, 1970). Speech directed toward another is an attempt at creating an intersubjective situation, an attempt to open the space that lies between. Sometimes, because we are afraid, we resist the pull of the other. One is afraid of the object of desire but even more afraid of oneself. "It is as if a horse shied away from its own shadow" (Reik, 1941, p. 140).[4]

Linschoten (1987) describes the very beginning of being with another *in love*:

> Two people sit there together, involved in a wonderful conversation of which an outsider cannot make head or tail. They lose the thread of their conversation and do not finish their sentences. The one says something, the other catches it and tries to understand it in a certain way, but does not feel sure of himself. Has he indeed understood the correct meaning? (p. 163)

These two persons, sitting across from one another, are able to speak, to open the space that is between them. They speak in phrases, however; their sentences are neither constructed nor complete. Lovers speak in fragments, Barthes says (1977/1978, p. 7). They repeat and contradict themselves. Their language is shaped by feelings, amorous feelings (Barthes, 1977/1978, p. 7). They are asking themselves: "What does she mean by that?" "What is going on in him?" These are important questions. We have to communicate our desire, our wish to move toward the other to them. Until we do, there is no encounter (Owens, 1970). "Eros requires speech" (Bloom, 1993, p. 25). The essence of this dialogue is its uncertainty.

Céline tries to remove uncertainty with a list of things to say. Her conversation with *him* is to be more like a play, with scripted dialogue. It is not intended as *play*. Play is a process that takes place *in between* (Gadamer, 1960/1990). The ease of play, that is, the absence of strain that is essential to a sense of play, is impossible. Céline is, as yet, afraid. She is afraid of what is revealed in her eyes. She is hesitant to reveal herself to herself, to everyone else, and most particularly to him. *He absolutely cannot know.* Uncertain of what to do, of what to say, of what is happening within her, she struggles. Fear and love go together, "so much so that if in the midst of our excitement we do not also feel afraid, it is a good sign we are not really in love" (Carotenuto, 1987/ 1989, p. 27).

Sometimes speechless lovers attempt to have others speak for them. They enlist a *go-between*. A go-between is an intermediary, "often in disreputable negotiations" (Thatcher, 1984, p. 371). Disreputable transactions are without honor, discreditable. To choose to speak through another person is to avoid an encounter. ("Two's company; three's a crowd," we say.) It discredits the message transferred. To speak loving words, one must be present to the other. Words through a third party are too distant. Sometimes this neutral third is a secret guest of one lover. His or her role is to provide one lover with his words, as Cyrano, hiding in the bushes, did for Christian (Rostand, 1951). This ploy, too, prevents an encounter. These words of love are *a speech.*

Teenagers, however, sometimes use a friend to go *before*, not between. Céline may get Angela to phone Bob, the friend of Tony—the boy Céline desires—to ask him what Tony thinks of Céline. Angela then calls Céline. If the news is good—Tony really likes Céline—she may be more confident before him the next day at lunch. The fear will not be gone, nor all the uncertainty, but she will know he is trying to speak too.

What happens if we stay too afraid to speak to the other, if we do not struggle like Céline to find the words and the courage to say them? Shakespeare (1994) gives us an image in these lines from *Twelfth Night*. It is the opposite of a blushing girl:

> *Duke*: And what's her history?
> *Viola*: A blank, my lord. She never told her love,
> But let concealment, like a worm i' th' bud,
> Feed on her damask cheek; she pined in thought
> And, with a green and yellow melancholy,
> She sat like Patience on a monument,
> Smiling at grief. Was this not love indeed? (2. 4. 108–114)

I never did speak to Sean. I found my courage years later with a different boy.

An Act of Imagination

Stephen Dedalus, the boy in Joyce's (1916/1992c) *Portrait of the Artist as a Young Man*, spends his evenings poring over the novel *The Count of Monte Cristo*. He builds in his mind "the bright picture of Marseilles, of sunny trellises, and of Mercedes" (p. 63). On the Sunday walks he takes with his father and grandfather they pass a house where he tells himself another Mercedes lives.

> Both on the outward and on the homeward journey he measured distance by this landmark: and in his imagination he lived through a long rain of adventures, marvellous as those in the book itself, towards the close of which there appeared an image of himself, grown older and sadder, standing in a moonlit garden with Mercedes who had so many years before slighted his love, and with a sadly proud gesture of refusal, saying:—Madam, I never eat muscatel grapes. (p. 63)

Stephen lives an entire lifetime during these Sunday walks. Unlike the confused but eager adolescent he is at present, he pictures himself in the distant future, world-weary but wise, a mature lover, beyond turmoil. This other Stephen, alone in a shadowy garden with a former love, can refuse her small offer of grapes with an elegant gesture. He *never* eats *muscatel* grapes. In this one phrase is revealed his sophisticated uniqueness. A luxury, perhaps, for others—certainly to the Irish boy Stephen now is—he does not eat them. His *never* implies countless other offers of grapes refused. And it is *muscatel* grapes he will not have. Mercedes might have tempted him with a different offering. How regretful Mercedes must be, knowing she had intentionally disregarded his attentions years ago. With the polish of experience, he has become a rare jewel of a man. What a fool she was to lose him. Stephen is now unmoved by her temptations.

Stephen imagines himself far beyond the adolescent anxieties he is living. Awakened to desire, he is struggling to make sense of himself and his feelings. He is stirred up by life; he is troubled. Girls arouse him. He wants to love and be loved, but it is all so strange and confusing. Though his father and grandfather are beside him on these walks, he does not look to them. He cannot imagine them feeling his passions. He wants a different future, an exciting one. He wants a heroic life like the Count of Monte Cristo's. In this story he reads at night by the fire; he relocates himself to a different world. It takes him far beyond his present self and everyday situation. It gives him ideas about whom he can be. *Reason* does not play a part in the story Stephen creates about himself:

> We can't ask reason to take us across the gulfs of the absurd. Only the imagination can get us out of the bind of the eternal present, inventing or hypothesizing or pretending or discovering a way that reason can then follow into the infinity of options, a clue through the labyrinths of choice, a golden string, the story, leading us to the freedom that is properly human, the freedom open to those whose minds can accept unreality. (Le Guin, 1989, p. 45)

It is his imagination that frees Stephen from the here and now and takes him to a world of possibilities. His vision of being a hero in his own life is giving impetus to his developing self. Like Stephen, in acts of imagination, we can conceive and perceive ourselves. The word *imagine* comes from the French *imaginer*, to think, which is derived from the Latin *imaginari*, to picture oneself (Skeat, 1993, p. 216).

In creating stories for ourselves, we create possible worlds. Stories help us assume a starring role in the creation of our lives, rather than accepting a minor role in the lives of others. Stephen uses a classic adventure story to take him away from the dreary demands of his everyday life. He uses the story to create one of his own. He makes himself a hero. Classic stories, like the one Stephen is reading, and like our great love stories, influence the way we think about life and love, give us words to speak about our experiences and to shape our own stories.

Rachel Brownstein (1994), in *Becoming a Heroine,* says that to want to be a heroine can promote a woman's aspirations to be someone who matters, someone who makes something special of herself. Brownstein credits romance novels with strengthening and shaping the self-concept of female readers. "Having an idea of becoming a heroine is a mode of self-awareness" (p xx–xxi).

"To learn to speak is to learn to tell a story" (Le Guin, 1989, p. 39). We make sense of our world by creating stories about it (Bruner, 1990). We order and reorder events that are relevant to us and determine our role in them. Making stories sets what happens to us in time and space. It enables us to remember the past, to dream of the future (Witherell, 1991). Our very sense of self is storied (Shotter & Gergen, 1989).

Stories, then, can be powerful in their influence. Powerful and dangerous. Stories can lead to unreason:

> He had filled his imagination with everything that he had read, with enchantments, knightly encounters, battles, challenges, wounds, with tales of love and its torments, and all sorts of impossible things, and as a result had come to believe that all these fictitious happenings were true; they were more real to him than anything else in the world. (de Cervantes, 1605/1987, p. 1183)

In Part I of *Don Quixote*, "I Know Who I Am, and Who I May Be if I Choose," readers are told that a certain gentleman of La Mancha has become so immersed in his reading that he spends his days from dawn to dusk and his nights from sundown to sunup reading until "finally, from so little sleeping and so much reading his brain dried up and he went out of his mind" (p. 1183). With wits that are beyond repair, the gentleman, Alonzo Quesada, conceives of putting into practice all that he has read in his books. He chooses to become Don Quixote and goes off to fight the ills of the world.

The *Quixote principle* refers to the shaping of identity through reading stories. As a reader, one comes to identify with a character in a story. Later, the reader enacts the aspects of this character in life. Narrative guides action, according to this principle (Hermans & Kempen, 1993). W. H. Auden (1952), writing of fairy tales, says the only danger to healthy self-development he can see for the readers of such tales is "the danger inherent in all works of art, namely that the reader is tempted to identify himself with the hero in his triumphs and withdraw from him during his sufferings" (p. xv).

Sufferings, however, may be exactly what the reader wants to hear about and understand. Sociologists have a term, the *Werther effect,* which they use to describe the effect of reading on suicidal behavior. Goethe's character, Werther, killed himself, in a noble and romantic gesture of unrequited love, and inspired a rash of suicides. Soon after the publication of *The Sorrows of Young Werther*, young men, dressed like Werther in yellow waistcoats and blue coats, shot themselves for love (Hermans & Kempen, 1993, p. 21). Stories, we can see, have the potential to lead us to act.

Paul Ricoeur (1991) explains how we take possession of ourselves as agents of action through imagination:

> it is indeed through the anticipatory imagination of acting that I "try out" different possible courses of action and that I "play" in the precise sense of the word, with possible practices.... Next imagination is involved in the very process of motivation. It is imagination that provides the milieu, the luminous clearing, in which we can compare and evaluate motives as diverse as desires and ethical obligations, themselves as disparate as professional rules, social customs, or intensely personal values. (p. 177)

Imagination, Ricoeur says, is the general function of developing practical possibilities. The identity of a person lies in self-narration. We constantly reinterpret our past, as we seek a sense of order and continuity. We then look to others to affirm the sense of identity that we are developing (Ricoeur, 1991).

To be open to acts of imagination seems necessary to love. In the 1956 movie *The Rainmaker*, Lizzie is a woman on the verge of spinsterhood. She lives on a farm in mid-western America with her father and two grown brothers. The men of her family want to help Lizzie get married. Being married and having children is her dream, so she cooperates as much as she can. She just can't seem to attract and flirt with men—her brothers tell her she scares men by being so smart, sensible and to the point. The family farm, like Lizzie, is in danger of drying up. There is a terrible drought in the area, and one night a rainmaker, named Bill Starbuck, comes to the door. He is full of magical promises about charming nature into raining. Common sense tells the family that Starbuck is a con man, but there is something of the shaman about him. Starbuck's philosophy is that if you imagine it strongly enough, with confidence and faith, you can make anything happen. They are intrigued with him and his views despite their own sense and agree to pay him a hundred dollars to bring rain.

The Rainmaker is a tale about the powers of the imagination. Lizzie has been afraid to imagine herself as a woman, to dream about falling in love and being loved in return. She is plain and that is that. Her life is to be defined by that point. Her brother Noah promotes this view. He wants her to be *reasonable*, to face facts and accept that she will become an old maid. He doesn't want to see Lizzie hope and be disappointed. Starbuck sees things differently. He weaves for Lizzie a wonderful story in which a girl like her is the heroine. He gives Lizzie a new name, Melisande. Melisande, he says, was the girl for whom King Hamlet sought a golden fleece. Lizzie knows his fantasy is a confusion of many, but it charms her anyway. She lets herself imagine being like the girl in Starbuck's story—soft, pretty, and loved as a woman. As she does so, Lizzie changes. She appears brighter, more alive and there's a glow about her. Her eyes shine; her hair comes down. Lizzie opens herself to the possibilities shown to her by Starbuck.

But the things Lizzie imagines for herself are not those of Starbuck. She doesn't want to be Melisande; she is Lizzie. She wants more than dreams or "lies." (When called "a liar," Starbuck is offended and replies, "I wasn't lying; I was dreaming.") Still, because Lizzie has allowed herself to see a vision other than spinsterhood, she will no longer accept the part Noah expects her to play. As the movie ends, the audience sees Lizzie with a new sense of herself and what her life can be. Her life will be lived somewhere between the hard "reality" of her brother and the dream world of the rainmaker.

It may be that to love, one needs to be able to dream and fantasize. Joe the participant in my study who isn't looking for love, wants a reasonable way to handle his desires. He wants to meet his needs for another in the least troublesome way. Joe says he doesn't want to bother with going through the motions of seeing someone, of building up a friendship, "of taking all this time." In other words, Joe doesn't want to create a love story with someone.

In Chekov's (1887/1982b) *The Kiss*, Ryabovich is an officer whose appearance seems to say that he is "the shyest, most modest and most insignificant officer in the whole brigade" (p. 34). Ryabovich has never allowed himself to dream; he has never been a hero to himself in any story. One night in a new town, his brigade is entertained at a country house:

> Ryabovich stood by the door with guests who were not dancing and watched. Not once in his life had he danced, not once had he put his arm around an attractive young woman's waist. He would usually be absolutely delighted when, with everyone looking on, a man took a young girl he hadn't met before and offered his shoulders for her to rest her hands on, but he could never imagine himself in that situation. (Chekov, 1887/1982b, p. 35)

And because he could never imagine it, Ryabovich never asks a girl to dance. That night, however, he gets lost and, confused, enters a darkened room. He stops, undecided as to what to do, when a girl suddenly puts her arms about his neck and breathes, "At last!" She kisses him. Immediately realizing her mistake, she gives a faint cry and draws back. Ryabovich rushes out of the room. He cannot get the incident out of his mind and goes over it again and again. This is a profound adventure for him. One evening, soon afterward, he decides to share his story with his fellow officers:

> He began to tell them in great detail about the kiss, but after a minute fell silent. In that one minute he had told them everything and he was astonished when he considered how little time was needed to tell his story: he had imagined it would take until morning. (pp. 44–45)

The literal story of the kiss is a brief one. It changes, nevertheless, Ryabovich's self-spoken life story and the image he holds of himself. Now, having a love story—even a fleeting one of mistaken identity—changes him, at least for a time:

> In the evenings, when his fellow officers talked about love and women, he would listen very attentively, sitting very close to them and assuming the habitual expression of a soldier hearing stories about battles he himself fought in. (p. 45)

Ryabovich is no longer on the sidelines, part of the crowd looking on. He is a man with his own story.

Dancing on the Brink of the World [5]

> Dances. That's where it [love] gets really obvious. Who asks whom to dance. It's junior high but there are lots of slow dances. I would ask him to dance all the time. What a rush! It was an ache to have to leave. (Céline)

At a dance one ventures out from being one of the crowd to being one with another. At a dance people *pair off,* and love, Céline says, becomes obvious. I attended my first dance when I was 12 years old and had just started junior high. Like most school dances, it was held in the school auditorium where the bleachers, the gym mats, and the volleyball nets had been put away. The auditorium was an enormous room, decorated for that night by a student committee, armed with crepe paper and balloons. As the dance started, the lights were dimmed, and the music, played by a hired "disk jockey," began. The place was transformed. Though I had been in the auditorium that morning during school, it felt strange and foreign to me—I was nervous like a tourist who wasn't sure of the right way to behave. I was wearing new shoes and a new dress, and my long hair was "up" instead of hanging freely. *I* felt strange to me too. I wasn't sure I really belonged there. That evening, when I was asked to dance by a Grade 9 boy, the president of the student council, I literally turned around to see the girl to whom he was speaking. I couldn't believe it was me. I took my first tentative steps toward becoming someone's "partner" that night.

That was the idea, of course. A dance is held with the blessings of parents, teachers, and the school administration because it is an opportunity for adolescents to meet, socialize, and learn how to form couples. For teenage couples at a school dance, dancing remains reminiscent of its history. Our dances in primitive times had either social aims—like celebrations—or magical/religious aims—like inspiring warriors (Murray, 1953). In the school auditorium, the social aims of a dance are actualized, and students learn in a public way how to meet each other. The dance has long been a means of allowing eligible men to meet marriageable ladies: It has been civilized, formalized, and managed for cultural ends. The magical, primitive aspects of the dance remain, however; hence the presence of adult chaperons at the school dance. The chaperons are there to ensure things stay proper and do not get out of hand.

Dancing quickens the blood, nevertheless. "What a rush!" Céline says of her school dances. She can ask *him* to be with her at a dance, at least for the length of a song. She chooses a slow dance, because in a slow dance he will "offer his shoulders" and she will put her arms about him. For the first moments of the dance, they will concentrate on synchronizing their movements but then they will find the rhythm of the song—and each other—and move more easily together. The music is loud; real conversation is impossible. Céline and her partner communicate by gestures, mouthed words, whispers in the ear, but mostly they relate to one another with the movements of their bodies. How close together do they move? How easily? How tightly does he embrace her? Does she put her head on his shoulder? In the rhythmic movements of a dance the body is used to express emotion and ideas. Dancing was used to communicate long before spoken language was born (Murray, 1953). The dance itself is language.

The image of a couple forming, embracing, and moving together across a crowded dance floor calls up the relation of two people in love to the rest of the world. They are part of the crowd but separate, facing one another, two bodies moving as one, caught up with themselves. The surrounding crowd is a foil for the intimacy of the two.

> At the still point of the turning world…
> Except for the point, the still point,
> There would be no dance, and there is only the dance…
> Desire itself is movement
> Not in itself desirable;
> Love is itself unmoving,
> Only the cause and end of movement, (Eliot, 1944, p. 15)

Falling in love, says Alberoni (1983), is a revolution of two. As such it belongs in the realm of the extraordinary. To be a lover one must break with everyday life. Immersed in day-to-day living, no one can reach the intensity of desire and will that is necessary for love. Love requires a venturing out from the ordinary.

> Every morning I lay on the floor in the front parlour watching her door. The blind was pulled down to within an inch of the sash so that I could not be seen. When she came out on the doorstep my heart leaped. I ran to the hall seized my books and followed her. (Joyce, 1914/1992a, p. 22)

He is in love with her, the older sister of his friend. Their families live on a street in Dublin where the houses, "conscious of the decent lives within them, gazed at one another with brown imperturbable faces" (p. 21). The closest he gets to her is when she comes out on the doorstep to call her brother into his tea.

> I did not know if I would ever speak to her or not or, if I spoke to her, how I could tell her of my confused adoration. … At last she spoke to me. When she addressed the first words to me I was so confused that I did not know what to answer. She asked me was I going to *Araby*. (p. 23)[6]

Araby. He is so startled he can hardly respond. When she finally speaks, the word is a wildly exotic one for his world. She tells him that *Araby* is the name of a charitable bazaar to be held soon in the city. She wants very much to go, but cannot as there is a retreat at her convent school. "If I go, [he promises], I will bring you something" (p. 24).

> At night in my bedroom and by day in the classroom her image came between me and the page I strove to read. The syllables of the word *Araby* were called to me through the silence in which my soul luxuriated and cast an Eastern enchantment over me. (p. 24)

He is going to *Araby* on a mission for his love. The imagined colors, noises, and smells of an Arabian bazaar become more real than the sounds and sights of his schoolroom:

> I answered few questions in class. I watched my master's face pass from amiability to sternness; he hoped I was not beginning to idle. I could not call my wandering thoughts together. I had hardly any patience with the serious work of life which, now that it stood between me and my desire, seemed to me child's play, ugly monotonous child's play. (p. 24)

Love takes him from the dull, brown, rain-soaked streets of Dublin to a sunny enchanting place, far away. Desire makes him chafe at his schoolwork. It seems senseless and foolish now. It is unreal—it is play, pretend—*Araby* is reality. He ventures impatiently toward it. This is a sweet, sad story—the boy arrives late at the bazaar; the stalls are closing, the hall is in darkness and there is a silence "like that which pervades a church after a service" (p. 16). In the story, Joyce captures the way falling in love takes the lover from what, before love, seemed the serious work of life.

When Nicole falls in love, she sits in class, copying notes dutifully from the board, but now she finds them of no real interest. What interests her, she writes in the margins of her notebook: a boy's name linked with hers inside a heart; a tiny sketch of his mouth; lines for a poem she is composing. It is the stuff of the margins that has significance. Like Céline, Derek, and Veronica, she lives for the time before, between, and after classes when the truly important events of the day take place. She gets to talk about *him* to her friends then. The most enticing part of the world, for her, is one that she has created with a boy over a telephone line. This is where she really lives.

Lovers move away from the civilized center of things. To realize their love, the lovers of our great stories flee to the wilderness, to the sea, to a cave or a tomb. The teenage lovers in this study were to be found in a darkened movie theater, a basement, a park, a doorway. Love stories are set at the edge of the world, and situated in moonlight, in a world of shadows. Mythical lovers, once the light of their communities, abandon the expectations of their families and the responsibilities of their position in life. To be together, they move away from all that. In the novels of Henry James, strong personal love occurs only in the margins of the novel because love, as James sees it, "requires a turning from the good of others and a request that others turn away their eyes" (Nussbaum, 1990, p. 346). It is at the margins that lovers find freedom. There is ambiguity and fluctuation at the edge of things (Titchkosky, 1996). To move together in a transition from one to two, lovers need the openness to move and create. They must go to the brink to make a world for themselves.

The world of lovers is a secret world, Nussbaum (1990) says, "dense with conversation, storytelling, ease and laughter, with magic spells and the charm of being understood and loved" (p. 352). At the brink of the world, everyday language cannot suffice. Lovers turn to the language of poetry, religion, and myth. This is the language of extraordinary experience (Alberoni, 1983). This is the space of the oxymoron: *beautiful terror; sweet madness; sorrowful joy; joyful sorrow.* The oxymoron is a mode of speech to be found in oriental religious texts, when pointing past the limits of logical thought (Campbell, 1968). Joseph Campbell (1968), writing of the mystery of the ultimate nature of being, quotes from the *Kena Upanisad* (1.3, p. 188):

> There the eye goes not;
> Speech goes not, nor the mind.
> At the brink where possibilities flourish,
> we find not only uncertainty but paradox.

The paradox of lovers' worlds is evident in language. Words fail lovers; they are left speechless, yet love makes poets of them all (Plato, 1956b). Individuals who never understood poetry, nor wanted to try, may be moved to use poetic language, to compose verse, to write songs, by the act of falling in love. H.L. Hix (1995), in *Spirits Hovering Over the Ashes,* says that love is a language that erases itself by becoming language. In his argument, Hix refers to a scene from Tolstoy's (1878/1978) *Anna Karenin.* In that scene, we may see how lovers go through and beyond words.

The setting is a party. Dinner is over and Levin and Kitty are sitting at a card table, surrounded by the other guests. Kitty gets up to leave but Levin tells her has wanted to ask her a question for a long time. He cannot *say* it but writes the letters w, y, t, m, i, c, n, b—d, t, m, n, o, t with a piece of chalk on the table.

> There seemed no likelihood that she would be able to decipher this complicated sequence; but he looked at her as though his life depended upon her understanding the words. (Tolstoy, 1878/1978, p. 422)

The letters stand for "When you told me it could not be—did that mean never, or then?" She looks at the letters, then at him, and flushes because she *does* understand. She writes back the initial letters i, y, c, f, a, f, w, h—meaning "if you could forgive and forget what happened." He, too, understands! Levin declares, in chalked initials, that he has never ceased to love her. Then he writes a long sentence and she writes back an answer.

> He could not fill in the words she meant at all; but in her lovely eyes, suffused with happiness, he saw all he needed to know. (p. 423)

When lovers come together to create a new place for themselves, they do so with a language all their own.

Excitement and enchantment are to be found at the margins of the world, but there is danger, too. It was not without cause that, in the margins of ancient maps, it was written: Hic sunt leones / Here be lions (Carotenuto, 1987/1989, p. 117). Lovers, undergoing a metamorphosis, call into question the status quo, something society considers as subversion (Carotenuto, 1987/1989). Lovers transgress expectations of loyalty and cohesion. They break away from their own group and become devoted instead to one who is *not kin*.[7] Lovers become outsiders. Outsiders are those whom society cannot trust to live by its rules (Titchkosky, 1996). As love is a collective movement of two people (Alberoni, 1983), it is often established in opposition to customary interests and institutions. For individuals to love and move together, they must enter a new region of values as important to them as those of societal institutions. Falling in love, in fact, challenges institutions on the level of their fundamental values (Alberoni, 1983, pp. 16–17). Eros, as some myths have it, is the offspring of Chaos.

Sometimes the courage necessary for a lover's challenge—for a revolution—is too great for potential lovers to find. Chekov (1887/1982a) in a story, "Concerning Love," shows how we can become enclosed by the demands of society and be unable to break free of it, even for love. Chekov's character Alyokhin has farmed the land left to him by his father ever since he left university. It is not the life he wants, nor what he was brought up to do, but he feels he must do it to repay family debts, no matter his aversion to it. Alyokhin is in love with Anna, who loves him in return. She is married, however, and they never speak of their love.

> I would go to the theatre with Anna—we always used to walk. We would sit side by side in the stalls, shoulders touching, and as I took the opera glasses from her I felt that she was near and dear to me, that she belonged to me, that we couldn't live without each other. But through some strange lack of mutual understanding we would always say good-bye and part like strangers when we left the theatre. In that town they were already saying God knows what about us, but there wasn't one word of truth in it. (p. 152)

During the opera they are together in a world of their own making, but it is a world they cannot sustain. Others do see them as apart—see them as lovers—but they themselves never venture further. Anna slowly turns inward, away from Alyokhin, away from her husband and children. She develops a nervous disorder and depression. It is not until her family is moving from the town and Anna herself is leaving for the Crimea for her health's sake that Alyokhin ventures to declare his love. In a small train compartment where they are briefly alone, they come together as lovers when he kisses her for the first and last time. He then continues much as before, "turning round and round in his huge estate like a squirrel in a cage, showing no interest in academic work or indeed anything that could have made his life more agreeable" (p. 153).

Alyokhin and Anna are afraid to become outsiders. The final movement toward one another and away from their everyday world seems too high in cost. It is likely that lovers, who do choose to endure whatever is necessary for love, arrive at a place where they see their critics as the real outsiders. From this place, they do not value or accept anyone else's interpretation of their situation as relevant (Titchkosky, 1996). Love forms its own rules.

There is nothing that is more symbolic of the turning of lovers to one another as the world falls away than the *kiss*. In three artistic expressions of this symbol of love—sculptures, all entitled *The Kiss*—this motion is revealed. In *The Kiss* of Brancusi, a primitive rectangular piece cut directly into stone, the lovers are differentiated only barely enough to be identified as separate beings. These lovers are innocent and anonymous (Janson, 1962). I find them a symbol of togetherness already achieved. *The Kiss* of Rodin, however, captures lovers on the brink. Rodin in this work shows the necessary venturing of lovers toward one another. Carved in white marble polished smooth as skin, this kiss is a personal kiss. There is movement in this piece: She reaches for him; he drops the book they were reading. They turn toward one another and away from the world. There is desire here and the daring that is necessary for love. This couple is Francesca and Paolo: Rodin made them for his piece *The Gates of Hell,* inspired by Dante's *Inferno.* But he could not leave them there, and removed them to stand apart, on their own (Janson, 1962). Vigeland's *The Kiss* is the kiss of adolescent lovers. One can imagine that they have been running toward one another and that the artist has caught the moment of their meeting The boy catches the girl in his arms and lifts her off her feet. Eyes closed, they are oblivious to all else:

> The world had disappeared at their boundaries,
> They were merely one another's partners
> Dreamless taking part in one another's members....
> The sweet birds fall silent. The world
> Withdraws up to the skin of the lovers.
> The last fire of the world forges together
> In the unspeakableness of their embrace.
> The universe becomes empty around their couch,
> Devoured by their nameless kisses,
> Devoured by their unity, breast to breast. (Aafjes)[8]

Love Is Becoming

In kissing lovers drink one another's life.
                              —*Aafjes*

"Love is becoming and offering up of the self," according to Karl Jaspers (1986, p. 116). Loving another moves us toward our own possibilities. In partaking of the existence of another being we are mysteriously more present to ourselves. We discover our own bodies in the touch of another. We see more clearly who we are and who we want to be in the eyes of this special person. Love takes us out of the crowd and moves us to create a world together, one that is more surely our own. Yet this, too, is a paradox. In becoming a lover, we give up ourselves. The gift of self is seen to be basic to love in many philosophies. For instance, in the ancient Hindu book of love, the *Kāma Sūtra* (Vātsyāyana, 1994), five characteristics of love are identified: the first is the *total gift of self* (p. 417).[9] To give the self away totally seems a fearsome thing. Reik (1941), in fact, finds that the deepest fear connected with love is the fear of losing our self-possession. In love, he says, there is always the deadly fear of surrender.

In considering this paradoxical relation of the self to the other in love, I remembered a story about a little mermaid who gives up everything to be with the human she loves.[10] In the Hans Christian Andersen (1871/1952) story "The Mermaid," the sacrifice of self that some lovers make is the major theme. I went looking for the original story—it's the Disney version most of us know now—and I summarize it here.

The youngest daughter of the sea king is allowed on her fifteenth birthday—as were her sisters before her—to rise above the waves and see the world that lies there. On that day, she falls in love with a human. He is a young prince whom she saves from drowning. After her rescue of him, the little mermaid goes often to secretly watch him. This young princess becomes very curious of the world above her. Asking her grandmother about it, she is told of the difference between humankind and those who live in the sea. "We can live to be 300 years old," her grandmother explains, "but when we cease to exist here, we are turned into foam on the water. We have not an immortal soul. Men, though they have a shorter life than ours, have a soul that lives on after the body becomes dust. It mounts up through the air to the stars." "Can I not do anything to win an immortal soul?" the little mermaid asks. The grandmother tells her, "No. Only if a man were to love you so that you should be more to him than father or mother; if he should cling to you with his every thought and with all his love,—then his soul would be imparted to your body and you would share in the happiness of mankind" (p. 666).

That night, there is a ball at the sea court. The little mermaid sings, and is happy for a while because she knows she has the loveliest voice of all in the sea or on the earth. But soon she thinks of the prince and is sad. In despair she goes to a sea witch and asks for help to be with the human she loves.

The sea witch prepares a potion for her. She is told to swim to land before the sun rises, to seat herself there and drink it. When she does this, her tail will shrivel and become legs. This metamorphosis will hurt her—it will seem as if she is cut by a sharp sword. The witch tells her, "You will keep your graceful walk but every step you take will be as if you trod upon sharp knives, and as if your blood must flow" (p. 668).

A great risk comes with this change, as well—she may never be a mermaid again. "If the prince loves another," the sea witch warns her, "your heart will break, and you will become foam upon the water."

There is a further cost: The witch must be paid for her services. She demands the greatest thing the mermaid possesses—her voice. The sea witch takes the mermaid's tongue. Now the little mermaid can neither speak nor sing. With a heart full of sorrow at leaving her home and family, she goes after her love.

In the morning the prince finds the little mermaid on the steps of his castle. He declares that she shall always remain with him, and she receives permission to sleep on a velvet cushion before his door. He grows fonder of her each day, but loves her as one loves a child. With her eyes she asks him if he does not love her best of all? He tells her she is dearest to him. He is in love, however, with the girl who saved his life when she found him lying on the beach after a great storm. "She is the only one in the world I could love." The prince is sent by the king and queen to visit a beautiful princess to see if he is willing to marry her. He goes, though he knows he cannot love her. To his happy surprise, the princess turns out to be the girl from the beach.

When she learns they are to marry, it seems to the little mermaid as if her heart will break. The prince's wedding morning will bring her death and change her into foam on the sea. As the ceremony approaches, the mermaid waits on the deck of the wedding ship for dawn, knowing the first rays of the sun will kill her. She suddenly sees her sisters rising out of the flood, their long beautiful hair no longer there to wave in the wind. They have cut it off. "We have given it to the witch, that we might bring you help, so that you may not die tonight" (p. 673). They explain that to live she must take the knife they give her and thrust it into the heart of the prince. When his warm blood falls onto her feet, it will turn again into a fish tail and she can return to the sea. She goes to where the prince sleeps and hears him, dreaming, call his bride's name. The little mermaid cannot harm him—she flings the knife into the sea. And then, looking upon the prince one last time, she throws herself into the water and feels her frame dissolve into foam.

When the sun shines and its rays fall on the cold sea, the little mermaid sees hundreds of glorious ethereal beings in the air. She finds herself rising more and more out of the foam. "Where am I going?" she asks aloud. Her voice has returned and is like that of these other beings, so lovely no earthly music can compare with it. "To the daughters of the air," she is told by them. By her good deeds and her endurance of suffering, she has raised herself to the world of spirits. Now she may gain an immortal soul.

This story is used at times to illustrate the foolishness of a woman who gives up everything for a man. This seems too easy an interpretation to me. We must ask, I think, *how could she be his beloved?* She is not herself. She, who once was a fledgling siren, cannot sing or speak. Her thoughts and feelings must be expressed through a gaze. She once moved quickly and surely through the sea; she could leap with joy into the air. Now, though she may still dance, there is no joy in it; the pain of movement in his world is too great. He cannot know her. She can neither tell nor show him who she is. "To love, one must be entirely oneself" (Reik, 1941, p. 144).

"At a certain moment all lovers must begin to speak" (Kern, 1992, p. 119), but the mermaid and the prince never achieve that moment. The dialogue of the little mermaid and her prince cannot occur, but it is not for the lack of a voice. (Mute human beings in love can encounter another individual.) A more fundamental encounter is denied them because they share no authentic discourse.

Lovers must be able to be open to one another, to become enthralled each with the other. This is what Heidegger terms *Rede,* authentic discourse.[11] Love, says Kern (1992), is possible because of *Rede. Rede* allows "a sharing that is a co-understanding of existential possibilities" (p. 119). The little mermaid, despite her love, cannot reach her prince in a genuine way because she cannot speak from her true self.

Love, nevertheless, has meant becoming for her. In venturing toward another in love, the little sea creature transcends her self. She goes beyond the world she knows and moves out to other possibilities. She does so freely, and with the knowledge that she is risking death. When the moment comes in which she may sacrifice another's life instead of her own, she chooses not to sacrifice the other. In this act, she gives *of her self,* her real self, rather than as before—then she *gives up*, abandons, herself. In bravely and consciously seeking what she loves, the little mermaid gains a chance for a soul. It is the act of loving that has mattered. I find in this children's story an illustration of love as Hegel suggested: Desire takes us beyond the self toward another self, and through that other, the self returns to itself at a higher level of consciousness (Kern, 1992).

Carotenuto (1987/1989) insists that "Love reveals us to ourselves" (p. 9). He paraphrases Joseph Conrad's remark that a man only knows himself in the moment of danger: "a person knows his or her true nature only through falling in love" (p. 9). Whom we love is a powerful clue in understanding ourselves. *Tell me who you love and I will tell you who you are and, more especially, who you want to be* (Steinem, 1992, p. 96). Loving one individual rather than another can feel, and be, like choosing certain values and a certain way of life over others. When we love, we are choosing to love and cultivate the elements of the beloved in ourselves (Nussbaum, 1990, p. 328).

We also want to make our gift of self to the other a worthy one. Love stimulates self-growth, in part, because the lover wants to recreate him/herself to merit the other's love. As lovers we imagine how the other would want us to be and then we attempt to become that. For Solomon (1988) the ultimate test for love is a role test, that is, whether one wants above all else to enhance himself in the eyes of the beloved.

When Havelock Ellis (Kiell, 1964), author of *Studies in the Psychology of Sex*, was 12 years old, a 16-year-old girl, Agnes, was a guest at his home for a week or two. Though he never saw her again, he considered her brief visit an epoch-making event in his life:

> I never saw Agnes again; I never made any effort to see her; I never mentioned her name; no one knew that I even thought of her. But for four years her image moved and lived within me, revealing myself to myself. I had no physical desires and no voluptuous emotions; I never pictured to myself any joy of bodily contact with her or cherished any sensuous dreams. Yet I was devoured by a boy's pure passion.... Under the stress of this passion I became a person, and, moreover, in temper a poet. I discovered the beauty of the world, and I discovered a new vein of emotion within myself. I began to write verse. I began to enjoy art, and, at the same time, Nature. ... The touch of this careless, vivacious girl had placed within me a new ferment which began to work through every fibre of my being. (p. 150)

Rilke (1989b) once asked poetically of lovers:

> And yet, when you have survived
> the terror of first glances, the longing at the
> window, and the first walk together, once only,
> through the garden: lovers, *are* you the same?

It would seem that the answer to his question must be *no*. Love is an inducement to ripen. Love is pure becoming (Alberoni, 1983).

Notes

1   Italics in original.

2   Sartre (1956/1994) does not disagree. He believes the fulfillment of desire is ultimately impossible because of this.

3   Italics in original.

4   Reik (1941) describes this fearful resistance of the other as something women sometimes do. He does not explain why he refers to women only.

5   From a dancing song of an extinct native people of California, the Costanoans (Le Guin, 1989, p. 48).

6   Italics in original.

7   This is beautifully portrayed in the 1996 movie *The English Patient*, where two people fall in love and break all the rules of family and society. In this story, the cave and the wilderness (here the desert) are once again the setting for lovers.

8   "In den beginne," quoted in Linschoten (1987, p. 192).

9   The other characteristics are "the fact of having mutual tastes, of doing what pleases the other, total trust, indifference to money" (p. 417).

10   I was walking on a beach at the time!

11   The other type of discourse he terms *Gerede*, idle talk.

10
The Sentimental Education

This work began with the question, *what is the experience of adolescent love?* In looking to answer it, I have considered influences that have shaped my own perception of love and the ways in which it is understood in my society. Scholars and philosophers have developed theories to explain it; psychologists have used scientific methods to measure, define, and predict it; and storytellers, grasping the power of love, have woven dreams about it. I have tried to create a description of amorous love as the adolescent experiences it and to evoke some of its essential aspects. It is time to ask a pedagogical question: How may we support the development of adolescents as they move toward the encounter of another through amorous love? And another: How may we help them be safe without diminishing the vulnerability and openness necessary for meaningful growth? Adolescence and love both involve a *rebirthing* of sorts (Alberoni, 1983, pp. 80–81). I believe these questions may be phrased as one: How may we attend this rebirth in a helpful way?

Attending the Rebirth

Acknowledge Their Experience
Rousseau (1762/1966) wrote in *Émile*:

> Those who desire to guide young people rightly and to preserve them from the snares of sense give them a disgust for love, and would willingly make the very thought of it a crime, as if love were for the old. All these mistaken lessons have no effect; the heart gives the lie to them. (p. 292)

Rousseau makes a crucial point here. Rational, reasonable admonishments to teenagers to study diligently, to plan for the future, to enjoy "safer sex," but to wait for "real" love are to no avail if the heart gives lie to them. Teenagers cannot wait if life does not wait for them. The lessons come whether we want them or not.

We need to recognize and acknowledge the profound effect amorous love may have on the adolescent. To dismiss it as superficial, comical, or trivial is to underestimate the power it has over the individual. We must admit that intimate connections between two adolescents may have lifelong significance. I received this anonymous letter in response to the *Edmonton Journal* article about my research. There was a notation at the top of the first page: "I'm way over the 18–24 group, but please read this":

> It started innocently in the late 1940s when a chance meeting took place on a country road—where my younger sister and I were picking wild raspberries. Two young boys in their teens, unknown to us at the time, came walking by and teased us.... One of the two seemed a bit more shy—his blond hair and blue eyes got my attention and I was immediately attracted to him or maybe it was his smile that left me with an unforgettable feeling. A few months later this same young man walked into the local cafe where I worked after school and one look at him made my heart jump for joy. He asked me to go to a show at our local Town Hall.... We walked there and back holding hands. It seemed so magical!

They continued seeing each other for two years until he went to work at a lumber mill and she went to college in the city. They grew apart and she met someone else. Six months later she married this new man.

> On my wedding day as my groom and I were walking out of the Hall, I saw "him" standing at the back. We exchanged a slight smile. Something inside of me said, "What have I done?" A pang tore through my heart and left me feeling sorry forever.

"He" married not long after. This marriage eventually ended in divorce.

> I went through the motions of living and have stuck it out for forty years this October. I have always kept him on my mind. We never met again. Every time his name was mentioned my heart leaped, every time I drove past his birthplace I thought about him. If I had troubled times—I'd wish he was at my side.
>
> I didn't try to contact him in any way all those years, but a year ago I heard he was terminally ill. I was devastated, it broke my heart and I immediately phoned him long distance to talk. He was shocked when I told him I still cared about him and did all those years. He said he thought about me a lot too.
>
> Two months ago while he was visiting family here in my city we arranged for a clandestine meeting between us. With my heart pounding we approached each other and embraced with overwhelming joy! Our love for each other is still there. We phone each other now whenever we can; I was able to have a week with him. We know we will never be together because of his illness.

She remains with her husband.

> First love definitely lasts and hurts too. I'm finding each day filled with sorrow at knowing I may never see him again, but I live with the thankfulness for the oppor-

tunity of meeting him initially and again now. He still has that same beautiful smile! He is 62 and I'm 60 years old.

Love can touch us profoundly at any age. Teenagers will find both joy and sorrow in love, and we cannot deny it to them nor protect them from it. We can teach them to respect love and its mystery, even in its initial stirrings.

Encountering a new desire for physical and emotional intimacy with another person is an awesome thing. This desire can lead to self-discovery and to life wisdom. It can lead to grief and to death. We need to acknowledge its presence and power in adolescence. A participant in this study, Jocelyn, says that

> I know from my experience that your feelings for this other person can make you go against everything you've ever been taught, the way you've been brought up to live your life. You will go against that and even your own better judgment. It is so powerful. You feel this is the person whom you cannot live without.

Jocelyn says she will pay close attention to this with her own children. If a relationship goes "bad," for them, she will want to understand how they are taking it:

> The sense of loss can be so great, it can be like a death. Just telling them, "You'll meet somebody else," "He wasn't right for you," "It isn't love anyway," doesn't work. Another person can't assume to make those judgments for you. Even your parents.

Jocelyn says she will listen to her children with an awareness for how powerful such feelings can be. She hopes she will be open to who they are and who they want to be. While Jocelyn will use her own adolescent love experience to help her understand the experiences of her teenagers, she knows that their encounters with love will be their very own.

The adolescent love experience of the gay teen was not addressed in this study. A gay friend has read this work and believes it to be, in most ways, a description of the adolescent gay experience as well. There are, however, some obvious differences. The concern of lovers that they will be thought mad or foolish if their feelings for the beloved are revealed has an added dimension for a gay teen. It may not be safe to disclose such feelings for someone of the same sex. The gay teen may be rejected, ostracized, and even considered immoral for being in love. Where may a gay teen go with his or her confusion? Where may such teens ask their questions about love? How do they learn how to make an amorous connection with another? If we picture two gay teens sitting side by side in a movie theater their issues become more apparent. Could they be open that this is a date? Would one feel that it is his or her place to initiate a connection, to be the one to place an arm about the other?

Should either dare? The disapproving *they* may be more dangerous. The experience of the gay teenager in love is one we need to understand. I hope such research will be forthcoming.

Acknowledge Your Experience

> No generation has learned from another to love, no generation begins at any other point than at the beginning, no generation has a shorter task assigned to it than had the preceding generation, and if here one is not willing like the previous generations to stop with love but would go further, this is but idle and foolish talk. (Kierkegaard, 1983, p. 121)

With regard to love, we need not expect the teens in our lives to learn from our "mistakes." They will make and learn from their own. Our amorous experience is important, nevertheless, as it is the place from which we perceive and understand their experience. We need to reflect upon ourselves as adolescents. How did we react as our bodies and our psyches readied for reproduction? Did we fall in love? If so, what was that like for us? If not, what was our relationship to amorous love? Were we waiting desperately for a true love or were we more like Joe, focused solely on a new sexuality? Did we wonder what all the fuss was about? Adolescence is not necessarily a comfortable space to revisit but, if we want to understand the adolescents in our lives, it seems a necessary trip.

A few years ago at a high school reunion, I walked into the school gymnasium and a flood of memories came back. Surprisingly, so did a lot of anxieties. Was I over- or underdressed? Where should I sit? Will I be remembered? If I sit over here with these friends, will those over there be annoyed? Being a teenager—or suddenly feeling like one—is tough. Sean was there, the object of my adolescent crush. He no longer affects the beating of my heart. I was going to speak with him (at last!) when my old friends began to loudly tease me about him. Just like old times. Again he kindly pretended not to hear. Later I noticed him looking at me; our eyes met and we both laughed, remembering the teens we use to be.

When discussing love with teens, it may help if we acknowledge our own amorous experience—or the lack of it. That doesn't mean we need to share the details of a love, but it may open up a dialogue if we admit to having been struck by Cupid's arrow ourselves. It is likely, of course, that the teens will assume their loves are deeper, truer, or more magical than ours have been. If one has never fallen in love, sharing that with the adolescent seems appropriate too. It may be important to accompany this admission with a sincere request for help in understanding what falling in love is like.

Keep the Questions Open

> I just turned 14, and plan to be an organic farmer of goats and ducks and Highland cattle, when I grow up. I remember when I started growing breasts; it happened suddenly and then I had to wear a bra and I didn't want anyone to see my chest. Then my hips and stomach and calves started getting bigger and I felt massive: I kept bumping into things. I was as prepared as anyone for my first period, but I wasn't prepared for having "crushes" on boys. They kept getting bigger, and lasted for months, and some were small and hardly anything. My question is, has anyone ever had such strong love that wasn't real? (Reid, 1997, p. 24)

This letter, written to the author of the "Dear Mother Dear" column in the Summer 1997 edition of *The Compleat Mother,* seems a good example of the questions adolescents ask about love. They are not easy questions to answer. A simple answer may be possible—for example, "Yes, some people have strong feelings that may not be love"—but a simple answer does not address all the confusion and subtle queries that underlie the question expressed.

Beyond the "Has anyone else felt like this?" question asked in this letter lie others. "What is happening to me?" "Is this normal?" "Am I normal?" "These feelings aren't real love, are they?" "How will I know when it is love?" The questions are colored by the physical changes this 14-year-old is experiencing—she's been embarrassed by new breasts and feels big and clumsy. She was expecting the physical changes but nobody told her about the emotional ones. Is it just she? How do we answer her and others' questions?

First, we need, I think, to admit that there are no generally correct answers. Alyokhin, a character in Chekov's short story "Concerning Love," says that

> Only one indisputable truth has been said about love up to now, that it's a "tremendous mystery," and everything else that's been written or said about it has never provided an answer and is just a reformulation of problems that have always remained unsolved. One theory that might, on the face of it, explain one case won't explain a dozen others. Therefore, in my opinion, the best way is to treat each case individually, without making generalizations. (Chekov, 1887/1982a, p. 145)

The most important aspect of such questions may lie in the search for answers, rather than the answers themselves. The fundamental question may be *how do I love?*

> And yet that question may even be such that it will never allow us to go through, but instead requires that we settle down and live within it. (Heidegger, 1954/1968, p. 137)

Heidegger wrote the above statement in a discourse on what is called thinking. It may be true for questions of love as well: We may need to dwell within them. What does this mean? In part, it means we need to have the words to think about *amour*, to raise questions and reflect upon them. Perhaps the sentimental education needs to be focused on the development of the imagination. Bloom's (1993) thesis that the young need to rediscover the words of love may have a fundamental truth to it.

Literature, movies, and music can be a source of dialogue for parents and others who are searching for a way to open a discourse on love with teenagers. The messages in the stories and songs can be discussed and queried. Adults need to know where teenagers are getting their information and ideas about romance. How is love portrayed in the lyrics of bands like the Smashing Pumpkins? What are television shows like *Baywatch* telling them? Understanding what is influencing their thoughts and emotions is not about monitoring sources for the purpose of censoring them. It seems to me it is about teaching teens to be aware of such influences and to critically examine them. Otherwise, we leave the discourse on love as a consumer product sold by the media.

Dwelling within the questions also means having courage. We like right answers. When we do not have them, we may be tempted to pretend we do or avoid the questions all together. We need to keep before us the recognition that the answers must be discovered by living. Heidegger (1954/1968) said:

> We shall never learn what "is called" swimming for example, or what it "calls for" by reading a treatise on swimming. Only the leap in the river tells us what is called swimming. (p. 21)

So, I think, it is with love.

Teach Them to Live into the Answers

> And we never stop asking ourselves questions when we love: is it honourable or dishonourable, clever or stupid, how will it all end, and so on. Whether that's a good thing or not, I don't know, but I do know that it cramps your style, doesn't provide any satisfaction and gets on your nerves.
>
> *—Chekov*

There is a good deal of frustration in the ambiguity of love, in the doubts that always rise. Love brings to life the dialectic that exists between nature and civilization, between desire and duty. There is a paradoxical transparency/secrecy to love. Though we hesitate to talk about it, it is, perhaps, as Singer (1984a) says, the only topic that interests everyone. Love challenges; its joys and sorrows are ongoing. Lovers dance on the brink of the world but they must go on to find a place within society.

We can teach teenagers that the frustrations and risks of love are worthwhile if they are used for growth and moving toward wisdom.

> There is no doubt at all that we must recognise in modesty, desire and love in general a metaphysical significance, which means they are incomprehensible if man's treated as a machine governed by natural laws, or even as "a bundle of instincts" and that they are relevant to man as a consciousness and as a freedom. (Merleau-Ponty, 1945/1962, p. 166)

Bloom (1993) says, "The lover's spirit is the goal of the psyche, the standard by which health is ultimately judged. A lover is foolish but not perverse, vulnerable but not naive, dis-armed but not impotent, hopeful but not optimistic, mystical but not disembodied" (p. 265). He ends his book on love with these words: "understanding love and friendship in their manifold experience is the key to self-knowledge" (p. 551). These are the things that love can teach.

The adolescent experience of love can certainly be an opening into a comprehension of adult love. It may allow amorous love to be uncovered, if only as a presentiment of something more to come. In Turgenev's (1950) *First Love*, Vladimir at 16 recognizes that Zinaida is in love because of his own experience. He can sense the change in her and her view of the world because of his own transformation. He recognizes that his love has been a prelude, perhaps, to an "other unknown something" (p. 102).

> During the past month I have suddenly grown so much older, and my love, with all its violent excitements and its torments, now seemed even to me so very puny and childish beside that other unknown something which I could hardly begin to guess at, but which struck terror into me like an unfamiliar, beautiful, but awe-inspiring face whose features one strains in vain to discern in the gathering darkness. (p. 102)

Perhaps the greatest wisdom about love that we can share with our teenagers is that the face of love may never be totally revealed to us. The question *what is love?*—if we ask it—is always in the process of being answered. The words to the young on love that I like best are those of Rainer Maria Rilke (1985):

> Be patient toward all that is unsolved in your heart and to try to love the questions themselves like locked rooms and like books that are written in a very foreign tongue. Do not now seek the answers, … you would not be able to live them. And the point is, to live everything. Live the questions now. Perhaps you will then gradually, without noticing it, live along some distant day into the answer. (p. 257)

References

Ackerman, D. (1994). *A natural history of love.* New York: Random House.

Alberoni, F. (1983). *Falling in love.* New York: Random House.

Amelang, M., & Pielke, M. (1992). Effects of erotica upon men's and women's loving and liking responses for their partners. *Psychological Reports, 71*(3, Pt.2), 1235–1245.

Anderson, H. C. (1952). The mermaid. In F. Jacobi (Ed.), *Tales of Grimm and Andersen* (pp. 658–675). New York: Random House. (Original work published 1871)

Archer, W. G. (1957). *The loves of Krishna in Indian painting and poetry.* London: George Allen & Unwin Ltd.

Ariès, P. (1962). *Centuries of childhood: A social history of family life.* (R. Baldick, Trans.). New York: Vintage Books. (Original work published 1960)

Aron, A. & Westbay, L. (1996). Dimensions of the prototype of love. *Journal of Personality & Social Psychology, 70* (3), 535–551.

Assiter, A. (1988). Romantic fiction: Porn for women? In G. Day & C. Bloom (Eds.), *Perspectives on pornography: Sexuality in film and literature* (pp. 101–109). New York: St. Martin's Press.

Auden, W. H. (1952). Introduction. In F. Jacobi (Ed.), *Tales of Grimm and Andersen* (pp. xii–xxi). New York: Random House.

Austen, J. (1976). Emma. In *The works of Jane Austen* (pp. 611–852). London: Hamlyn. (Original work published 1816)

Austin Hurtig, W. (1992). *Love is the subject: A content analysis of "Top 10" songs.* Unpublished manuscript.

Barritt, L., Beekman, T., Bleeker, H., & Mulderij, K. (1983). The world through children's eyes: Hide & seek & peekaboo. *Phenomenology and Pedagogy, 1*(2), 142–161.

Barthes, R. (1978). *A lover's discourse: Fragments.* (R. Howard, Trans.). Toronto: McGraw-Hill-Ryerson. (Original work published 1977)

de Beauvoir, S. (1989). *The second sex.* (H. M. Parshley, Trans.). New York: Vintage Books. (Original work published 1949)

Becker, C. (1986). Interviewing in human science research. *Methods, 1,* 101–124.

Bergin, T. (1968). *Dante.* New York: American Heritage Press.

Bergman, A., & Bergman, M. (1983). The way he makes me feel. *Yentl:* CD. Scarborough: Columbia.

Bergmann, M. (1987). *The anatomy of loving.* New York: Fawcett Columbine.

Bergum, V. (1991). Being a phenomenological researcher. In J. Morse (Ed.), *Qualitative nursing research: A contemporary dialogue* (pp. 55–71). Newbury Park, California: Sage.

Berscheid, E. (1988). Some comments on love's anatomy: Or whatever happened to old-fashioned lust. In R. Sternberg & M. Barnes (Eds.), *The psychology of love* (pp. 359–374). New Haven, Connecticut: Yale University Press.

Bertocci, P. (1982). The search for meaning in adolescent sexuality and love. *Teachers College Record, 84*(2), 379–390.

Bierhoff, H. (1991). Twenty years research on love: Theory, results, and prospects for the future. *The German Journal of Psychology, 15*(2), 95–117.

Bloom, A. (1993). *Love and friendship.* New York: Simon & Schuster.

Bownas, G., & Thwaite, A. (1964). *The Penguin book of Japanese verse.* Baltimore: Penguin.

Branden, N. (1980). *The psychology of romantic love.* New York: Bantam.

Brehm, S. (1992). *Intimate relationships* (2nd ed.). New York: McGraw-Hill.

Brown, N. (1966). *Love's body.* New York: Random House.

Brown, R. (1987). *Analyzing love.* Cambridge, New York: Cambridge University Press.

Brownstein, R. (1994). *Becoming a heroine.* New York: Columbia University Press.

Bruner, J. (1990). *Acts of meaning.* Cambridge, Massachusetts: Harvard University Press.

Burton, R. (1977). *The anatomy of melancholy.* New York: Vintage Books. (Original work published 1621)

Buss, D. (1988). Love acts: The evolutionary biology of love. In R. Sternberg & M. Barnes (Eds.), *The psychology of love* (pp. 100–118). New Haven, Connecticut: Yale University Press.

Buxton, M. (1987). Adolescent couples in a psychiatric hospital: I'll never forget what's her name. *Residential Treatment for Children and Youth, 4*(2), 75–83.

Byrne, D. (1971). *The attraction paradigm.* New York: Academic Press.

Campbell, J. (1968). *Creative mythology: The masks of God.* London: Penguin.

Campbell, J. (1972). *Myths to live by.* Toronto: Bantam.

Campion, K. (1983, February). Intimate stranger: The readers, the writers, and the experts. *MS,* 98–99.

Carotenuto, A. (1989). *Eros and pathos.* (C. Nopar, Trans.). Toronto: Inner City Books. (Original work published 1987)

Carroll, L. (1971). Alice's adventures in wonderland. In D. Gray (Ed.), *Alice in wonderland* (pp. 1–99). New York: W. W. Norton & Company. (Original work published 1865)

Carter, S. C. (1998). Neuroendocrine perspectives on social attachment and love. *Psychoneuroendocrinology, 23*(8), 779–818.

Cavell, S. (1984). *Themes out of school.* Chicago: The University of Chicago School.

de Cervantes, M. (1987). Don Quixote, Part I. (S. Putnam, Trans.). In M. Mack et al. (Eds.), *The Norton Anthology of World Masterpieces* (5th ed.) (pp. 1181–1270). New York: W. W. Norton & Company. (Original work published 1605)

Chang, J. (1991). *Wild swans: Three daughters of China.* New York: Doubleday.

Chanter, T. (1995). *Ethics of eros: Irigaray's rewriting of the philosophers.* New York: Routledge.

Chekov, A. (1982a). Concerning love. In *The kiss and other stories* (pp. 145–153). (R. Wilks, Trans.). London: Penguin. (Original work published 1887)

Chekov, A. (1982b). The kiss. In *The kiss and other stories* (pp. 31–48). (R. Wilks, Trans.). London: Penguin. (Original work published 1887)

Chetwynd, T. (1982). *A dictionary of symbols.* London: Palladin Grafton Books.

Christian-Smith, L. (1990). *Becoming a woman through romance.* New York: Routledge.

Curtin, M. (Ed.). (1973). *Symposium on love.* New York: Behavioral Publications.

Davies, M. (1996). EPQ correlates of love styles. *Personality and Individual Differences, 20*(2), 257–259.

Dermer, M., & Pyszczynski, T. (1978). Effects of erotica upon men's loving and liking responses for women they love. *Journal of Personality and Social Psychology, 36*(11), 1302–1309.

Dickinson, E. (1960). Poem 293. In T. Johnson (Ed.), *The complete poems of Emily Dickinson* (p. 136). Toronto: Little, Brown and Company. (Original work published 1890)

Donne, J. (1994). *The works of John Donne.* Ware, UK: Wordsworth Edition.

Drabble, M. (1975). *The realms of gold.* New York: Penguin.

Eastman, A. (Ed.) (1970). *The Norton anthology of poetry.* New York: W. W. Norton & Company.

Ehrenreich, B., Hess, E., & Jacobs, G. (1986). *Re-making love: The feminization of sex.* New York: Doubleday.

Eliot, T. S. (1944). *Four quartets.* London: Faber & Faber.

Eliot, T. S. (1987). Little Gidding. In M. Abrams (Ed.), *Norton Anthology of English Literature* (5th ed.). New York: W. W. Norton & Company.

Evans, R. (1968). *B. F. Skinner: The man and his ideas.* New York: Dutton.

Evans, R. (1981). *Dialogue with B. F. Skinner.* New York: Praeger.

Evola, J. (1983). *Eros and the mysteries of love.* Rochester, Vermont: Inner Traditions International. (Original work published 1969)

Ewen, D. (1963). *Encyclopedia of the opera.* New York: Hill & Wang Publishers.

Fallon, E. (1984). *Words of love: A complete guide to romantic fiction.* New York: Garland.

Faulder, L. (1994, January 10). Love letters. *The Edmonton Journal*, p. C1.

Fehr, B., & Russell, J. (1991). The concept of love viewed from a prototype perspective. *Journal of Personality and Social Psychology, 60* (3), 425–438.

Fiedler, L. (1992). *Love and death in the American novel.* New York: Anchor Books.

Firestone, S. (1971). *The dialectics of sex.* New York: Bantam.

Fischer, C., & Alapack, R. (1987). A phenomenological approach to adolescence. In V. Van Hasselt & M. Hersen (Eds.), *Handbook of adolescent psychology* (pp. 91–110). New York: Pergamon Press.

Fisher, E. (1975). *Woman's Creation.* New York: McGraw-Hill.

Fisher, H. (1992). *Anatomy of love.* New York: W. W. Norton & Company.

Fisher, H. (1993, March/April). After all, maybe it's biology: The natural history of monogamy, adultery and divorce. *Psychology Today*, pp. 40–45, 82.

Flaming, D., & Morse, J. (1991). Minimizing embarrassment: Boys' experiences of pubertal changes. *Issues in Comprehensive Pediatric Nursing, 14*, 211–230.

Foucault, M. (1965). *Madness and civilization: a history of insanity in the Age of Reason.* (R. Howard, Trans.). London: Tavistock Publications.

Frank, A. (1952). *The diary of a young girl.* NewYork: Doubleday & Co.

French, M. (1992). *The war against women.* New York: Summit Books.

Freud, S. (1961). *Civilization and its discontents.* (J. Strachey, Trans.). New York: W. W. Norton. (Original work published 1930)

Fromm, E. (1956). *The art of loving.* New York: Avon Press.

Gadamer, H-G. (1990). *Truth and method.* (J. Weinsheimer & D. Marshall, Trans.). New York: Crossroad. (Original work published 1960)

Gergen, K. (1991). *The saturated self: Dilemmas of identity in contemporary life.* New York: Basic Books.

Gergen, K., & Davis, K. (1985). *The social construction of the person.* New York: Springer.

Gibran, K. (1992). *The Prophet.* New York: Alfred A. Knopf.

Gonzalez-Crussi, F. (1988). *On the nature of things erotic.* New York: Harcourt Brace Jovanovich.

Gould, T. (1963). *Platonic love.* London: Routledge & Kegan Paul.

Green, P. (1982). Introduction. In Ovid, *The erotic poems.* (pp. 15–81). London: Penguin.

Greene, M. L. (1972/1936). *The school of femininity: A book for and about women as they are interpreted through feminine writers of yesterday and today.* Toronto: Musson.

Greer, G. (1971). *The female eunuch.* London: Paladin.

Gregory, T. (1978). *Adolescence in literature.* New York: Longman.

Haas, A., & Haas, K. (1990). *Understanding sexuality.* Toronto: Mosby.

Hall, G. S. (1920a). *Adolescence: Its psychology and its relations to physiology, anthropology, sociology, sex, crime, religion and education (Volume I).* New York: D. Appleton & Company.

Hall, G. S. (1920b). *Adolescence: Its psychology and its relations to physiology, anthropology, sociology, sex, crime, religion and education (Volume II).* New York: D. Appleton & Company.

Halliburton, D. (1981). *Poetic thinking: An approach to Heidegger.* Chicago: University of Chicago Press.

Handley, H. (Ed.). (1986). *The lover's quotation book.* New York: Penguin.

Hatfield, E., & Berscheid, E. (1988). Passionate and companionate love. In R. Sternberg & M. Barnes (Eds.), *Psychology of love* (pp. 191–217). New Haven, Connecticut: Yale University Press.

Hatfield, E., Brinton, C., & Cornelius, J. (1989). Passionate love and anxiety in young adolescents. *Motivation and Emotion, 13*(4), 271–289.

Haule, J. (1990). *Divine madness: Archetypes of romantic love.* Boston: Shambhala.

Heidegger, M. (1962). *Being and time.* (J. Macquarrie & E. Robinson, Trans.). New York: Harper & Brothers. (Original work published 1927)

Heidegger, M. (1968). *What is called thinking?* (J. G. Gray, Trans.). New York: Harper & Row. (Original work published 1954)

Heidegger, M. (1971). *Poetry, language and thought.* (A. Hofstadter, Trans.). New York: Harper Press.

Heidegger, M. (1977). *The question concerning technology and other essays.* (W. Lovitt, Trans.). New York: Harper & Row.

Hendrick, C., & Hendrick, S. (1989). Research on love: Does it measure up? *Journal of Personality and Social Psychology, 56*(5), 784–794.

Hermans, H., & Kempen, H. (1993). *The dialogical self: Meaning as movement.* New York: Academic Press, Inc.

Highwater, J. (1990). *Myth and sexuality.* Markham, Ontario, Canada: Penguin.

Hix, H. L. (1995). *Spirits hovering over the ashes: Legacies of postmodern theory*. New York: State University of New York Press.

Horton, D. (1957). The dialogue of courtship in popular songs. *The American Journal of Sociology, 62*, 567–578.

House, E. (1991). Realism in research. *Educational Researcher, 20*(6), 2–9, 25.

Howe, K., & Eisenhart, M. (1990). Standards for qualitative (and quantitative) research: A prolegomenon. *Educational Researcher, 19*(4), 2–9.

Huesmann, L. R. (1980). Toward a predictive model of romantic behaviour. In K. Pope & Associates (Eds.), *On love and loving: Psychological perspectives on the nature and experience of romantic love* (pp. 152–171). San Francisco: Jossey-Bass.

Hultgren, F. (1995). The phenomenology of "doing" phenomenology: The experience of teaching and learning together. *Human Studies, 18*, 371–387.

Hunt, M. M. (1959). *The natural history of love*. New York: Alfred A. Knopf.

Infobusiness. (1993). *Mega movie guide*: CD. Orem, Utah: Infobusiness, Inc.

Irigaray, L. (1989). Sorcerer love: A reading of Plato's Symposium, Diotina's speech. *Hypatia, 3*(3), 32–44.

Irigaray, L. (1996). *I love to you: Sketch for a felicity within history* (A. Martin, Trans.). New York: Routledge.

It was love at first sight. (1995, November 19). *The Edmonton Journal*.

Jacob, J. (1992). Facilitators of romantic attraction and their relation to lovestyle. *Social Behavior and Personality, 20*(3), 227–233.

James, W. (1987). *Essays, comments and reviews*. Cambridge, Massachusetts: Harvard University Press. (Original work published 1887)

Jankowiak, W., & Fisher, E. (1992). A cross-cultural perspective on romantic love. *Ethnology, 31*(2), 149–155.

Janson, H. (1962). *History of art*. Englewood Cliffs, New Jersey: Prentice-Hall Inc.

Jaspers, K. (1986). Esistence—existenz (Selection 8). In E. Ehrlich, L. Ehrlich, & G. Pepper (Eds.), *Karl Jaspers' basic philosophical writings* (p. 62). Athens, Ohio: Ohio University Press. (Original work published 1932)

Johnson-Laird, P. N., & Oatley, K. (1989). The language of emotions: An analysis of semantic fields. *Cognition & Emotion, 3*, 81–123.

Johnstone, J. (1974). Social integration and mass media use among adolescents: A case study. In J. Blumer & E. Katz (Eds.), *The uses of mass communications: Current perspectives on gratifications research* (pp. 35–47). London: Sage.

Joyce, J. (1992a). Araby. *Dubliners* (pp. 21–28). New York: Penguin Books. (Original work published 1914)

Joyce, J. (1992b). The Dead. *Dubliners* (pp. 175–225). New York: Penguin Books. (Original work published 1914)

Joyce, J. (1992c). *The portrait of the artist as a young man.* Ware, UK: Wordsworth Classics. (Original work published 1916)

Kakar, S., & Ross, J. (1986). *Tales of love, sex and danger.* London: Unwin Paperbacks.

Kazak, A., & Reppucci, N. D. (1980). Romantic love as a social institution. In K. Pope & Associates (Eds.), *On love and loving: Psychological perspectives on the nature and experience of romantic love* (pp. 209–227). San Francisco: Jossey-Bass.

Keen, S. (1983). *The passionate life: Stages of loving.* San Francisco: Harper & Row.

Keene, D. (Ed.). (1955). *Anthology of Japanese literature.* Tokyo, Japan: Charles E. Tuttle.

Kelley, H., & Thibaut, J. (1978). *Interpersonal relations: Theory of interdependence.* New York: Wiley & Sons.

Kern, S. (1992). *The culture of love: Victorian to moderns.* Cambridge, Massachusetts: Harvard University Press.

Kiell, N. (1964). *The universal experience of adolescence.* New York: International Universities Press.

Kierkegaard, S. (1959). *Either/Or.* (D. Swenson & L. Swenson, Trans.). Princeton, New Jersey: Princeton University Press. (Original work published 1843)

Kierkegaard, S. (1983). *Fear and trembling.* Princeton, New Jersey: Princeton University Press. (Original work published 1843)

Kirkman, M., Rosenthal, D., & Smith, A.M.A. (1998). Adolescent sex and the romantic narrative: Why some young heterosexuals use condoms to prevent pregnancy but not disease. *Psychology, Health & Medicine, 3*(4), 355–371.

Klemm, D. (1983). *The hermeneutical theory of Paul Ricouer: A constructive analysis.* London: Associated University Presses.

Kockelmans, J. (1989). *Heidegger's "Being and Time": The analytic of Dasein as fundamental ontology.* Washington, D.C.: University Press of America.

Kolbenschlag, M. (1979). *Kiss sleeping beauty good-bye.* Toronto: Bantam.

Kostash, M. (1987). *No kidding: Inside the world of teenage girls.* Toronto: McClelland and Stewart.

Kristeva, J. (1987). *Tales of love.* (L. Roudiez, Trans.). New York: Columbia University Press. (Original work published 1983)

Kvale, S. (1983). The qualitative research review. *Journal of Phenomenological Psychology, 14,* 171–196.

Labahn, K. (1995, July 26). Voices. *The Edmonton Journal,* p. A2.

Laframboise, D. (1996). *The princess at the window.* Toronto: Penguin.

Lakoff, G., & Johnson, M. (1980). *Metaphors we live by*. Chicago: University Press.

Lalonde, R. (1982). *Sweet madness*. (D. Homel, Trans.). Toronto: Stoddart Publishing. (Original work published 1981)

Lazarus, R. (1991). Progress on a cognitive-motivational-relational theory of emotion. *American Psychologist, 46*(8), 819–834.

Leary, D. (1987). Telling likely stories: The rhetoric of the new psychology, 1880–1920. *Journal of the History of the Behavioral Sciences, 23*, 315–331.

Lee, J. (1973). *Colours of love*. Toronto: New Press.

Lee, J. (1988). Love-styles. In R. Sternberg & M. Barnes (Eds.), *Psychology of love* (pp. 38–67). New Haven, Connecticut: Yale University Press.

Lee, J. (1998). Ideologies of lovestyle and sexstyle. In V. de Munck (Ed.). *Romantic love and sexual behavior: Perspectives from the social sciences* (pp. 33–76). Westport, Connecticut: Praeger Publishers.

Le Guin, U. (1989). *Dancing at the edge of the world*. New York: Harper & Row.

Leonard, V. W. (1994). A Heideggerian phenomenological perspective on the concept of person. In P. Benner (Ed.), *Interpretive phenomenology*. London: Sage Publications.

Lerner, J. (1956). *My fair lady: A muscial play in two acts*. New York: Coward.

Lewis, C. S. (1936). *The allegory of love*. Oxford: Oxford University Press.

Lewis, C. S. (1960). *The four loves*. Glasgow, Scotland: Collins & Sons.

Liebowitz, M. R. (1983). *The chemistry of love*. Toronto: Little, Brown & Company.

Lindseth, A. (1986). On the possibility of a metascientific foundation for psychoanalysis. In L. Mos (Ed.), *Annals of theoretical psychology: Vol. 4* (pp. 59–97). New York: Plenum Press.

Linschoten, J. (1987). Aspects of the sexual incarnation: An inquiry concerning the meaning of the body in the sexual encounter. In J. Kockelmans (Ed.), *Phenomenological psychology* (pp. 149–194). Boston: Martinus Nijhoff Publishers.

Livingston, K. (1980). Love as a process of reducing uncertainty. In K. Pope & Associates (Eds.), *On love and loving: Psychological perspectives on the nature and experience of romantic love* (pp. 133–151). San Francisco: Jossey-Bass.

Longus. (1953). Daphnis and Chloe. In M. Hadas, Trans., *Three Greek romances*. Indianapolis: Bobbs-Merrill Educational Publishing.

Loudin, J. (1981). *The hoax of romance*. Englewood Cliffs, New Jersey: Prentice-Hall.

Love. (1991). In P. Edwards (Ed.), *The encyclopedia of philosophy* (Vol. 5, pp. 89–94). New York: Macmillan Company and Free Press.

Lowery, S., & DeFleur, M. (1988). *Milestones in mass communication: Media effects*. New York: Longman.

Lowndes, L. (1997) *How to make anyone fall in love with you*. New York: McGraw-Hill.

Lubek, I. (1979). A brief social psychological analysis of research on aggression in social psychology. In A. Buss (Ed.), *Psychology in social context* (pp. 259–306). New York: Irvington.

MacKinnon, C. (1989). *Toward a feminist theory of the state*. Cambridge, Massachusetts: Harvard University Press.

Mack, M. (Ed.). (1987). *The Norton anthology of world masterpieces*. New York: Norton.

Mandeville. (1986). Teenager en amour. In *Comme un teenager*: cassette. St.-Laurent, Québec: Janvier Musique.

Marazziti, D., Akiskal, H. S., Rossi, A., & Cassano, G. B. (1999). Alteration of the platelet serotonin transporter in romantic love. *Psychological Medicine, 29*(3), 741–745.

Marcel, G. (1950). *The mystery of being: Reflection and mystery*. (G. S. Fraser, Trans.). Chicago: Gateway.

Márquez, Gabriel García. (1988). *Love in the time of cholera*. (E. Grossman, Trans.). New York: Penguin Books. (Original work published 1985)

May, R. (1969). *Love and will*. New York: Dell.

McGraw, J. (1994). Love: Its universe and universality. *Dialogue and Humanism, 2–3*, 11–21.

Mellen, S. (1981). *The evolution of love*. Oxford: W. H. Freeman & Co.

Merleau-Ponty, M. (1962). *Phenomenology of perception*. (C. Smith, Trans.). London: Routledge & Kegan Paul. (Original work published 1945)

Mitchell, J. (1984). *Women: The longest revolution*. London: Virago Press.

Mitchell, J. J. (1979). *Adolescent psychology*. Toronto: Holt, Rinehart & Winston.

Mitchell, J. J. (1986). *The nature of adolescence*. Calgary, Alberta, Canada: Detselig Enterprises Limited.

Modleski, T. (1982). *Loving with a vengeance: Mass-produced fantasies for women*. Hamden, Connecticut: Archon Books.

Montgomery, M. & Sorell, G. (1998). Love and dating experience in early and middle adolescence: Grade and gender comparisons. *Journal of Adolescence, 21*(6), 677–689.

Morehead, A., & Morehead, L. (1981). *The new American Webster handy college dictionary*. New York: Signet.

Morehead, P. (Ed.). (1978). *Roget's college thesaurus*. New York: Signet.

Morgan, K. (1986). Romantic love, altruism, and self-respect: An analysis of Simone de Beauvoir. *Hypatia, 1*(1), 117–148.

Murasaki, S. (1955). *The tale of Genji*. (A. Waley, Trans.). Garden City, New York: Doubleday.

Murray, A. (1953). Dance. In *Encyclopedia Americana* (Vol. 5, pp. 447–450). (Canadian ed.). Montreal, Canada: Americana Corporation of Canada Limited.

Murray, S. (1999). The quest for conviction: Motivated cognition in romantic relationships. *Psychological Inquiry, 10*(1), 23–34.

Murstein, B. (1988). A taxonomy of love. In R. Sternberg & M. Barnes (Eds.), *The psychology of love* (pp. 13–37). New Haven, Connecticut: Yale University Press.

Neemann, J., Hubbard, J., & Masten A. (1995). The changing importance of romantic relationship involvement to competence from late childhood to late adolescence. *Development and Psychopathology, 7*(4), 727–750.

Nelson, M. (1983, February). Sweet bondage: You and your romance habit. *MS*, 97 –98.

New Book of Knowledge. (1968). (Vol. 19). New York: Grolier Incorporated.

Nijō, Lady. (1973). *The confessions of Lady Nijō*. (K. Brazell, Trans.). Stanford, California: Standford University Press.

Nizami. (1966). *The story of Layla and Majnun*. (R. Gelpke, Trans.). London: Bruno Cassirer.

Nussbaum, M. (1990). *Love's knowledge: Essays on philosophy and literature*. Oxford: Oxford University Press.

Ortega y Gasset, J. (1957). *On love: Aspects of a single theme*. (T. Talbot, Trans.). New York: Meridian. (Original work published 1941)

Ortega y Gasset, J. (1971). Man's vocation. In D. Norton & M. Kille (Eds.), *Philosophies of love* (pp. 21–31). Totowa, New Jersey: Chandler.

O'Toole, M. (Ed.). (1992). *Miller-Keane encyclopedia & dictionary of medicine, nursing, & allied health sciences* (5th ed.). Toronto: W. B. Saunders Co.

Otto, A. (1991). *The American quilt*. New York: Harper-Collins.

Ovid. (1982). *The erotic poems*. (P. Green, Trans.). London: Penguin. (Original work published 15 B.C.)

Owens, T. (1970). *Phenomenology and intersubjectivity: Contemporary interpretation of the interpersonal situation*. The Hague: Martinus Nijhoff.

Pagels, E. (1988). *Adam, Eve and the serpent*. New York: Random House.

Pann, Y., & Stearns, L. (1992). *Love: A Caravan storycard*. Boulder, Colorado: Caravan International Inc.

Parry, A., & Doan, R. (1994). *Story re-visions: Narrative therapy in the postmodern world*. New York: The Guilford Press.

Pascal, B. (1966). *Pascal Pensées* (A. J. Krailsheimer, Trans.). London: Penguin.

Peele, S. (1988). Fools for love: The romantic ideal, psychological theory, and addictive love. In R. Sternberg & M. Barnes (Eds.), *Psychology of love: Psychological perspectives on the nature and experience of romantic love* (pp. 159–190). New Haven, Connecticut: Yale University Press.

Person, E. (1988). *Dreams of love and fateful encounters: The power of romantic passion*. London: Penguin.

Philbrick, J., & Stones, C. (1988). Love-attitudes of white South African students. *Psychological Reports, 62*, 17–18.

Plager, K. (1994). Hermeneutic phenomenology. In P. Benner (Ed.), *Interpretive phenomenology* (pp. 65–83). London: Sage.

Plato. (1956a). Phaedo. In E. H. Warmington & P. G. Rouse (Eds.), *Great dialogues of Plato* (pp. 460–521). New York: New American Library.

Plato. (1956b). Symposium. In E. H. Warmington & P. G. Rouse (Eds.), *Great dialogues of Plato* (pp. 69–117). New York: New American Library.

Prilleltensky, I. (1990). Enhancing the social ethics of psychology: Toward psychology at the service of social change. *Canadian Psychologist, 31*(4), 310–319.

Proust, M. (1954). *Swann's way*. (C. K. Moncrieff & T. Kilmartin, Trans.). London: Penguin.

Rabine, L. (1985). *Reading the romantic heroine*. Ann Arbor: University of Michigan Press.

Ramsdell, K. (1987). *Happily ever after: A guide to reading interests in romance fiction*. Littleton, Colorado: Libraries Unlimited.

Reid, A. (1997, Summer). Dear mother dear. *The Compleat Mother*, 82.

Reik, T. (1941). *Of love and lust*. New York: Farrar, Strauss & Giroux.

Restak, R. (1979). *The brain: The last frontier*. New York: Warner Books.

Ricoeur, P. (1991). Imagination in discourse and in action. *From text to action: Essays in hermeneutics (II)* (pp. 168–187). (K. Blamey, Trans.). Evanston, Illinois: Northwestern University Press.

Ridley, M. (1991, February). Science: Wielding the axe. *The Economist*, 3–22.

Rilke, R. (1985). Learning to love. In J. Welwood (Ed.), *Challenge of the heart* (pp. 257–265). Boston: Shambhala.

Rilke, R. (1989a). Exposed on the cliffs of the heart. In S. Mitchell (Ed.), *The selected poetry of Rainer Maria Rilke* (p. 143). New York: Vintage International.

Rilke, R. (1989b). The second elegy. In S. Mitchell (Ed.), *The selected poetry of Rainer Maria Rilke* (p 157–161). New York: Vintage International.

Rizley, R. (1980). Psychobiological bases of romantic love. In K. Pope & Associates (Eds.) *On love and loving: Psychological perspectives on the nature and experience of romantic love* (pp. 104–113). San Francisco: Jossey-Bass.

Robitaille, L., & Lavoie, F. (1992). Le point de vue des adolescents sur leurs relations amoureuses: étude qualitative. [The point of view of teenagers on their love relationships: A qualitative study]. *Revue Québecois de Psychologie, 13*(3), 65–89.

Rolfe, W. J. (1904). Introduction to Romeo and Juliet. In W. J. Rolfe (Ed.), *Shakespeare's tragedy of Romeo and Juliet* (pp. 9–25). New York: American Book Company.

Rose, S. (1985). Is romance dysfunctional? *International Journal of Women's Studies, 8*(3), 250–265.

Rostand, E. (1951). *Cyrano de Bergerac.* (B. Hooker, Trans.). New York: Modern Library.

de Rougemont, D. (1956). *Love in the western world.* (M. Belgion, Trans.). New York: Harcourt, Brace & Company. (Original work published 1940)

Rousseau, J.J. (1966). *Émile.* (B. Foxley, Trans.). London: J.M. Dent & Sons Ltd. (Original work published 1762)

Rubin, Z. (1970). Measurement of romantic love. *Journal of Personality and Social Psychology, 16,* 265–273.

Ruggiero, J., & Weston, L. (1983). Conflicting images of women in romance novels. *International Journal of Women's Studies, 6* (1), 18–25.

Rumi. (1992). *A garden beyond paradise: The mystical poetry of Rumi.* (J. Star & S. Shiva, Trans.). New York: Bantam Books. (Original work written ca.\1260)

Sarano, J. (1966). *The meaning of the body.* (J. Farley, Trans.). Philadelphia: Westminister Press.

Sarason, S. (1981). An asocial psychology and a misdirected clinical psychology. *American Psychologist, 36*(8), 827–836.

Sarsby, J. (1983). *Romantic love and society.* Harmondsworth, Middlesex, England: Penguin Books.

Sartre, J-P. (1994). *Being and nothingness.* (H. Barnes, Trans.). New York: Gramercy Books. (Original work published 1956)

Saul, J. R. (1995). *The doubters' companion: A dictionary of aggre.sive common sense.* Toronto: Viking.

Sayles, G. P. (1994). *How to marry the rich.* New York: Berkley Publishing Group.

Schopenhauer, A. (1966). *The world as will and idea.* (R. B. Haldane & J. Kemp, Trans.). New York: Scribner's Sons. (Original work published 1818)

Scott, J. (1983). The sentiments of love and aspirations for marriage and their association with teenage sexual activity and pregnancy. *Adolescence, 28*(72), 890–897.

Sebald, H. (1992). *Adolescence: A social psychological analysis.* Englewood Cliffs, New Jersey: Prentice-Hall.

Seidman, S. (1991). *Romantic longings: Love in America, 1830–1980.* New York: Routledge.

Shakespeare, W. (1904). *Romeo and Juliet*. In W. J. Rolfe (Ed.), *Shakespeare's tragedy of Romeo and Juliet* (pp. 27–154). New York: American Book Company.

Shakespeare, W. (1994). Twelfth night; or, what you will! In the Shakespeare Press Edition. The complete works of William Shakespeare (pp. 641–669). Hertfordshire, UK: The Wordworth Editions Ltd.

Shotter, J., & Gergen, K. (Eds.). (1989). *Texts of identity*. London: Sage.

Simon, R., Eder, D., & Evans, C. (1992). The development of feeling norms underlying romantic love among adolescent females. *Social Psychology Quarterly, 55*(1), 29–46.

Singer, I. (1984a). *The nature of love: Plato to Luther* (2nd ed.). Chicago: University of Chicago Press.

Singer, I. (1984b). *The nature of love: Courtly and romantic*. Chicago: University of Chicago Press.

Singer, I. (1987). *The nature of love: The modern world*. Chicago: University of Chicago Press.

Skeat, W. (1993). *An etymological dictionary of the English language*. Oxford: Clarendon Press.

Soble, A. (1989). Analysing love. *Philosophy and Social Science, 19*, 493–500.

Soble, A. (1990). *The structure of love*. New Haven, Connecticut: Yale University Press.

Solomon, R. (1988). *About love: Reinventing romance for our times*. New York: Simon & Schuster, Inc.

Spiegelberg, H. (1972). *Phenomenology in psychology and psychiatry: A historical introduction*. Evanston, Illinois: Northwestern University Press.

Steinem, G. (1992). *Revolution from within*. Toronto: Little, Brown and Co.

Stendhal (1957). *Love*. (G. Sale & S. Sale, Trans.). New York: Penguin. (Original work published 1822)

Sternberg, R. (1995). Love as a story. *Journal of Social and Personal Relationships, 12*(4), 541–546.

Sternberg, R. (1998). *Cupid's arrow: The course of love through time*. New York: Cambridge University Press.

Sternberg, R., & Barnes, M. (Eds.). (1988). *The psychology of love*. New Haven, Connecticut: Yale University Press.

Sternberg, R., & Grajek, S. (1984). The nature of love. *Journal of Personality and Social Psychology, 47*(2), 312–329.

Stuart, G. W., & Sundeen, S. (1995). *Principles and practice of psychiatric nursing* (5th ed.). St. Louis, Missouri: Mosby Yearbook, Inc.

Sullivan, H. S. (1953). The interpersonal theory of psychiatry. New York: W. W. Norton & Co.

Sutton, J. (1974). *Lovers and others.* Toronto: Clarke, Irwin & Company.

Su Tung Po. (1989). We share the moon. (L. J. Steams, Trans.). (Greeting card). Boulder, Colorado: Caravan International. (Original work published ca.\ 1075 A.D.)

Synder, S. (1992). Interviewing college students about their constructions of love. In J. Gilgun, K. Daly, & G. Handel (Eds.), *Qualitative methods in family research* (pp. 43–65). Newbury Park, California: Sage.

Tennov, D. (1979). *Love and limerence.* New York: Stein & Day.

Thatcher, V. (Ed.). (1984). *The new Webster encyclopedic dictionary of the English language.* New York: Avenel Books.

Theweleit, K. (1994). *Object choice (All you need is love).* (M. Green, Trans.). London: Verso.

Thomas, D. (1971). *The collected poems of Dylan Thomas 1934–1952.* New York: New Directions.

Titchkosky, T. (1996). *The primacy of between-ness: A hermeneutics of marginality and art.* Unpublished doctoral dissertation. York University, Ontario, Canada.

Tolstoy, L. (1978). *Anna Karenin.* (R. Edmonds, Trans.). London: Penguin. (Original work published 1878)

Townsend, S. (1982). *The secret diary of Adrian Mole aged 13 3/4.* London: Methuen.

Tsagaan Sar. (1992). *Ianlin Huar, White Moon: Traditional and popular music from Mongolia*: CD. Los Angeles: Pan Records.

Turgenev, I. (1950). *First love.* (I. Berlin, Trans.). London: Penguin.

Turgenev, I. (1961). *Five short novels.* (F. Reeve, Trans.). New York: Bantam.

Valency, M. (1958). *In praise of love.* New York: Macmillan.

Valentines. (1968). In *The new book of knowledge* (Vol. 19, pp. 266–268). New York: Grolier Incorporated.

van Manen, M. (1990). *Researching lived experience: Human science for an action sensitive pedagogy.* London, Ontario, Canada: Althouse Press.

van Manen, M., & Levering, B. (1996). *Childhood secrets: Intimacy, privacy, and the self reconsidered.* New York: Teachers College Press.

Vanyperen, N., & Buunk, B. (1991). Equity theory and exchange and communal orientation from a cross-national perspective. *The Journal of Social Psychology, 131*(1), 5–20.

Vātsyāyana. (1994). *The complete kāma sūtra.* (A. Daniélou, Trans.). Rochester, Vermont: Parkstreet Press.

von Straussburg, G. (1960). *Tristan.* Harmondsworth, Middlesex, England: Penguin Books. (Original work published 1210)

Walsh, A. (1991). *The science of love*. Buffalo, New York: Prometheus Books.

Ward, P. (Ed.). (1986). *A love story from nineteenth century Québec: The diary of George Stephen Jones*. Toronto: Broadview Press.

Weiner, M. (1980). Healthy and pathological love—Psychodynamic views. In K. Pope & Associates (Eds.), *On love and loving: Psychological perspectives on the nature and experience of romantic love* (pp. 114–132). San Francisco: Jossey-Bass.

Wells, T. (1995, November 9). Letters of eternal love epitaph for two teens. *The Edmonton Journal*, p. A12.

Welwood, J. (Ed.). (1985). *Challenge of the heart*. Boston: Shambhala.

Wertz, F. (1984). Procedures in phenomenological research and the question of validity. In C. Aanstoos (Ed.), Exploring the lived world: Readings in phenomenological psychology. *Studies in the Social Sciences, 23*, 29–48. Atlanta: Darby.

Witherell, C. (1991). The self in narrative. In C. Witherell & N. Noddings (Eds.), *Stories lives tell*. New York: Teachers College Press.

Wittgenstein, L. (1961). *Notebooks, 1914–1916*. Oxford, UK: Blackwell.

Wolkstein, D. (1991). *The first love stories*. New York: Harper Perennial.

Wollstonecraft, M. (1975). A vindication of the rights of woman. In C. H. Poston (Ed.) *Mary Wollstonecraft: A vindication of the rights of woman: An authoritative text, backgrounds, criticism*. New York: W. W. Norton & Company. (Original work published 1792)

Woolf, V. (1977). *A room of one's own*. Glasgow, Scotland: Grafton. (Original work published 1929)

Yancey, G., & Berglass, S. (1991). Love styles and life satisfaction. *Psychological Reports, 68*(3), 883–890.

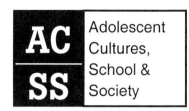

Joseph L. DeVitis & Linda Irwin-DeVitis
GENERAL EDITORS

As schools struggle to redefine and restructure themselves, they need to be cognizant of the new realities of adolescents. Thus, this series of monographs and textbooks is committed to depicting the variety of adolescent cultures that exist in today's post-industrial societies. It is intended to be a primarily qualitative research, practice, and policy series devoted to contextual interpretation and analysis that encompasses a broad range of interdisciplinary critique. In addition, this series will seek to provide a pragmatic, pro-active response to the current backlash of conservatism that continues to dominate political discourse, practice, and policy. This series seeks to address issues of curriculum theory and practice; multicultural education; aggression and violence; the media and arts; school dropouts; homeless and runaway youth; alienated youth; at-risk adolescent populations; family structures and parental involvement; and race, ethnicity, class, and gender studies.

Send proposals and manuscripts to the general editors at:

Joseph L. DeVitis & Linda Irwin-DeVitis
College of Education and Human Development
University of Louisville
Louisville, KY 40292-0001

To order other books in this series, please contact our Customer Service Department at:

(800) 770-LANG (within the U.S.)
(212) 647-7706 (outside the U.S.)
(212) 647-7707 FAX

or browse online by series at:

WWW.PETERLANGUSA.COM